P9-DYZ-484

EIGHT
STEAMBOATS

To Sue[PL],

Fair Winds &
Best Wishes

Patrick Livingston

GREAT LAKES BOOKS

A complete listing of the books in this series can be found online at http://wsupress.wayne.edu

PHILIP P. MASON, Editor
Department of History
Wayne State University

DR. CHARLES K. HYDE, Associate Editor
Department of History
Wayne State University

SANDRA SAGESER CLARK
Michigan Bureau of History

LARRY B. MASSIE
Allegan, Michigan

JOHN C. DANN
University of Michigan

NORMAN MCRAE
Detroit, Michigan

DE WITT DYKES
Oakland University

WILLIAM H. MULLIGAN, JR.
Murray State University

JOE GRIMM
Detroit Free Press

GORDON L. OLSON
Grand Rapids, Michigan

DAVID HALKOLA
Hancock, Michigan

MICHAEL D. STAFFORD
Milwaukee Public Museum

LAURIE HARRIS
Pleasant Ridge, Michigan

JOHN VANHECKE
Wayne State University

SUSAN HIGMAN
Detroit Institute of Arts

JOELLEN VINYARD
Eastern Michigan University

LARRY KULISEK
University of Windsor

ARTHUR M. WOODFORD
St. Clair Shores Public Library

EIGHT STEAMBOATS

SAILING THROUGH THE SIXTIES

STEAMBOATS

PATRICK LIVINGSTON
FOREWORD BY NEAL SHINE

WAYNE STATE UNIVERSITY PRESS
DETROIT

Copyright © 2004 by Wayne State University Press,
Detroit, Michigan 48201. All rights are reserved.
No part of this book may be reproduced without formal permission.
Manufactured in the United States of America.
08 07 06 05 04   5 4 3 2 1

Library of Congress Cataloging-in-Publication Data
Livingston, Patrick.
  Eight steamboats : sailing through the sixties / Patrick Livingston.
    p. cm. — (Great Lakes books)
  ISBN 0-8143-3175-0 (pbk. : alk. paper)
  1. Livingston, Patrick.   2. Sailors—Great Lakes—Biography.   3. Lake
steamers—Great Lakes—History—20th century.   4. Shipping—Great Lakes—
History—20th century.   5. Great Lakes—Navigation—History—20th century.
I. Title.   II. Series.
  VK140.L59A3 2004
  386′.5′097709046—dc22
                                                            2004006486

"The Times They Are A-Changin'" by Bob Dylan, © 1963 by Warner Bros. Inc.
Copyright renewed 1991 by Special Rider Music. All rights reserved.
International copyright secured. Reprinted by permission.

1969 (a.k.a. "Nineteen Sixty Nine") by David Alexander, Scott Asheton, Ronald
Asheton, James Osterberg, Jr. © 1969 (Renewed) Warner-Timberlane Publishing
Corp. & Stooge Staffel Music. All Rights Reserved. Used by permission. Warner
Bros. Publications U.S. Inc., Miami, FL 33014

The excerpt from *A River Runs through It* by Norman Maclean appears courtesy of
the University of Chicago Press, © 1989 University of Chicago Press.

∞ The paper used in this publication meets the minimum requirements of the
American National Standard for Information Sciences—Permanence of Paper for
Printed Library Materials, ANSI Z39.48–1984.

This book is dedicated to
JANET LOUISE
my consort on endless Sunday river cruises
and my beacon through many a midnight storm . . .

And to
BRIDGET, PATRICK, *and* BRENDAN
as you catch the virtual mailboats to your own ships . . .

I sat there and forgot and forgot, until what remained was the river that went by and I who watched. On the river, the heat mirages danced with each other and then they danced through each other and then they joined hands and danced around each other. . . .

Eventually the watcher joined the river, and there was only one of us. I believe it was the river.

NORMAN MACLEAN, *A River Runs through It*

CONTENTS

CONTENTS

ILLUSTRATIONS

ACKNOWLEDGMENTS

This is my first go-round in the world of publishing and I can honestly say that had I known what I was getting into those many years ago when I decided to begin recounting my life experiences both on and off steamboats, I probably wouldn't have let that stop me. As it is, I have learned that there is a great deal more to publishing a book of this nature than simply sitting down and putting pen to paper. For a non-practicing Luddite, I must first credit the advent of the computer and the software program that taught me to type well enough to make my words readable. From that point on, it becomes infinitely easier. There are a number of people who exercised great patience in connecting me to the pictures that I felt would really enhance these adventures both afloat and ashore. They include Frank Ripley, Roger LeLievre, Bill Hoey, John Truscott, Peter Werbe, and Lee Rusetzke. Rick McEvoy was good enough to allow me to use his letters from 'Nam. From an institutional standpoint, Elizabeth Clemens of the Walter Reuther Library at Wayne State University, Julie Herrada of the University of Michigan Special Collections Library, and Bob Graham of the Institute for Great Lakes Research at Bowling Green State University guided me through their archives. John Polacsek, Curator of the Dossin Great Lakes Museum on Belle Isle, helped me to think and rethink the publishing process from several perspectives—not to mention the incredible pictures he was able to pull from his archives. I also relied heavily on the Marine Historical Society of Detroit publication *Ahoy and Farewell* for information about the ships.

Neal Shine has graciously put aside the fact that I am an (almost) alumnus of St. Bernard's and written a foreword to make any eastsider proud to be born there. His foreword replaced one put together by westsider Marshall Tate twenty years ago when *Eight Steamboats* was still a novel.

Jane Hoehner, Danielle De Lucia Burgess, and Jennifer Gariepy of the Wayne State University Press have been incredibly supportive

ACKNOWLEDGMENTS

of my advent into their world. Their positive words, as well as like support from their entire staff have made me wonder why I didn't do this sooner. I am looking forward to working with them on future projects.

Finally, I must acknowledge the shadow contributions of my parents, Jack and Hazel, and my older sibs, Bob, Jim, Cathy, Walt, and Larry who, unbeknownst to them, kindled and rekindled my fascination with the river with tales of their never ending encounters with that ever changing shape in our midst.

As I write this, I am aware that only three people have read through the first draft of this book. Aside from two Wayne State University Press reviewers, I must acknowledge the support of my wife Janet, first editor, who has patiently and wisely nurtured me through the thousand questions I brought to her and helped me deal with them one at a time.

FOREWORD

Neal Shine

Whatever else that neighborhood of factory workers and shopkeepers might have lacked, there was always the river. At a time when change there was frequent and sometimes unhappy—renters moving in and out of the narrow frame houses, children being born, people dying, owners walking away from failing stores and being replaced by new owners with a better plan but not better odds—the river was the only constant. Steady, alive, unchanging.

It was a close community, serious and hardworking. Tucked into a tidy corner of Detroit's southeast side, it was homogenous only to the extent that most of the people who lived there had come from another part of the world. It was a place whose existence was defined largely by its institutions—the schools that did their best to educate us, the churches that nourished us spiritually and the factories—Chrysler, Hudson Motor Car Company, Motor Products, Briggs Body and Zenith Carburetor—that sustained us economically. It was its own place, hemmed in on the north by the small businesses on East Jefferson—bars, grocery stores, butcher shops, movie theaters, drug stores. There were noisy diners with narrow counters and low stools and men speaking Greek through half-doors to faceless people in the kitchen we never saw. There was a candy store or two, a couple of beauty shops, the fire station, and places where you could get your shoes resoled, your shirts laundered, your pants pressed, your hair cut, your hat blocked, buy a bag of nails, send a telegram or mail a package. And when the time came, there were the funeral homes: Doherty, DeSantis, and the one we considered the most appropriately named, DeKay. On the east the unofficial corporate boundary was the tracks of the Detroit Terminal Railroad, and on the west, Waterworks Park. Although it was a stretch to include as part of the neighborhood every block between us and Waterworks, the park seemed to provide the kind of obvious natural boundary that would certainly excuse what we considered a harmless exercise in urban annexation. And on the south, there was the river.

We lived at 635 Beniteau, a block from the river. In my room at night I could lie in bed and hear the whistles as the boats signaled each other. Passing to port, passing to starboard, until sleep came.

To us it was always "the river," never "the Detroit River." Since it was our only river there existed no chance that it would ever be confused with another. Growing up on those streets in the 1930s and 1940s, the river was such a condition of our existence that we simply took it for granted. It was as much a part of our lives as streetlights or paved sidewalks and, we assumed, it had always been there and always would be. Rushing out of the house to play each afternoon after school the shouted maternal instruction that always followed us out the door was, "Stay away from the river!" It was a warning that was universally ignored. In a neighborhood whose color scheme was shades of gray, the river was our rainbow. The river always had its own magic.

At every opportunity we headed to its banks, ranging through the broken concrete and discarded building material that grew in uneven piles on the open land along its shores. We climbed mounds of hard, pale yellow dirt that sprouted exotic arrays of hardy urban foliage and looked out at the river, across to the east end of Belle Isle and beyond that to Canada. It was the place we called "The Dumps," and if others saw it as a hazard created by unscrupulous truckers who came by night to defile the empty fields, it was to us a place of high adventure. We walked in single file along the banks of the river, each carrying a stick to ward off danger or, in the absence of danger, to lop off the tops of milkweed plants, dandelions, Queen Anne's Lace, or any other under-growth foolish enough to get in our way. Whoever led the column was responsible for probing the ground as we walked and whenever soft, mushy earth gave way beneath his stick, to call out to the rest of us the warning, "Quicksand!" If the kids who lived north of Jefferson taunted us as "River Rats," we must have decided at some point that it was a designation we could embrace because we ended up naming our unaf-filiated baseball team "The Beniteau River Rats." We indulged in the rich fantasies that were inspired by our proximity to the river and the availability of scores of dry-docked boats stored in the boatyards at the water's edge over whose decks and bridges we scrambled endlessly. If being called bad names was part of the price for believing on one day that we were pirates preying on fat merchantmen in the Caribbean and on the next, the crew of a British man-of-war getting ready to engage the Spanish fleet, it was something we had no difficulty accepting. But then there were the real boats. The dull red ore carriers that pushed past low in the water, the river parting white before the stubby bows, trailing tendrils of steam and the deep rhythmic pounding of the engines that drove them. When one passed we would suspend the fantasy at hand and watch without talking until it had moved out of sight on its way up toward Lake Huron or down to Lake Erie, resuming our imaginary adventures only when the wash from its passing made a soft splashing sound on broken stone that lined the riverbank. And sometimes we saw a crewman on deck walking toward the bow past the expanse of flat hatch covers, the movement of the boat turning his steps into a giant's stride. We always knew that the romance of high adventure lay somewhere beyond the confines of our neighborhood, someplace where the waters ended at exotic destinations. Not in "the old country," that universal port of embarkation so dear to our parents and grandparents, but in places like Zanzibar, Cathay, Madagascar, Mandalay, the Spice Islands, or the Horse Latitudes. Places of story and poem. Places of Kipling and Masefield. If the boats that slid past us on the river had lettered on their stern home ports like Cleveland or Ashtabula, Alpena, or Rogers City, we knew that was only a technicality. And if we knew in our hearts that their holds were filled with crushed iron ore for the furnaces of the downriver steel mills, it was easy enough to suspend reality.

They would be, if we wished it so, scows and clippers, galleons and schooners. A quinquireme of Nineveh from distant Ophir, rowing home to haven in sunny Palestine, or a dirty British coaster with a salt-caked smokestack butting through the channel in the mad March days. And we could imagine, with little difficulty, cargoes of ivory, apes and peacocks, sandalwood, cedarwood, and sweet white wine.

There were evenings in my life when I went to the river's edge, often to try and deal with the confusion of adolescent romance. And when a boat moved past in the darkness, its portholes yellow circles of light, I would again wonder what it might be like to sail aboard one of them, to sail away from all my troubles.

One of the young men who showed up at Harp's Pool Hall from time to time claimed to be a Great Lakes sailor. He was a few years older than we were and wore peg pants and had brilliantined hair combed slickly back into a duck's tail. He was the kind of guy we called a "zoot." Between snooker shots he would tell us about life aboard the boats, about the abundance of good food, the good pay, the fellowship, and the fascinating ports of call. I don't remember his ever mentioning Alpena or Rogers City. Although we secretly envied him and longed for that kind of adventure, none of us ever had the initiative to do what was necessary to make it happen. One day we put aside fantasy and did sensible things with our lives. Went to college, learned trades, worked in the auto plants or delivered mail, got married, had children. But most of us never really managed to put the river out of our lives.

Even now, on quiet nights when sleep won't come, in the dark silence of my room I sometimes think I can still hear, across the years, the faint, lonely rasp of a steam whistle. Boats passing in the night.

Neal Shine is the retired publisher and president of the Detroit Free Press *and is currently a professor of journalism at Oakland University where he teaches feature writing and media ethics. He and his wife still live on the east side in a condominium on the shores of Lake St. Clair.*

INTRODUCTION

Take Me to the River

SPRING 1949: DETROIT, EAST SIDE

Mid-May. A Sunday with strong hints of the beautiful summer to come. With church and dinner past, thousands of Detroiters young and old alike are energized to become a part of the beauty by getting outside. And so they head out to local lakes and parks, with a good many of them ending up somewhere near the straits that give the city and the river rolling past it its name.

Along the river, the brilliant skies have illumined the waters, fresh and rolling with a pleasant breeze. It seems as though the white-caps and sailboats bob as one. Fluffy white cumuli roll across the sky slow enough to entertain but fast enough to evade the warm rays of the sun pouring down into each moment. A steady parade of ships has provided day-long entertainment for the multitude of families enjoying the one time of the week when most factories are closed and people can be together. The constant notes of their steam whistles as they signal their intent to pass one another continually draws attention from those otherwise engaged in picnicking, fishing, sunbathing, and playing ball in the many parks that line the banks along both the U.S. and Canadian shores.

As evening rolls around, folks quit the river and gather back in their houses and flats. Time to think about the new week of school and work to come. But the day has been so beautiful and the early evening light so full of promise that the parental inclination is to let the kids run around the neighborhood a little more to get the most out of this perfect moment. Parents of newborns pop the babes into the buggy for one more stroll around the block while the older siblings run whooping ahead and behind, skipping and performing cartwheels on the grass

1

Detroit docks, circa 1950 (Walter P. Reuther Library, Wayne State University)

flush with new growth. The sidewalks pass so closely to the houses that the murmur of radios can be heard through open curtained windows.

These radios are attended by the older folk who have had their perfect moments in the past and cannot think of a Sunday evening without Jack Benny. And so it is that those who are out walking have the best of two worlds: the day itself and the entertainment that flows from the windows of every house they pass, allowing them to anticipate the Walkman by several decades.

On the near east side, along the corner of Pennsylvania and Mack Avenue, one slightly altered family is also enjoying its walk. The father is distracted and the kids are preoccupied with a contest to come up with suitable names. The alteration is due to the fact that their mom isn't along with them pushing the stroller. She is in nearby East Side General Hospital pushing for both herself and for a new life. The hospital is small and surrounded by houses so that the laughs from the Jack

Benny show filter into the rooms that are fronting McClellan Avenue. It is also located just a few blocks from the river so that the melodious and harsh whistles from steamboats often compete with the sounds from the large wooden cabinets that house the receivers.

While all of those sounds may be unwanted background to those of the mother intent on listening to the doctor's commands to "Push. Push!" they are probably among the first noises that greet my ears as I successfully kick my way out into the world.

SPRING 1953: ON THE WATERFRONT

A soul-chilling murky Saturday morning along the riverfront. A sunless, windless, shrouded day rendered invisible by the weather. With no change in store and time standing desperately, endlessly still, I am walking with my mother, holding her hand. We are downtown. How we got there and why we are here I have no idea. Perhaps my father has taken my brothers to the barber college for their monthly haircuts and my mother, simply wanting a day out of the house with her baby, told him to drop us here. Or perhaps we took the Mack streetcar downtown for some shopping and simply ended up here as part of the trip. The point is I am barely four years old and don't know.

We are walking along the wooden docks in the area of what must be Third Street. At my mother's prompting, I strain to catch a view of the Bob-Lo boats docked a few blocks away at the foot of Woodward. I can barely make out the canvas covered stern of one of them, nestled in its winter berth. It blends in with everything else that makes up this colorless moment. My attention reverts to watching my shoes move along the worn planks of the dock. The wood of the dock is shiny black with the mist that permeates the air. When I breathe, it feels as if I'm not breathing in anything at all—just mist that mingles with the steam coming out of my mouth. My gaze follows the grain of the wood to its end at the river. The water is grey and dull. The river itself is dull with a single seagull sitting on it and no ship traffic save for an old car ferry sidewheeler rumbling noisily into a slip in Windsor on the Canadian shore opposite. The echoes of the ferry hitting the dock and the gates crashing down are muffled by the air and sound hollow. I worry about catching an earache, which lasts longer than a stomachache. A few ice floes bob listlessly in the still waters, giving no sign that the river is flowing in any direction at all.

3

But then my mother directs my attention back to the dock itself. I look up to see her pointing at the nearby wooden pilings right in front of me against which a huge ship has somehow silently appeared. It takes me a moment to connect this lifeless vessel to the large brown ropes I have been appreciating on the dock. Now I see that the ropes are coming out from the ship and are connected to the dock itself. They are wrapped around large, round iron posts. My eyes return to the ship itself. It is painted white, but not even this colorless day can hide the blemishes where the paint has peeled to reveal splotches of brownish wood along the sides of the hull and even along the sides of the first and second decks. My gaze follows the ship all the way to its end far along the dock. Then it goes up to its top high above my head. Higher even than the top of the Bob-Lo boat's top deck that I cried to come down from only last summer.

My mother is talking. She is pointing to the gangway that leads onto the ship and saying, "*Eastern States*. That's the boat we all went on to Niagara Falls when you were a baby." I have no idea what she's talking about. As I was saying, it's enough for me to get on the Bob-Lo boat for an endless hour-and-a-half cruise with its blasting whistle and roaring engines scaring the bejeebers out of me. I decide to pay no attention and instead concentrate on the entranceway to the ship in front of me. There, right in front of my eyes, just the other side of the gangway and on board the ship, I stare at a pair of gumball machines. They stand alone and forlorn, their red paint chipped and brown showing through. They are connected to the mottled grey deck by cobwebs and a rusty chain. I strain my eyes to convince myself that I can see the round candies of brilliant reds, yellows, and blues begging to be released for a penny. My mother ignores my little hand tugging for a closer inspection of the machines. When I seek out her face I can see that she's gazing right through the ship into some other place.

"That was a good time," she says out of nowhere. "Maybe someday we'll go again." We go back to our silent explorations of the desolate vessel—she to the ship of her memory and I to the ship of my imagination.

FALL 1953: THE BURNING OF THE *PUT-IN-BAY*

A dark breezy night with a chill in the air. The black kind of sky I associate with Up North on the camping trip we took this past sum-

The *Put-In-Bay* burns in Lake St. Clair (Dossin Great Lakes Museum)

mer. Except there are no stars here. I'm with my father and brothers and we've driven a long way after supper from the city to get out to wherever this is on Lake St. Clair. When they said Metropolitan Beach, I imagined the place we visited on a hot summer day and splashing in the water along the sandy beach before we got the fudge-sicles. But this place in the dark bears no resemblance whatsoever to that summer playground.

We park the black '48 Plymouth in what seems to be the middle of nowhere. It's a long walk from the parking lot to the beach itself and along the way I clamor for my dad to carry me. But since he's already carrying my brother Larry I have to be content with a hand to hold. Lake St. Clair is just another word to me. Even more remote and less concrete than Metropolitan Beach. Because of my summer experience I know it's a lake that is so big you can't see across it to the opposite shore. But I don't connect it with the more familiar Detroit

River, in part because I've rarely been here and in part because I've never seen a freighter on its waters. As far as I'm concerned, it's just another place. And, on a night like this, with only darkness around me, not a place I would recommend to friends.

After a while, we arrive at the beach and scuffle along the sand before joining a cluster of people. The rustling of the fresh breeze almost masks the sounds of waves lapping up on the nearby shore. The crowd seems subdued in keeping with the atmosphere around us. There are one or two people with flashlights that occasionally are flipped on to reveal the wavelets as they arrive from the dark lake. It is difficult to tell how big they really are. All I know is that I probably wouldn't want to get too near and have to walk back all that way in wet clothes.

Then someone says, "You can see the lights of the tug out there." And there is a lot of commotion and straining of bodies all around me as people try to see what the voice has described. My father finally picks me up so that I can join the others as they peer into the blackness. I follow my father's finger out into the void where my eyes pick up a couple of tiny pinpricks of what must be lightbulbs on the alleged tug.

"They'll be setting her on fire any time now," another voice from nowhere prophesies.

Fire. Now that's got my attention. I forget about the chill breeze and concentrate my attention on the bouncing points of light.

"When she goes we'll have plenty of light," someone else says.

This draws chuckles from the crowd until a sober voice responds, "There were a lot of beautiful days and nights aboard that ship."

To which someone adds, "Lots of good times with friends. Cruising past Bob-Lo into Lake Erie."

"And moonlights out here to the Flats too," another voice reminds us all. "Too bad for it to go this way."

And then those in the group fall silently into their individual memories of either being on the soon-to-be-inflamed ship or having seen it cruise by on warmer evenings.

After a while of this, someone observes, "Taking them a while to get it goin', ain't it?"

And there is a general restless murmuring of assent that the show should be getting on the road. For my part, I have tired of focusing my eyes on the tiny lights in the darkness and my father has tired of holding me up in support of that task.

Then another voice enters the scene and soon the word is going around that it's too windy out there and the tug crew can't set the fire. There is a general groan of disappointment that sweeps over our group until reality sinks in and someone says, "This could take all night."

"Or longer," another voice adds. "Supposed to be some rain coming later. Hell, they might not do this for a couple more days."

The breeze and accompanying chill have, if anything, intensified, leaving little hope for a change for the better. After a few more moments hanging on and hoping for the forecasters to be disproved, we make the long trek back across the sand toward the parking lot, leaving the hard core to continue the wait.

I recall nothing of the ride home, having fallen asleep in the back seat.

SUMMER 1955: THE BROWNIE COASTER

Full summer. Brilliant blue sky. Warmth all around. Embraced by this beauty we quit our house at 3731 Pennsylvania, hop the streetcar downtown and make it down to the foot of Woodward in time to scramble up the gangplank onto the gleaming *Ste. Claire.*

The band is playing from the third deck, the whistle blows three frightening long blasts and the midget mascot Captain Bob-Lo does a little dockside jig as we scurry to find our friends and seats on the second deck. Then, as our moms settle in, it's a race down to the bottom deck to look at the huge triple expansion engine as it lays at rest in anticipation of the bells that will bring its pistons into throbbing life for the eighteen-mile trip downriver. The roar of the whistle can be heard even from down here and, as the ship casts off, our time is spent running from one deck to the next. From the engine room we go to the third deck to hear the band play "Anchors Aweigh." Then it's to the top deck where we enjoy the view and watch the wheelsman steer the ship watching for any sign that the whistle will be blown, sending us all screaming for the stairway with our hands covering our ears. We ultimately rejoin our family on the second deck where the band has established itself on the bandstand and the wooden floor has become crowded with dancers. Even with all this divertissement, the hour and a half trip drags by until someone yells, "I can see the island." Then it's back to the front of the third deck where we watch for the familiar shape of the boat dock angling out into the river. And then the ship slows to a crawl past Fort Malden in Amherstburg and begins its swing around so that its port side lines up with the dock. At this point, all the rides are revealed in their glory and we are beside ourselves with the possibility of soon being among them.

Of course, we are admonished to stay with our parents, except for my older siblings who are allowed to run ahead if they are fortunate enough to have the dime for admission to the island. So we wait for the crowd to thin out and ever so slowly make our way along the dock to the island itself. Once past the admission taker, we are steered to the nearest picnic area where—wouldn't you know it—it's time for lunch. Precious minutes are squandered over sandwiches and fresh tomatoes before we are brought to the restroom and are escorted to the midway. Of course my siblings have by this time had several hours head start on us, and my peers and I tug our moms to kiddie land, steering clear of the more daunting big rides like the Moon Rocket and the Bug and the Whip.

But this year is a little different. For aside from the usual rides on the kiddie cars, the little boats, and the carousel, it is the Brownie Coaster that becomes my challenge. The Brownie Coaster is a very miniature coaster that features a bobbing elf on its front. The ride covers a series of tiny hills no more than five feet in height around a track about 200 feet in length. And yet it becomes the first ride that allows me to claim it as my personal favorite. Through the afternoon I also lay claim to several other rides while my mom waits patiently nearby. But my idyll comes too soon to an end as the great white swan of a ship—the *Columbia* this time—glides back into the dock and the boarding announcements commence. As I am swept along with the multitudes back onto the *Columbia*, I revel in the realization that I now possess my own reason-for-being on Bob-Lo. I am moving beyond the vagaries of existentialism and establishing a true identity of my own on the waters of the Great Lakes.

On the ride back I make it my business to follow the big kids up to the top deck and take pains to keep my hands away from my ears as the *Columbia*'s whistle roars over everything to signal an approaching lake ship. As the old vessel passes I am comfortable enough to admire its cabins and portholes and notice the crewmen lounging over the rails and enjoying the afternoon sun.

In the autumn of that year, as the Yankees and Brooklyn Dodgers give way to street football games, I discover an old white

The whistle of the
Columbia (Dossin
Great Lakes Museum)

The Brownie Coaster (Dossin Great Lakes Museum)

Bob-Lo souvenir captain's hat. That, coupled with a pair of weak binoculars and an enclosed front porch with full size storm windows provides me with my first pilot's house and I become a captain for the first time.

SUMMER 1959: ISLAND EPIPHANY

Detroit. July. A sultry evening at the end of a hazy, heat-filled day. Saturday. The hour after the last languid supper dish has been put away and before the bars attract their second wave of serious patrons. The air hangs like a damp cloth over the houses and the tired factories sigh in anticipation of entering their final hours before the Sunday holiday. Somewhere in the lingering still heat parents are encouraging sleep and laying out clothes for the kids to wear to church on the morrow.

At the McIntyre house on Beniteau things are different. Nine kids, fun-loving parents, and friends can do that. There is no talk or thought of tomorrow's mass time. Now is all that matters. Kids are in the backyard, shooting hoops at a basket attached to half of an old kitchen table fastened to the garage roof. The driveway court is illuminated dimly by the faraway kitchen lights. A gaggle of barely pubescent girls collects on the porch for aimless discussion while the older teens are dispersing to places that teens go when they become too old to hang around the house on nights full of promise like this.

Out of the blue, jolly Mr. McIntyre rumbles out the back door followed by the missus and announces, "Okay, everyone in the car. We're going to Belle Isle!" And with that, everyone is jostling for seats or floor space in the Plymouth station wagon.

Belle Isle is a special place for all Detroiters but even more so for those who have grown up on the lower east side within walking distance of the river and earshot of the moaning whistles of the steamships as they lumber and chug to their various ports of call around the Great Lakes. Places named Black Rock, Ashtabula, Allouez, and Escanaba. Port Arthur-Fort William, Lackawanna, Rogers City, and Buffalo. Near and through places called the Straits of Mackinac, the Thousand Islands, the Welland Canal, and Soo Locks. To places as distant as Duluth to the west and Montreal and the great ocean to the east. The never ending stream of ships halted only by the occasional spring fog and the winters that freeze most everything from January until the thaw in early April.

Thus stuffed into the nooks and crannies of the wagon, the extended family car flows down Jefferson to the Boulevard (Grand Boulevard) and crosses the MacArthur Bridge, leaving the steamy mainland to its own devices. From the bridge, the river opens itself up all the way past downtown. We gaze at the twinkling lights of Windsor, the foreign country to the south, home to little that interests us save that blinking Canadian Club sign that seems to blanket the river with its neon flashing—first red, then blue covered by white. The blinking red lights of the CKLW broadcast tower can be seen looming over the river just past downtown. Inspired by the sight, someone turns up the car radio to pick up the strained voice of a rock and roll DJ from WJBK ranting about the latest Bobby Freeman song. As soon as the import of his words are registered, his voice is quickly overridden by the resumption of the many conversations taking place throughout the spacious car.

The Plymouth tools its way slowly through the island traffic intent on the same escape that much of the city is seeking tonight. The outer road that rings the island's circumference is full of desolate, desperate, thrill-seeking and angst-ridden Detroiters out to forget the heat of the city. On the river, the Bob-Lo steamer *Ste. Claire* appears, heading up toward Lake St. Clair. Its decks are full of moonlight revelers hoping that association with the water will bring them a breath of relief. But even the pleasure ship seems bound by the spell of summer that has blanketed the entire Great Lakes region. Flags that would snap and flutter in the breeze are now invisible, drooping listlessly around their poles on the top deck. At best, on a night like this, boaters will count themselves fortunate to catch even a slight, saving breeze wafting down from air-conditioned soirees of the yacht clubs nestled along the shores of the Grosse Pointes on the lake.

Undaunted by the sauna-like conditions, we kids ride along comforted slightly by the soggy breeze created by the car's momentum. We take for granted the canals, promenades, and statues that have provided frequenters of this island the same status afforded the people who this same night are seeking similar relief in Manhattan's Central Park. Indeed, Belle Isle—once known as Hog Island for the animals placed there by the French colonists to rid it of snakes—has been transformed by none other than the designs of Frederic Law Olmsted, creator of Central Park, to its designation in Detroit Chamber of Commerce brochures as "Jewel of the River."

The Plymouth cruises along the shore facing Canada, leaving the *Ste. Claire* and its glowing yellow lights behind. Past the majestic casino and the lowly pavilion, the Remick Band Shell and the carillon tower, the peninsula that holds the remains of the schooner *J. T. Wing*, the broad athletic fields, and the flagpole memorializing Francis Scott Key. The car comes to a halt near the Coast Guard station and out tumble seven or eight kids starved for this chance to stretch legs and arms. We float about, now toward the dark river, now to the comforting shelter of the listless willows as the stillness of the night envelops and forces us to play by its rules.

A game of tag breaks out and the night air is split with laughter as we scramble from tree to tree and around their massive trunks with shouts of "You're it" and "Missed." Yet for me, all of ten years old, the game is suspended as I take a breather to gaze out at the black water and a vision passing dreamily before my eyes. It is an old laker hissing through the night air, its dark midbody silhouetted against the grey haze that shrouds the river. The forward housing rises three stories above the deck, culminating in a darkened pilot house. A green running light gleams dully through the heavy air. A couple of portholes emit weak glimmers of light. As the ship slides past, I make out more yellow lightbulbs that illuminate the stairways and back of the bow housing and pilot house. Oblivious to the sounds of my friends, I am mesmerized by the silent passing of this awesome huge thing. As the decklights slide past, I am treated to the sight of the stern housing. Not as tall as the bow, this part of the ship features two white painted houses full of portholes and doorways out of which rises a tall black smokestack with a large red "C" that is lit by a single floodlight, the ship's only concession to vanity. As I drink in the fullness of this vision, my attention is drawn to the area directly below the housing where a wide door is open near the waterline. It takes me a moment to recognize the deep chuffing sound and to realize that the doorway is the gangway opening to the engine room. The place where resides the mammoth combusting beast that keeps the coal-eating ship sliding forward. The glow from the doorway accompanied by the steady throb of the engine moving the shaft tells me that here is a place full of life, heat, mystery, and danger. The heart of the ship. Right there. Before my eyes. I stare until convinced that I've seen the silhouetted upper body of a man, forearms resting on the gangway as he leans out to drink in what is for him the cool night air.

As the vision chugs along at ten miles an hour and slowly recedes into the haze of the river, it is all I can do to watch. I drink in the full impact of the fact that, while everyone else in the world is on Belle Isle and the streets of the city trying to be somewhere else, there are men out there making that ship move through these dark waters. And those same men will be there all through this night and keep on sailing tomorrow too. I gaze, oblivious to the game going on around me. Mesmerized at the vision, questions form in my mind. What do those people on those ships do? Where do they sleep—in those white houses on the front and back? And what do they eat? Where are they going? Do they ever get off?

As the Plymouth joins the caravan back to the reality of Detroit in the still hot night, I am possessed by the image that the ghostly ship has burned into my mind and the questions it has raised. What began as an innocent game of tag under the willows has left me a changed person. I will not look at this river the same way again.

SUMMER 1962: LOST AT SEA

Another full summer. This time August. Late Thursday night watching reruns of *The Untouchables*. And suddenly the program is interrupted by a bulletin that a ship has collided with a barge in the river and is sinking near the Ambassador Bridge. The name of the ship is the *Montrose*—she is a salty and has struck a lowly river barge with no home nor recognizable name.

At first it seems like my brother Walt is excited enough to break a grounding and hop in the car and tool down there to witness the drama. But he decides against it and so I content myself by gleaning all I can from the TV before retiring to a late night of listening to CKLW's on the spot recaps and updates on my tiny transistor radio in bed, all the while figuring how I can manage to coerce someone into getting me over there as early as possible tomorrow.

My interest in shipping has only grown over time. I have graduated from Christmas presents of comic books to a subscription to *Telescope* magazine from the Great Lakes Maritime Institute. I find myself identifying some of the more recognizable ships on the lakes as they pass Belle Isle, downtown Detroit, or as I pass them while aboard the *Ste. Claire* or *Columbia* that I now try to ride more than once a summer.

I actually get a thrill when I see the *Cliff's Victory* or one of the awesome 730 footers as they sail past. I also follow Stoddard White's shipping column in the *Detroit News* and the notation of the vessel passages. I am becoming a frequent visitor to the newly constructed Dossin Great Lakes Museum on Belle Isle that has replaced the ancient *J.T. Wing* schooner museum. More importantly, I have discovered in the Walker branch of the library books titled *Ghost Ships of the Great Lakes* and *Lore of the Lakes*. I find myself being drawn ever more deeply into the world of ships on the lakes.

A few days later I am standing on the Ambassador Bridge that links Detroit to Windsor. As huge semis lumber by inches away, I stare, oblivious to everything except the black and brown hull laying on its side directly below me covered almost entirely by the river. I am transfixed at the site made even more interesting by the opportunity to watch the mailboat *J. W. Westcott* as it makes its runs to deliver mail and whatnot to ships as they pass within a hundred yards of the sunken vessel.

I manage to get to this vantage point a couple of times over the next couple of weeks. On one occasion, a Sunday, I watch from the bridge as the *Aquarama*, a nine-deck passenger carrier on the Cleveland run, makes a swift turn from its Detroit dock and swings past the *Montrose* as she begins her jaunt toward Lake Erie. I have read accounts of her Captain Howell and his daredevil antics behind the helm of the swift liner. He has been accused of breaking the river speed limit of ten miles per hour on a number of occasions and swamping numerous small craft in the process. I watch the ship make her swing at what seems like an incredible speed (she is reputedly capable of twenty miles per hour) and imagine what kind of trouble the captain is heading for this time. The captain, according to certain sources, enjoys the title "Madman of the Lakes."

I enter my freshman year at St. Bernard's with my hair swept up in the style of everyone's hero, JFK. Pictures of the sunken *Montrose* and the streamlined *Aquarama* are taped to my bedroom wall. My dreams of becoming a sports legend are slowly being supplanted by

The *Montrose* (Dossin Great Lakes Museum)

my continuing fascination with the lives of sailors and the still unanswered question of just what it is they do all day. While the familiar port-to-port passing whistles continue to routinely interrupt my bedtime prayers, records indicate that the ships are not as numerous as they were in the mid-50s, when it was estimated that a ship passed Windmill Pointe every sixty seconds. The old creeping rustbuckets built at the turn of the century are beginning to be replaced by a newer, larger generation of ships.

WINTER 1965: THE NATIONAL MARITIME UNION HALL

March. The deadest and absolutely longest month of the year—especially when St. Bernard's has been eliminated in the first round of the district basketball playoffs.

But I am saved by a yellow postcard that I have placed atop the china cabinet in the dining nook. The card is a response from a letter I wrote to the NMU Hall in Detroit inquiring about what I would need to do to get a job on a freighter.

The card, which arrived within a couple of weeks of my letter, is proof of my existence and recognition that my dream can become reality. The hand-scrawled reply reads simply, "Have work for you. Come to hall."

This is the break I have been impatiently waiting for. A week later, I am on the Mack bus headed downtown after school in the late-winter gloom. Patches of dirt encrusted snow along the route bear mute witness to the enduring cold. My buddy Roger has agreed to accompany me and it is he who spies the red brick two-story building on Fort Street just before the Ambassador Bridge. We walk back to the unassuming entrance and climb worn stairs to a dingy second floor. The crusty old steamboats I have closely watched over the years have prepared me for this scene. I open a plywood panel door onto a room that occupies most of the floor. The floor is covered in a checkered pattern of black and rust linoleum with a multitude of burn marks visible at least in the rust squares. There is an old TV on a stand in one corner with its screen blank. A number of empty aluminum-framed chairs are scattered throughout. They are pretty much covered with the same light green hide with cracks and cuts resplendent. The two windows overlooking the alley out back show streaks of dirt where the rumpled brown curtains allow a bit of light to come through. A few standing ashtrays, most of them empty, are located here and there in a sort of random pattern. In spite of the fact that no one is around, the smell of smoke and sweat permeates the stagnant air.

After a few moments of looking, I find the office tucked into a corner of the room. While Roger hangs back, I approach the window, postcard in hand, and succeed in getting the attention of a man who is hunkered down over a desk reading a magazine. He sees me and takes his time in pushing his chair away, rising, and strolling the five steps necessary to get to his side of the counter. He is a squat middle-aged man dressed in a white short-sleeve shirt with yellow stains visible under the armpits. His dark hair is receding and smack in the middle of his mouth is the stump of an unlit cigar. It takes him all of three seconds to size me up.

"Whaddya want?"

I thrust the postcard through the hole in the glass for him to see. "I'm looking for Mr. Streho."

He strains to decipher the writing on the card and responds, "That's me. Now whaddya want?"

Nonplussed, I press the card into his hand and answer, "I want to work on a ship."

Louis Streho snorts and the cigar threatens to come out of his mouth as he spits, "How old're you anyway?"

"I'm gonna be sixteen in May," I stammer, trying to meet his stare.

"Sixteen!" he snorts again, this time removing the cigar from his mouth. "Sixteen. Why the goddamn hell didn't you say so when you sent me your letter?"

"I . . . I didn't know it would make any difference," I manage, my confidence quickly ebbing.

"Sixteen. Jesus Christ." And now he's coming through the door that connects the office to the rest of the hall. "You're way too young of a sonofabitch to even be here. You've gotta be eighteen to ship out."

And now he's herding Roger and me back toward the door we entered.

"You can't come back here for anything for two years. So don't bother until then."

And just like that we're back on the street in the gathering dusk.

As we scuff along toward the bus stop, Roger breaks out his harmonica and plays part of a Beatle's song. I recognize the words coming through the tune: "Baby's in black and I'm feeling blue."

On the long ride back, he breaks my reverie as I stare out the window by asking, "What're you gonna do now that you can't become a sailor?"

"Geez, man. I dunno. Two years is a long time to wait." But what can I do? While he plays one tune on his harmonica, the song buzzing through my mind is "Leaving Here" by Eddie Holland.

1967: THE SUMMER OF LOVE, PEACE, AND RIOTS

Come gather 'round people
Wherever you roam
And admit that the waters

Around you have grown
And accept it that soon
You'll be drenched to the bone
If your time to you
Is worth savin'
Then you better start swimmin'
Or you'll sink like a stone
        —Bob Dylan, "The Times They Are A-Changin'"

It is the wildest of times. Filled with fast cars and pretty blonds with wild reputations. The word is that there is a chick with a Vette cruising Woodward with a "Beat me you can eat me" sign posted in her rear window.

After graduation wears down, there is still time for a few more parties before the reality of life has a chance to assert itself. And with the threat of the Vietnam war happening all around us, there is less time than we think. So our celebrations are tinged with the reality of the news of the world. And the news of the world is being made both at home and in rice paddies ten thousand miles away.

After midnight. A warm May evening. I'm lying in bed reading and casually listening to a program called Kooler World playing on WJLB. It's all about the new music coming from the coasts. Then this one song grabs me and I turn up the radio to listen, not having heard anything like this before. After the long song careens to a close, I strain to hear the announcer rasping over the weak AM signal "Light my Fire. The group is known as the Doors."

As my eighteenth birthday and high school graduation draw near, I find that the world is opening dramatically, increasing in scope and allure in inverse proportion to the slow unfolding of my eyes. The once tame Beatles, every parent's friends, are now viewed with suspicion as they travel to exotic places and have strange adventures in places like India that I follow closely. Their new album *Sgt. Pepper's* is rumored to be far out there, beyond where rock and roll has gone before.

To add to the excitement, a happening on the last day of April that will bring the world of "Light My Fire" and *Sgt. Pepper's* to Detroit is announced. The first ever Detroit Love-In—to be held on Belle Isle (where else?).

18

Resident head hippie, John Sinclair, and company at the Artists'
Workshop near Wayne State have announced this event as the beginning of a new era in our environs. As far as I and my friends can gather,
love-ins are experiences where people gather to listen to music and
just bop around and watch each other do things. Of course, there is
the prevalent rumor that suggests that the drugs marijuana and LSD
might make their sinister presences felt as well.

As the big Sunday rolls around, I pack my buddies into the blue
'56 Plymouth and we cruise down Jefferson to a cousin's apartment
where we park and begin the walk over the bridge to the island. The
day is exquisite, warm and full of sunshine. We stroll across the newly
risen green grass toward the band shell. The scene unfolds in small
tableaus: here a rock band called the Seventh Seal playing an endless
version of Dylan's "Like a Rolling Stone"; there a group of black guys
in the street singing an a cappella version of "Ain't Too Proud To Beg"
with a small white dude hitting the impossibly high notes; everywhere
young people smiling and dancing among the big trees, some passing
out cookies and dandelions, others bottles of beer.

We have walked into Golden Gate Park in the midst of our own
Detroit. And the feeling is of being one with the magic. Sinclair and
friends have managed to bring the vibe of peace to this island in our
river. To make the scene even more pleasurable, I only have to glance
over to the river to see freighters passing in the brilliant sun, the
incense laden air punctuated by the sonorous blasts of their whistles
en passant.

In the late afternoon, I wander over to the picnic shell that has
served as the informal headquarters for the day. Glancing up, I recognize Roxanne, a classmate from Osborn, perched on the roof with
a serape draped around her granny dress. She looks so beautiful and
unattainable up there it is all I can do to watch her and sigh my teenage
lungst (lust+angst). But her brow is troubled as she looks over the
throng that extends into the distance. I follow her gaze and notice that
there appears to be disruption snaking its way through crowd. There
is a definite parting of the masses highlighted by the occasional body
thrown into the air. The motion is accompanied by a buzzing sound
that is definitely becoming noisier by the instant.

Then the crowd opens to reveal a black-clad, long-haired motor-
cyclist grinning maniacally through his bristles as he guns his bike and
spins his wheels in the soft grass turning for another run through the

The Love-In on Belle Isle (The *Fifth Estate*, C. T. Walker)

"Faces of the Love-In" (The *Fifth Estate*, Richard Stocker, Norm Koren, C. T. Walker; collage by Ovshinsky)

now rapidly dispersing partyers. The back of his jacket labels him as a "Devil's Disciple." Not to be outdone, some of the biker's buddies have decided to follow his lead and begin chasing him through and over the crowd. I watch in awe, thinking that these must be the dudes that Sinclair has proclaimed as part of his vision of peace and love. To create an alliance of countercultures he has asked members of various motorcycle gangs to serve in the antipolice capacity of peacekeepers for the love-in. He has suggested the term "Psychedelic Rangers" to more appropriately fit their anticop, good shepherd role.

Unfortunately, someone unthinkingly takes offense at being almost run down and retaliates by hauling one of the bikers down. That is the signal that a host of his beer guzzling peers have been waiting for. I watch from the comparative safety of the shelter as all hell commences to break loose. Within a minute the scene of the love-in has been transformed to that of maelstrom. The bikers roll into the crowd, intent on moving everyone on their feet away from their fallen brethren. Panic sets in as the innocent flower children begin to run away from the impending violence. Rocks and beer bottles fill the air, targeting the bikers who seem energized by this opposition.

It is about here that my buddies and I begin to take our leave of the area, glad that we have the option of walking away rather than being tied to one of the thousands of cars trying to get off the island at the same time. As we make our way back across the bridge, a seemingly endless line of cop cars full of flashing lights begins to make its way onto the island. That night I watch the rest of the melee via the magic of TV in my living room. I have witnessed the best of the new age and discovered that there's no place like home.

So it is with a new view that I approach graduation from Laura F. Osborn Public High School in Detroit, made possible by the premature closing of St. Bernard's (after forty years) and my family's move from Pennsylvania Avenue to the city's northeast side. For the first time in my life, I am out of whistle range. Aside from adjusting from a school of 100 students to one of 3,000, I find that I have enjoyed my two years at Osborn and have made a lot of new friends in the process. I have even managed to fall in love with a girl who barely knows I exist. Due to a lousy chemistry grade coupled with a reluctance to start dorm life, I have turned down a caddy scholarship to a Big Ten school and have decided to accept an offer to attend Monteith, a small college that is part of nearby Wayne State University.

Graduation comes and goes with its flurry of parties and highway crashes. As the big night arrives and I parade across the stage of Ford Auditorium, I find myself depressed at finally being the right age but no closer to attaining my dream job before starting Monteith in the fall.

A school buddy introduces me to a friend named Tony who actually worked on freighters for the past year. One day I meet him at the Coney Island across from school. Over some great hot dogs, Tony talks about his life aboard the *Sylvania*, an old coal hauler. He talks about the great food—steak and eggs, the night lunch, all you can eat all the time. He tells me about the cramped rooms that get hot as hell in the summer. Then he lights a cigarette and casually says, "Yeah. I was on her that night in Port Huron when she sank." I recall the news accounts vividly. The *Sylvania* is the ship that sank at her dock along the St. Clair River a few weeks back.

"Yeah. We got the word she was sinking and just had time to grab a few things and get off before she settled down there. Lucky the water wasn't real deep. After she was on the bottom, you could still climb back on her and get to the upper cabins where the captain and mates' stuff was. All of our stuff got soaked and ruined."

I recall it took a while for the *Sylvania* to be raised.

"Yeah. It is kind of a drag," Tony recounts. Then they found me a berth on another Tomlinson boat. Engine room job. Didn't like it even though the boat was a little bigger and newer. Better food. Next I think I'm going to the West Coast. Want to catch a ship to Japan."

I decide to get to the point and ask, "So how can I ship out?"

Tony takes a drag on his Camel and says, "They don't make it easy. I'll tell you that. First you gotta get a letter from the union hall saying you have a job on a ship. Then you take that to the Coast Guard and they give you this "Z" card for the Merchant Marine. With that you can get on any U.S. ship anywhere."

Thinking to myself that doesn't sound too hard I say, "Well, I already know this guy at the hall. Louie Streho's his name."

Tony considers this, takes another drag, and asks, "What hall you talking about?"

"The NMU hall—National Maritime Union hall—near the bridge."

"NMU? I don't know about them. I ship SIU—Seafarers International. My uncle got me in. They say SIU's cleaner about who they let on their ships. Better ships."

We part company leaving me with a fair amount to think about. While I am exhilarated at the thought that my dream is a little closer to my grasp, I am still without a clue as to how to go about that critical first step. Sensing my lack of direction, my mother suggests that I go down to the docks of the Georgian Bay Line and see if they are hiring crew for their passenger ship *South American*.

CHAPTER 1

Steamboat 1

Last of the Queens:
The SS *South American*

Having nothing to lose, I follow my mother's advice. As I park my '56 blue Plymouth at a meter below Jefferson, I am comforted to see the *Ste. Claire* at its berth, preparing for the eleven o'clock sailing. As if in recognition, the large white steamer sends out three full-throated blasts that echo off the City-County building across Jefferson Avenue. I am thrilled by the sound, recognizing it as the ten minutes to departure signal. As I approach the dock and its familiar smells of popcorn, coffee, and stale beer, my attention is caught by the less familiar sight of the cruise ship *South American*. Significantly larger than the *Ste. Claire*, the *South American* was designed as an overnight passenger steamer. I recall having seen her underway a number of times and even having photographed her at dock several years before with the family Kodak Brownie.

But the intent of my being here this time is not to hang out on the familiar Bob-Lo boat. Instead I walk with a sense of purpose toward the larger vessel and its dockside offices at the foot of Bates Street. The offices are located in a brown brick building, this one also two stories and dwarfed by the large white ship adjacent. On a billboard that sits atop the building painted in white on a red background are the words

SS *North American*
SS *South American*
Georgian Bay Line

The Georgian Bay Line's Detroit dock (Dossin Great Lakes Museum)

Now, without thinking, I am drawn to the red-and-white striped awning that serves as a canopy for piles of suitcases and steamer trunks destined for staterooms aboard the white-hulled ship. As I approach the building, I realize with a rising excitement that I have never been so close to this ship in my life. I stop to simply drink in the enormity of her beauty, as she hisses steamy breaths and gushes water through outlet pipes near the waterline while she rests in her berth. My eyes slowly rise up the portholed sides to the top deck, much higher than that of my frame of reference, the nearby Bob-Lo boats. Now I am looking at a real ship, I think. The kind that they all talked about on those Sunday afternoons on Pennsylvania. And I am finally here.

Having nothing and everything to lose, I take a breath, open the building's screen door and approach the wooden counter. I ask the secretary in my most mature voice if there are any positions, expecting the catch-22 routine. To no surprise, she tells me that I will first need to have a physical and be certified by the Coast Guard before they can hire me. But then, to my amazement, she thrusts a letter into my hand that is the long sought for promise of employment that the Coast

Guard has mandated before they could begin the process of issuing the almighty "Z" card. She directs me to go to the Marine Hospital where the physical will be administered. Once I have a clean bill of health, I can return to the office and they will see if there are openings. In response to my wondering gaze, the woman smiles and says, "Don't worry, sonny. There's always plenty of openings around here."

I waste no time in racing to the ancient grey hospital located on the river adjacent the Windmill Point lighthouse on the city's eastern border. There I sit in an institution-green waiting room for an eternity with a handful of older patients. Finally I am administered a pretty routine physical that consists of the usual hernia test, answering a bunch of questions with the word "no" and having a blood and TB test taken. The plain-looking nurse tells me that it will take five days to process and I should check back in that time. Thus begins one of the longest weeks of my young life.

I go through the motions of pretending it is just another summer hanging around with my friends but, in the back of my mind, I know I should be elsewhere. And it is with a strong sense of relief that I am finally able to get back to the hospital, pick up the letter and bring it down to the Georgian Bay office. The secretary reviews it cursorily, goes into a back room to confer with someone, comes back and says, "You should report here tomorrow around one. The ship will be in and the steward will know if there are any openings. Make sure you pack a bag because, if there is a job, the ship sails at four."

I don't know if I slept that night, but I do know that I left home with an old battered suitcase the next day at noon. When I get to the dock, the ship is already there, looking incredibly majestic in her superstructure of gleaming white paint and striking twin smokestacks striped with black, red, and amber. I stand at the dock, in the midst of the bustle of loading and unloading, momentarily mesmerized at the vision before me. I am comforted by the familiar hissing and pouring-forth of the ship itself. After a few moments, I gather my courage and suitcase and shyly enter the office. The secretary directs me to wait in an open storeroom at the rear of the small building. Presently, a man comes back. He is older—in his forties—and wears glasses. He is dressed in a black uniform with gold rings around the sleeves. Over his breast is a hard white plastic name tag that spells "Beauregard" in rigid black. He gives my hospital papers a quick once over, asks if I've ever sailed before and then directs me to a bench, telling me to sit tight, that he'll know in a while if there are to be any openings today.

The day is warm, the room airless and still and the wait arduous. As I clutch the battered suitcase I know that, no matter what, I want to be on that ship more than anything in the world. Over the next half hour, two more guys join me with their suitcases and hopes in that room. We talk a little about where we've come from and where we're going. Chris is the same age as I am and has just gotten off a bus from Yellow Springs, Ohio. He says, "I sure as heck hope they give me a job today" in a voice tinged with fear and potential anger. "It's too long a ride and too much money to go back home tonight." The other fellow is heavyset and oafish in his appearance. His name is Chuck and he introduces himself by stating, "All I wanna do is get the hell away from here this summer. My old man says I'll have to go to Dodge Main if this don't work out."

After forever, Beauregard comes back in, brushing bread crumbs from his pants leg. He is obviously in a hurry and says to the three of us, "Okay, I've got two for sure." Because I am first there, I am surprised to see him pick out Chris first. But I figure it has to do with his distance from home more than anything. But I am shocked when he then chooses Chuck who is a local like myself. I sit there impatiently, watching my dream vanish as the two of them gather their suitcases and scamper aboard after Beauregard.

I have almost given up hope when Beauregard reappears about fifteen minutes later and beckons me to follow saying, "Another spot just opened up. You're on. Follow me." It is all I can do to follow him across the crew's narrow gangway without falling in the river in my rapture. I am on board the *South American* as a crew member. The dream sparked so many summers ago is being brought to life!

As I cross onto the magical world beyond the gangplank, my heart is beating a mile a minute. The cloyingly sweet smell of engine oil is my first breath of *South American* air. I follow Beauregard to a door that leads down a flight of stairs. "This is your new home, son," he says pointing to hand-painted lettering above a doorway. I have to look closely and a couple of times before I can make out the letters that spell out "FLICKER."

In my excitement, I think the letters spell out something else and have one of those *jamais vu* experiences that makes me wonder for an instant if I haven't truly crossed over into another dimension. But as

I descend the narrow stairway, I encounter a scene I know I have never seen before. The Flicker is a large dimly lit space, full of disheveled bunks and dented lockers. Some of the bunks are filled with blanketed bodies. In spite of the warm day outside, the climate in this room is a chilled clamminess.

I look around and finally find what appears to be an empty upper bunk. After tossing my suitcase onto the stained yellow mattress and taking one more quick look around, I head back up the stairs. When I reach the daylight of the corridor, Beauregard gives me, Chris, and Chuck a quick appraisal tinged with disdain and says, "The three of you'll work the dishes down below. Report to Freddie down there. Your uniforms and bedding are from Clarence around the corner. If you have any questions, ask him." And then he vanishes through the gangway.

While my two new shipmates head toward the linen closet, I am drawn toward the rest of the ship. I wonder where the corridors lead and decide to head down one along the port side. After passing a few doorways to inside cabins, I come to the main lobby of the first deck. The cozy room reminds me of the lobby of the Hotel de Ville in Rome encountered on a trip with my parents a couple of years before when visiting my brother Bob. In the corner near the entrance from the dock is a small desk where a couple of college-aged guys dressed in natty white outfits with gold trim are handling the room assignments of oncoming passengers. The floor of the lobby is tiled in black and white one-inch squares and create a dazzling effect. A few steps from the desk is a closet bar discreetly tended by a motionless black man dressed in white. There are a couple of tables and chairs to accommodate those who feel like enjoying a drink while watching for new faces to arrive on board. I study the scene for a few moments before determining to see more.

I take note of the grand staircase leading from the lobby to the upper decks and in a few strides find my feet walking up the red carpeted steps. I discover only corridors leading to passenger cabins on the second deck and continue up the now narrowed stairway to the third deck. This is where the outside deck begins and I slowly saunter around the ship enjoying the experience immensely in the midst of porters lugging tons of baggage and new passengers settling into their shipboard life. I continue my journey to the top deck and stop only when I run out of space to cover. I slowly work my way back down the stairs until I regain the decidedly plebeian confines of the linen locker. While waiting to receive my linen from an old black man named Clarence, I casually say, "Man, those upper decks are cool. So many people and so many neat places."

Clarence throws my bedding at me and snorts, "Don't you know that crew aren't allowed up there? Beauregard catch you and you offa here a lot faster than you got on. Gotta know the rules. Only place crew can go above is the top deck at the stern. And that's only for you white folks. Now take this and get back down and make your bunk before somebody steals it. Your uniform's there too. I gave you double cause you're a dishwasher. Won't get no more for a week so take care of it."

"Okay, man. I will. I'll be cool," I answer as I carry the pile down the Flicker stairway. I locate the upper bunk with my suitcase still on top and begin to throw the sheets and pillow case on the excuse for a bed. I don't really notice the ragged condition of the bedding because I am too excited at the overall ambience of the Flicker itself. In addition to the rows of bunks I noticed the first time down, my attention is now drawn to a corner that is partially covered from ceiling to floor by sheets and a couple of coarse grey blankets. From the other side of the temporary wall comes the murmur of voices that indicate to my sharp ears that a card game is in progress.

With the bed made, I begin to look around to find a place to stow the suitcase. There is a row of shabby grey lockers at the end of the bunks, but every one of them has a lock on it. As I puzzle over this, a large black man comes out of a side room and says, "You must be one of the new ones. Won't be no space till somebody gets off. Best to just throw that shit under the bed. Hang onto your wallet. Sleep with it. That's the best." And he drifts off behind the linen curtain toward the game.

I decide to follow the advice and stow the suitcase beneath the bunk. I then determine that I want to see more of the ship so I search out the stern route indicated by Clarence. I quickly become lost and am fortunate to bump into a burly crew-cut guy who invites me to follow him. This path takes us past a bank of toilet stalls located in a large room full of chains and hissing, rattling boxes. "Steering gear boxes," my guide explains. We clamber up a series of ladders and discrete stairways and finally emerge on an upper deck amidst a row of passenger cabins. My guide takes the turn and walks the deck toward the stern until the only way to go is up one more ladder. As I begin the short climb, I am taken by the large-windowed room next to the ladder that is labeled "Ballroom." He motions me up and explains, "This is the only part of the passenger decks we can walk on. There's no other way to get to this ladder to the fantail." By the time we reach the exposed top deck that is directly over the ballroom, I am surprised to discover that the *South American* has cast off its lines and is already underway in the river. I quickly orient myself to the parkland and docks of Windsor and the Canadian shore just before the Ambassador Bridge and exult in the fact that I am actually onboard a ship on a voyage that will take me into the Great Lakes for the first time. No longer will I have to sit and marvel at the recounting of my older siblings of the trips they've taken aboard the Detroit and Cleveland Navigation Company steamers to places like Put-In-Bay or Buffalo on Lake Erie. Now I will be able to tell my own Great Lakes stories, ones that will extend beyond the smallest of the lakes to include the Welland Canal and Lake Ontario and the St. Lawrence Seaway itself, all the way to Montreal, where no one I know has even been.

As we stare at the passing shoreline, I say to my guide, "I can't believe it. Going all the way into Lake Erie tonight. This is so cool."

The other, who finally introduces himself as Johnny, says, "You think this is cool. Just wait till after supper when everyone gets together up here for the night. That's when the fun starts."

"This whole deck is just for the crew?" I gasp, unable to contain my excitement.

"All ours," says Johnny grandly. "And it really gets to be fun later when the chicks get off work."

After a few more minutes of silent gazing, Johnny says, "Okay. You know how to get up here. I've gotta get back to the game down below. See you around."

"Yeah. Thanks, man. This is great," I respond as I drink in the view and feel the warm summery breeze of the river on my face.

I amble over to the railing and simply peer at the passing shoreline. The *South American* is making good time I note while admiring the foamy wake astern. We are already passing the salt mines outside Windsor and approaching the Livingstone Channel for downbound shipping. The dozens of times I had been down the river, I have never taken this channel. Another first, I think with mounting excitement.

The afternoon is still full of sun and warm breezes as I relax into a deck chair. I wonder idly why more crew aren't up here enjoying the

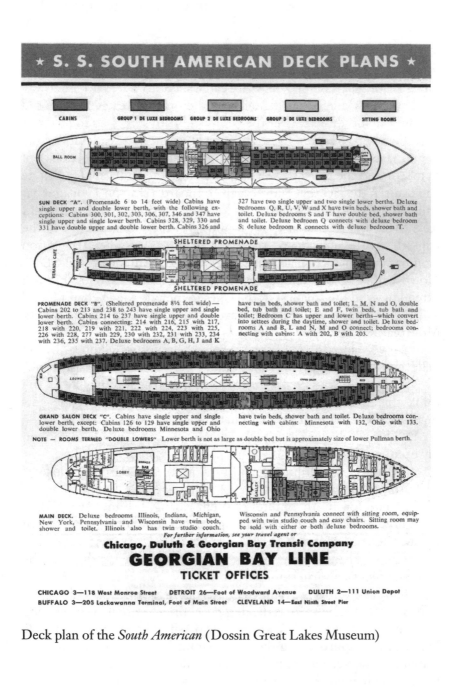

★ S. S. SOUTH AMERICAN DECK PLANS ★

CABINS   GROUP 1 DE LUXE BEDROOMS   GROUP 2 DE LUXE BEDROOMS   GROUP 3 DE LUXE BEDROOMS   SITTING ROOMS

SUN DECK "A". (Promenade 6 to 14 feet wide) Cabins have single upper and double lower berth, with the following exceptions: Cabins 300, 301, 302, 303, 306, 307, 346 and 347 have single upper and single lower berth. Cabins 328, 329, 330 and 331 have double upper and double lower berth. Cabins 326 and 327 have two single upper and two single lower berths. Deluxe bedrooms Q, R, U, V, W and X have twin beds, shower bath and toilet. Deluxe bedrooms S and T have double bed, shower bath and toilet. Deluxe bedroom Q connects with deluxe bedroom S; deluxe bedroom R connects with deluxe bedroom T.

PROMENADE DECK "B". (Sheltered promenade 8½ feet wide)— Cabins 202 to 213 and 238 to 243 have single upper and single lower berth. Cabins 214 to 237 have single upper and double lower berth. Cabins connecting: 214 with 216, 215 with 217, 218 with 220, 219 with 221, 222 with 224, 223 with 225, 226 with 228, 277 with 229, 230 with 232, 231 with 233, 234 with 236, 235 with 237. Deluxe bedrooms A, B, G, H, J and K have twin beds, shower bath and toilet; L, M, N and O, double bed, tub bath and toilet; E and F, twin beds, tub bath and toilet; Bedroom C has upper and lower berths—which convert into settees during the daytime, shower and toilet. De luxe bedrooms A and B, L and N, M and O connect; bedrooms connecting with cabins: A with 202, B with 203.

GRAND SALON DECK "C". Cabins have single upper and single lower berth, except: Cabins 126 to 129 have single upper and double lower berth. Cabins bedrooms Minnesota and Ohio have twin beds, shower bath and toilet. Deluxe bedrooms connecting with cabins: Minnesota with 132, Ohio with 133.

NOTE — ROOMS TERMED "DOUBLE LOWERS" Lower berth is not as large as double bed but is approximately size of lower Pullman berth.

MAIN DECK. Deluxe bedrooms Illinois, Indiana, Michigan, New York, Pennsylvania and Wisconsin have twin beds, shower and toilet. Illinois also has twin studio couch. Wisconsin and Pennsylvania connect with sitting room, equipped with twin studio couch and easy chairs. Sitting room may be sold with either or both deluxe bedrooms.

For further information, see your travel agent or

Chicago, Duluth & Georgian Bay Transit Company

GEORGIAN BAY LINE

TICKET OFFICES

CHICAGO 3—118 West Monroe Street   DETROIT 26—Foot of Woodward Avenue   DULUTH 2—111 Union Depot
BUFFALO 3—205 Lackawanna Terminal, Foot of Main Street   CLEVELAND 14—East Ninth Street Pier

Deck plan of the *South American* (Dossin Great Lakes Museum)

scenery on such a beautiful day. The only other people up here are a couple of girls stretched out reading novels while trying to perfect their tans in the sun's long slanting rays. I casually wander over and say, "Nice day."

The dark-haired one lowers her book long enough to give me the once over and respond, "You new crew?"

"That's me," I answer, shaking my head and smiling. "I never dreamed I'd actually be out here on this river today. This is great."

"Yeah, it's okay," the dark-haired one replies.

"Beats the hell out of working in the city," her blond companion tosses in.

"So what do you do on here?" I ask.

"We do the room service for the rich people."

"Yeah, we're the housekeepers."

"That's cool," I respond. "Sounds better than being a dishwasher."

"That's what you do?" the blond asks, turning her head enough to give me a cursory once over.

"Yep."

"Uh, I hate to tell you, but aren't you supposed to be in the galley a half-hour ago?"

My heart flips a beat at this news. "Uh, I dunno. No one told me."

"I think you're right," the dark-haired girl confirms. "I heard first sitting called about then."

I blanch at this confirmation and say, "I guess I'd better get back down there."

"Nice meeting you," the dark-haired girl offers nonchalantly with a laugh at my embarrassment.

"Yeah. Same here. Maybe I'll see you later," I respond, already turning to go down the ladder.

I hustle all the way down, barely remembering the turns in the labyrinth of below decks. Back at my bunk, I quickly don my work trousers and white tunic, stiff with starch. I ask directions from one of the guys entering the card game to the galley. I follow a passage on the first deck to a long flight of stairs that takes me down to a steamy cacophonous room filled with bodies flurrying every which way. I notice that tons of dishes are being piled in one location near the corner. There I recognize the two other new crew members who signed on with me, Chris and Chuck. They are in the midst of stacking dirty dishes into a huge basket that is on a conveyor belt into a giant grey pass-through dishwasher with "Hobart" engraved on it. On the other end of the washer is a short, stumpy black man who is streaming with sweat. He notices me and yells, "Man, where the hell you been?"

I stammer "I, I didn't know I was . . ."

"Man, don't matter. Just better be here when you supposed to from now on. Now get these dishes out of here and stack 'em like this. No. You got to move faster. Look at all them dishes waiting to come through. You wanna be here till midnight? Yeah, that's right. You gotta stack 'em in these racks like this. Okay, that's all you gotta do for now. Just keep doing that job every time a basket comes through. But you gotta work fast."

I quickly lose myself in the fevered pace of the work. After a few minutes, I am absorbed in trying to work my way through basket after basket to keep from being buried in the volume of dishes pouring from the dryer. When I am just about immersed in the pile before me, I glance up to see the man, Chris, and Chuck all staring at me with big grins on their faces. Perplexed, I stop to try and figure out what they are looking at. When their smiles explode into laughter, I have a pretty good idea. The black guy is the first one to talk, saying, "Yeah, I guess you gonna have to do. Name's Freddie. What's yours?"

"Pat"

"Pat?" Hear that John?" he yells to a grey-haired, frazzled-looking man working away at the glass cleaner. "You got Pat and Chuck and Chris and Freddie on this trip. I think we're on our way to a good time."

The man pauses only long enough to turn his grizzled head up to grunt something that sounds like, "Yeah. Real good." He is absorbed in his task which involves taking dirty glasses, one in each hand, and plunging them onto two rotating brushes in a tub of soapy water. He then takes the glasses and puts them in a drying rack. We all stare at John for a few silent seconds before Freddie yells, "C'mon, dishes pilin' up again. Let's get at 'em before they get us."

After another ten minutes have passed, I notice the flow of incoming dishes has slowed to a crawl and we are caught up. I think that this isn't so bad when Freddie turns to us pulling off his rubber gloves and says, "Break time, boys. You can all go up for some air if you want."

"Break?" I ask. "You mean we're not done?"

"We're about halfway done," says Chuck, who has tied a white rag around his sweating head. We three new crew climb the long flight of iron steps to the fresh air of the summer evening. There is still a lot of daylight pouring through the top half of the open gangway and I immediately peer through the railing for a glimpse of the familiar river. I am both disappointed and elated for I see only the open water of what must be Lake Erie with no land in sight. I have missed the trip out of the river past Bob-Lo Island, my previous land's end, and I am adrift in the smallest of the Great Lakes. I cling to the railing and say to my companions, "Wow. Lake Erie."

"Yeah, man. We're on the way to Montreal," exclaims Chuck, pronouncing the word "moan-ray-owl" in an affected French-Canadian accent. "That's the way they say it." He repeats it for our benefit, rolling the "r."

Before we have had too much time to look at the water and enjoy the relatively cool breeze of the deck, Freddie appears at the top of the steps and yells, "They're comin' in again. Time to get back at it." And we troop back down the steps into the heat of the kitchen, our sweating clothing sticking to our backs and legs. Soon we are again awash in a sea of dishes and struggle to stay afloat against the filthy incoming tide of crockery, glass, and silverware.

Beads of sweat drop from our brows to mingle with the sudsy dishwater while the racket of the Hobart—as we refer to the dishwasher—makes it all but impossible to communicate other than by shouting.

Just when it seems that we will never get out from under the flood brought forth by the straining busboys and waitresses, there is a respite and the pile is lessened to almost realistic proportions. The Hobart begins to gain ground on the pile and the finished and reracked gleaming stacks of plates once again assert their presence. John continues to work away at the glasses and soon has them nestled in their plastic racks of twenty-four. Freddie begins to show us how to clean up and put the machines to sleep for the night. This time, when we drag ourselves up to the deck, the sun has set and twilight is upon us.

Leaving the professionals, Freddie and John, to their routines, Chris, Chuck, and I make our way back down to the Flicker where the still, warm air makes us peel our soaked uniforms away from our skin. "I'm gonna shower before I do anything, man," groans Chuck.

"Yeah," agrees Chris. "But what do we do with these clothes? Mine are soaked."

"Mine too," I echo. "Maybe we can hang them up somewhere."

"Yeah. Maybe there's a place down here," says Chuck, looking around.

We search in vain, unable to locate a clothesline. Finally, Freddie, passing through, says, "Find wherever you can for those. Just make sure they don't cover anything of anyone else's. If you do, they'll just throw 'em overboard and Clarence'll charge you for 'em."

Encouraged by this, we become more practical. Chuck hangs his from the top of the locker he was fortunate enough to secure. Chris and I are forced to hang ours from the railings of our bunks.

We then retreat to the showers, a dubious rigging of pipes and dripping, lukewarm water in a narrow tiled room that is the best the aging vessel can do for the crew. We wash the sweat from our skin with little bars of soap we find in the racks. The thin white towels we have been issued are enough on a warm night to dry us but they become another soaked item to hang.

Back in casual clothes, Chuck ventures, "What say we head up to the top deck?"

Chris chimes in with, "Yeah. That's where all the waitresses are."

"So let's go," I agree.

We reconnoiter the route back through the windlass and steering cable room and negotiate our way up the system of ladders and stairs to the top stern deck. To climb the last flight of the ladder, we have to pass the ballroom. I note that the ship's orchestra is in full swing and the room is full of dancing passengers.

Up above on the open top deck, there are about twenty-five of the ship's young crew. They are assembled in small groups and chatting among themselves. A few are holding Cokes and some are smoking, but the more outrageous of the lot quickly distinguish themselves by their loud humor. Many of the waiters and waitresses that I noticed earlier in the kitchen are clustered together and have the clean-cut looks of college brothers and sisters. For the first time, I note that most don't have the Beatle-inspired look I had become used to seeing the previous winter and spring. The frat gang seems to be modeled more on the Kingston Trio and appears a closed circle anyway. The girls are harder to peg as anything different from the Jackie Kennedy lookbook. And, worst of all, no one notices the newest crew members except for a few waitresses who give us a quick once-over before going back to their sorority-laced conversation around the railing. Toward the stern is another collection of females gathered around a girl with a guitar who is singing the Scarborough Fair canticle from the latest Simon and Garfunkel album.

The night is still warm and the ship's progress through the dull darkness is marked by a pleasant breeze, cooling to the skin. Chuck lights up a cigarette, exhales, and chuckles to himself. "Finally out of the city," he wheezes. "We made it."

"I don't know about you, but those dishes kicked my butt," says Chris.

"Freddie said to be back there at seven for the breakfast dishes," I say, feeling the ache in my arms from all the dishes I lifted.

"Yeah," says Chris. "That means we've gotta get up in time for our own breakfast before that."

"Yeah, I'm gonna head down and see what my bunk's like," says Chuck, flicking his cigarette over the railing into the darkness and stretching his arms.

As we head down through the ladder system that leads us through the ship's entrails, I say aloud, "Wonder where we'll wake up tomorrow."

My new shipmates are too fixated on their bunks to answer.

In the Canal

Morning comes to the dark Flicker with no light. My first vision is of Freddie's face when he appears as an apparition from nowhere and tells me to get up. I groggily shake the sheet off my clammy body and then work my way out of the bunk and down to the floor. I rummage through my suitcase for a change of underwear and then grope for my work uniform. Disappointed, I let it fall back to its spot. Still soaked. I rummage again for the only spare that Clarence provided, recalling the warning that this would have to last me for a week.

Pulling on my still damp tennis shoes, I catch Chris on his way to the crew's mess toward the port bow on the main deck. We walk down a corridor that takes us by some windows that allow us to look down on the sweating engine room with its throbbing pistons. We pass a few cabins and then enter a galley full of pots and pans and a few steam tables that lead us to the crew's mess, a tiny box of a room that contains five long tables with four stools per side. About half of the seats are taken and the assembled eaters are at various stages of their breakfasts. As soon as we are seated, the lumpish waiter in a white mess jacket appears at the doorway and looks at us expectantly. After a moment of blank staring he says, "You must be the new guys."

I return the greeting, saying, "Yeah."

The kid says, "Well, the first thing is that the first three tables are reserved for deck and engine crew. You guys have to move to the last two tables." After he confirms that we have relocated to the sanctioned spot, he nods to a black board on the wall and says with a smirk, "Now you're supposed to tell me what you want for breakfast so I can bring it to you."

"Don't waste your time," pipes up a guy, also in dress whites. "Whatever you ask for, he brings everyone the same stuff. Wouldn't quite call it food," he adds, going back to his toast.

"So whaddya got?" I ask.

He reads the board as if to a moron, glaring at me. "Toast and eggs. French toast. If you want cereal, you get it on the way in. Boxes are out there."

"I'll have the French toast," I say and Chris holds up two fingers. Getting the message, the kid disappears and returns in seconds with two plates, each with three pieces of French toast. "Everything you need's on the table," he grunts, putting the dishes down in front of us.

The breakfast is a pretty subdued affair with a lot of scraping, slurping, and chewing but little conversation. No one lingers over a second cup of coffee. Chris and I find the mess not that comfortable a place. As crew members finish, they simply get up and leave. If they are with a companion, we hear a murmured "See you later" but not even that with most. As we finish our breakfasts, we simply follow suit and exit the stark spot.

We climb back down below decks to the dishwashing area and are somewhat relieved to find that the pace, though steady, is nowhere near as frantic as the night before.

"No sittings at breakfast," Freddie explains. "Folks just come and go as they want between seven-thirty and nine. "Lottsa folks just wanna sleep in. Catch something in the tea shop and hold out for dinner at noon. Then we get busy again."

With the slower pace, I have a chance to get to talk a little to Freddie. True to my desire, I follow my inclination to discover anything I can about this ship and other cruise ships on the Great Lakes. I ask him if he has sailed on many ships and he answers, "Nope. Just this here *South American*. And the *North*." He indicates John, the glass-washing specialist. "You wanna talk to somebody's been on a lotta these boats, you talk to him. Hell, he was on here when this ship went missing in Lake Superior for a week. They thought she went down for sure."

But when I pursue the question with the slow-talking John, he brushes it off as no big thing. His only response is "Yeah, I've been on all those D&C boats and C&B boats all around the lakes. All they are to me is one big galley after another. I'll tell you something though. With those night boats to Cleveland, you'd get guys who come on in Detroit and get off in Cleveland with enough money to get drunk for a couple days and then catch another boat going the other way. You never knew what shape they'd be in. And you had to watch out for the thieves." This gives me a whole new perspective on those beautiful ships I had envisioned cutting smartly through the sparkling lakes and rivers.

At a break up on deck, I say to Chris, "You know, I was so busy getting on board yesterday, I never even asked about how much we had to work."

"Six days a week," snaps Chuck, eager to provide information. "Get a day in Montreal. That's what Beauregard said."

"Beauregard don't know shit," interjects Freddie. "You get a day, but you gotta split it with the five of us. In Montreal we always need three of us for dinner at noon and three for supper in the evening. There's five of us. You figure," he concludes with a leer.

While I ponder that, Chris says, "Wow, so that's about ten bucks a day."

"Yeah," snorts Chuck. "Sixty-five a week and all the leftovers you want." To emphasize the point he waves a plate with smeared egg yolk and half a sausage under our noses before dumping it into the large trash can beneath the dishwasher.

"C'mon, we got another load to get in then we're about done for now," says Freddie.

After the cleanup, Chris, Chuck, and I spend some time finding locations on deck to hang our soggy clothing. "Gotta air-dry it," says Chuck "It'll just get mildewed down there in that still air."

I wander over to the half-open loading gangway and, resting my arms on the bottom of the doorway, observe, "There's a lighthouse. We're coming into land."

"Port Colborne," says a crew member who joins us. "Beginning of the Welland Canal."

"What do you do?" asks the upwardly mobile Chuck.

"I'm a deckhand," the man replies.

"So how long does it take to get through?" asks Chris.

The man snorts and says, "It all depends. They say we get right-of-way as a passenger ship. Normally takes about eight hours. But I've seen us take a lot longer. Almost overnight."

"So then we go through Lake Ontario and then through the Seaway," I conclude, having long ago committed the Great Lakes to memory. "But when do we get to Montreal?"

"If things go like they want them to, we go through the canal today and Lake Ontario overnight," explains the man patiently, finding a fleck of tobacco leaf on his lip. "Then we hit the Seaway and the Thousand Islands tomorrow afternoon and stop in Ogdensburg for a little visit. Then we spend that night going down the Seaway and locking through some more in New York state. We should wind up in Montreal sometime around early afternoon day after tomorrow, if we're lucky," he concludes, lighting a cigarette and watching as the *South*—as we have learned to call her—begins to move slowly through the waterway and toward the first lock.

I am thrilled beyond belief. I have seen ships lock through in the Welland and at the Soo in the Upper Peninsula of Michigan but I have never before been on a ship going through a lock. And I know that before we are through this canal, the *South* will have gone through eight locks until she is released into Lake Ontario.

As I bask in the wonder of being a part of this, I am mesmerized at the rapidity at which the *South American* slips into a waiting lock. I see the man we were just talking to on the dock. He is carrying a thick line along the side of the slowly moving ship. At someone's command, he places the looped end of the line over a bollard on the dock. Then he steps back and watches as another deckhand likewise secures a line from the stern of the ship. Then the *South American* is at rest until, in a matter of a couple minutes, it begins to slide down the walls of the lock. I am transfixed as the drenched cement walls slide by inches from my face as the *South* descends. There is silence as we are completely in the shadows of the vault. The silence is broken by one short blast of the ship's whistle—the signal to throw off lines—and we are once again moving forward out of the lock and back into the canal.

"Let's head up to the fantail for the next lock," I yell excitedly. "I've gotta see it from up there."

"It's either that or lunch, you guys," says Chuck.

"Already?" asks Chris incredulously.

"Remember, we have to eat before we go to work or all we get is their leftovers," says Chuck. "And, personally, that stuff they give us is just a little bit better. At least more filling."

"Yeah," I agree reluctantly. "We should have all afternoon to still be going through. We can go up to the fantail after dinner cleanup."

And we trudge back to check on the dryness of our mess clothes and prepare for the dinner shift.

It is approaching two o'clock when Chris and I mount the final rung of the ladder to the fantail. It is a scorchingly brilliant summer day and the crew are lounging all over the deck. The girls take turns splashing suntan lotion and water on their skin while the guys play cards, read magazines or books or just talk in small groups. Farther ahead toward the bow, separated from us by fifty feet, the ship's passengers are likewise engaged. From my perspective, it looks like the crew could be having more fun. It is hard to imagine a more perfect day. Chris points out as we casually observe the scene that the waitresses are younger and far more attractive than the passengers.

The *South* cruises languidly through the blazing afternoon, stopping every so often to allow a lock to clear before entering the next one and continuing its passage toward Lake Ontario. I marvel at the closeness of the ships we pass heading up into Lake Erie. There are salties and lake freighters alike but no other passenger ships. I recall hearing one of the engine room gang saying that the *South* is the only remaining passenger ship on the Great Lakes, and I am at once saddened and elated at the realization that I am here on this incredible day as the *South American* sails toward Montreal.

The idyllic afternoon becomes a bit intense as the heat of the day takes its toll on the denizens of the totally exposed fantail. The flat scenery of the canal, broken occasionally by other ships, becomes monotonous and the dank smell of the water at the bottom of the locks makes everyone just a trifle nauseated. It is almost with a sense of relief

S.S. *South American*

Built	1914
Builder	Great Lakes Engineering Works, Ecorse, Michigan
Owner	Chicago, Duluth and Georgian Bay Transit Company
Length	321'
Beam	47'1"
Draft	18'3"
Capacity	521 passengers; 160 crew
Engine	Quadruple expansion steam
Boilers	Three Scotch oil-fired
Events	Burned to waterline at dock in Holland, Michigan, 1921

that the fantail deck is cleared for everyone to head down to prepare for supper.

Still overwhelmed at the simple amazing fact that I am on board, I pull myself into my still damp uniform. I head down the alleyway and the iron stairs to the ever-hungry Hobart machine that eats the ships' dishes, glasses, and silverware brought to us by the white-suited, clean-cut busboys who burst through the door from the large dining room. Tonight there are remnants of one of the cruise specialties— frog legs—for us to scrape.

After another grueling session, I am too weary to even consider climbing back up to the fantail for the evening. A glance through the gangway is enough to let me know that we are still in the canal. I shower in the decaying, tiny stall and then lay down to rest. Within minutes I am wrestling the boogeymen of the engine room as the ship's whistle signals the deckhands to cast off toward the final lock in the system. I sweat through sleep in my bunk as the ship finally breaks free into the cooling breeze of Lake Ontario.

THE THOUSAND ISLANDS

Another morning and I am becoming used to the routine: rise and tug on the soggy white galley outfit; walk to the crew mess; take whatever

The lobby of the *South American*, where passengers were greeted as they entered the ship (Dossin Great Lakes Museum)

is on the menu; eat and head down to the galley; sweat it out with Freddie, John, Chuck, and Chris; head up to the fantail; find a lounge chair and collapse for a while, notice the grey waves of Lake Ontario as they meet the overcast sky on the tropical day; BS with the guys; banter with and ogle the girls; head back down and pull on the still wet galley outfit for dinner. . . .

It is early afternoon on the fantail when I notice that we are once again approaching land. I am amazed to hear the ship's PA begin a taped tour of the Thousand Islands that we are beginning to sail through. For the next couple of hours, I am entertained by the corny monologue telling of the history of salad dressing as well as the area's castles and romantic past.

By mid-afternoon, the *South* is approaching a wide river spanned by a large steel bridge. The ship is going to dock at a nearby town called Ogdensburg for an hour of offshore fun for the passengers.

Chris grabs me and says, "Let's go. This is our chance to hit a bar." For, as I hardly need to be reminded, the drinking age in New York state is eighteen, an age that I have recently attained. So I throw

The *South American* in
the St. Lambert lock,
approaching Montreal
(Dossin Great Lakes
Museum)

on a shirt and we follow the passengers a couple of blocks up the street.
My first stop is a local five-and-dime where I acquire an alarm clock
to help me wake up. Freddie has warned me for the last time about
being late. Next time he says he will go right to Beauregard and they'll
dump me in Montreal. Our next stop is a seamy sort of bar unfre-
quented by any of the passengers or crew that we can recognize. In
keeping with my working-class upbringing, I order a shot and a beer
and nurse the combo. Brooke, one of the waitresses, has joined us and
she orders a Seven and Seven. Chris orders a Genesee and we settle
into the novelty of being where we are. But that quickly wears off, the
place is so unremarkable, a bar of wood and brick exterior, occupied
by a few half-crocked locals, that we are relieved to hear the ship's
whistle as an excuse to head back and prepare for supper dishes.

As we take our evening break at the gangway, I note that the ship has entered another lock—the Snellnois, somebody says. And we will be passing through more through the night as we descend to sea level along the St. Lawrence Seaway. Facing the blackness of the night as I finally emerge from the galley almost two hours later, my mind is focused only on the bunk.

MONTREAL

The third morning out from Detroit finds the *South* steaming down the seaway approaching Montreal. The excitement mounts through-out the morning and the sittings at the midday meal are light and somewhat hurried as passengers opt to spend as much time on deck as possible. By early afternoon, Chris, Chuck, and I are stationed on the port side of the fantail as the *South* begins to cruise by the islands adjacent the city. We marvel at the skyline and then try to identify the various pavilions on the Expo 67 site itself. We can agree only on the Buckminster Fuller-designed geodesic dome. Most of the rest of the crew take the sightings in stride, having already witnessed this a few times. But a deck below, the passengers are drinking it all in as eagerly as we are. Along the way, we hear cries of "There's La Ronde" and "Check out the Habitat 67."

Within an hour, the *South* has negotiated her way through the St. Lambert Lock into a slip at Quai 57 beneath a tall clock tower. Almost immediately, passengers begin to disembark through the same starboard-side gangway that they had used to enter the ship some sev-enty-two hours before. As we watch them stream away from our spot on the fantail, Chuck says, "Here's where we get a break. Forty-eight hours in old Moan-ray-owl."

"And hardly anyone to feed," seconds Chris.

"Freddie says we each get three meals off now. But not all at the same time."

"Yeah. He says three people have to do the galley at dinner. But only two at the breakfast and lunch."

"And him and John get first dibs on when."

"So what do we do?" I ask.

"Well, I wouldn't mind working tonight if I can get all day tomor-row," says Chuck.

"I wouldn't mind a full day either," says Chris, upping the ante.

The *South American* passing Expo 67 and the Russian Pavilion (Dossin Great Lakes Museum)

"You mean we actually get three meals off?" I ask incredulously. "Heck, I don't care when, I'll just take 'em."

With the *South* snuggled in her berth, passengers continue to stream off for a big night on the town, leaving the ship almost deserted.

"You kids might as well run up the street," says Freddie as we finish up another paltry load of dishes and the second sitting fails to materialize. Within seconds we are down in the Flicker throwing on our best street clothes, combing our hair, and joining the throng of crew heading across the dirt road, across railway tracks, and toward town. But we only get as far as the bar of a union hall on the far side of the street where we become enamored of the heavy ales proffered by the bartender in what is obviously a labor hangout. From my seat on a rickety wooden chair, I can see the sign on the nearby Molson brewery just down the block. Bartender, one more *s'il vous plait*.

And so, a few heavy ales later, we wheel ourselves back across the tracks to our warm bunks and another night aboard the ship.

The next morning brings news of a crew picnic up on Mount Royal. It is determined by Freddie that he and John can handle the lunch dishes, the few that are expected, so I pile into a cab with a bunch of others and we tool up onto Mount Royal high above the city. At the picnic are guitars and even some food that a couple of the waitresses have squirreled away from somewhere. The day is pure high summer, full of dazzling sunlight and frisbees, a guitarist again singing Scarborough Fair, and someone passing out bottles of ale. Most impressive are the beautiful young crew women. Chris and I spend a lot of the afternoon with them just trying to make conversation and our efforts meet with some success.

As I wheel down the mountain in the late afternoon with my new-found friends, I begin to realize the benefits of the sailing life. And, stopping for one last one on my way back to the ship at the local, I begin to think I might be able to tolerate the dishes for a while longer.

With the ship scheduled to depart the next afternoon, I wheedle one last break from Freddie to go and see Expo 67. I find my way to the Metro station and quickly figure out the maps to get me where I am going. The trains are sleek, new, and smooth, hissing on a cushion of air into the clean new station. We are at Expo in no time. With only the morning and part of the afternoon to spend, I need to prioritize my visit. The dome is first on the list but the wait is formidable. I decide against that and the equally popular Soviet exhibit. I wander until I come to La Ronde and determine that, if nothing else, I will ride the vaunted Gyrotron. This line is long too, but I persevere and am rewarded with a seat on a car riding a track into the sky toward a huge structure that emits strange sounds. At the top, the car enters the darkened cavern and I see planets and worlds coming together. The car proceeds slowly down a curving track that takes me deeper into the solar system and then beyond to deep space. By the time I reemerge into daylight I am a little disappointed that there are no real speed hills or thrills, just strobe-lit visuals. But I quickly forget that as I reengage with the Expo itself. I spend the rest of the time wandering the grounds, visiting the less-trafficked pavilions and gawking at the beauty of the site itself. But then I realize that I need to get back to the *South*, that the afternoon is already well on its way and that I don't really want to be stranded in this expensive place with no money.

So I race back across town on the Metro and run the last few blocks back to Quai 57, passing on the chance to catch one more ale before departure. As it is, I am back with sufficient time to clamber back into my galley clothes and amble down to the galley where Freddie, John, Chris, and Chuck are patiently waiting for the dishes from the first sitting to begin rolling in.

With a few blasts of her beautiful steam chimes rolling off the adjacent warehouses, the *South* begins a slow turnaround maneuver that will take her back into the homeward channel. I hypnotically attend to the Hobart, knowing that I have one great adventure under my belt. I am pleasantly surprised to find that this has only whetted my appetite for more.

The return trip to Detroit is full of work on the Hobart as the sultry days of summer overtake the *South*. The card game continues in the Flicker. The evenings on the fantail become casual get-togethers that bring to a close another sweltering day in the galley. This time, when the ship stops in Ogdensburg, several of the crew take this opportunity to dive off the end of the dock into the surprisingly cold waters of Lake Ontario.

As the *South* crawls across tepid Erie toward home, I look forward to seeing the old world from a totally different perspective. Aside from some summer camp experience, this is my maiden voyage from the home. I have been away for the first time by myself. I have a world to relate to that no one from the world I left has touched. And I am surprised at how I have not stopped to give it a moment of thought until now.

When the ship docks in Detroit, it is a Saturday morning around ten o'clock. I call home to find that everything is going well. I am comforted by the news that no one has died or even been injured in my absence. Even more importantly, no one has had a comparable adventure. There have been no more love-ins or even good parties according to my sources.

I take advantage of a few hours off to take Chris and Al, a crew member from Ohio, to see the city and visit my cousin on the west side. On the way we stop at the SIU hall on Jefferson to check out the positions available. We are given pretty short shrift by the union people to whom we are now paying dues and leave feeling like second-class members. Al, who is going to be a junior at Ohio State and has been on the *South* for a few trips already, tells us that we are considered such because the Georgian Bay Line and the union have agreed to exempt us from the regular pay scale. This is due to the fact that we have so many crew members that it would be impossible for the company to stay afloat financially. The licensed crew, including deck-hands and engine room help, get their union scale while the rest of us get something approaching minimum wage. But I am at a point in my sailing career where I am overjoyed at simply being considered a crew member aboard the *South*.

When we get back to the ship, Beauregard corrals us with a promise of some overtime hours if we will help load ship's stores. The promise of more money brings the three of us quickly back into uniform and we begin dollying caseloads of canned goods and produce onto the ship. The route takes us from the dock along a narrow gangplank and through a wide hatchway where we deposit our loads in a staggering pile on the deck.

The process is haphazard at best with a dozen or more crew negotiating their way through the narrow gangway and along the increasingly congested deck. At one point, I twist a load the wrong way and trip over a stray box. I go down on my back with a full box of cans crashing into the side of my knee. I lay there stunned on the deck as my leg begins to throb and I see blood seeping through my white pants. I manage to get to my feet and out of the way of the caravan marching through oblivious to my injury. I limp to the side and manage to catch Beauregard's attention. He glances dismissively at my wound and then, seeing the pain in my eyes, says, "Better get the ship's doctor to look at that." This is news to me. I had no idea there was a doctor on board. I follow the command toward the front of the ship until I come to a tiny door marked "doctor." I am further surprised to find a man inside. He brings me in and conducts a quick exam of my injury. He assures me that nothing is broken. As he staunches the blood with a large bandage, he asks if I've had a tetanus shot and releases me to rest in the Flicker.

But no sooner do I exit his cabin door than I am accosted by Beauregard. He says, "Nothing broken, right?" to confirm the doctor's finding. At my acknowledgment, he continues, "You know, we really need to get these stores on board. If you were able to keep on helping, you might get that promotion to the night gang you requested." In no time at all, I'm on my feet and back struggling to drag yet another dolly full of cans across the gangway and onto the *South*.

I don't know if I am delirious and have imagined this scene or not. All I know is that, if it's true, I won't have to report to the galley for dishwashing tonight. Instead, I can join the night gang and spend all night cleaning the ship, whatever that means. Most important, it means freedom from the Hobart and the drenched uniforms that I have had to climb into three times a day for the past eight days. This is enough to make me ignore the pain in my leg and carry on until all the supplies are on board.

As my reward, I receive three hours OT and then Beauregard's much awaited words, "Report to the ship's boatswain at 11:30. He'll show you the job."

On the Night Gang

At 11:30 sharp, Chris, Chuck, and I join the boatswain for an orientation to our new assignment on the night gang. Our duties take us through the now darkened galley where we train streams of water from high pressure hoses onto the pipes that crisscross the high ceiling, the walls, and down to the floor where the water gurgles through the large drains.

Then we are given permission to wander the carpeted hallways of the otherwise forbidden guest decks to vacuum and clean the floors and polish the brass rails of the grand staircase. After that we are directed to the promenade decks again with the hoses and an admonition to miss no speck of dirt. The *South* must be made to gleam in the first light of fast-approaching morning. By 5 AM we drag our exhausted carcasses to the crew's mess where we are allowed to order an early breakfast before disappearing to our bunks for the remainder of the morning.

The altered schedule makes this trip to Montreal pass even faster than the first. While the night gang work is a sight easier than the dishwashing chores, I find that I'm sleeping through some of the best parts of the trip. But the evenings on the fantail help compensate. With the guarantee of full July warmth, the crew ascends the single ladder to the topmost deck of the *South* with a unified purpose to escape into the relaxing breeze of the canal, lake, or islands—to whatever point the progress of the ship has brought us. There is nothing remarkable about these evenings. The usual conversations take place as the guys compare sports and frat notes and a clique of girls gathers around one of the waitresses who has brought her guitar to the scene. What is worthwhile is simply the fact that we are all young and together and that is really all we need. The fact that we are on a cruise ship heading to Montreal on a warm night as opposed to heading for a prison camp in the Gulag does help us to enjoy ourselves just a trifle more. What I enjoy even more is, when the rest of the crew have yielded to the reality of the rapidly-approaching morning and abandon the deck for their bunks, Chris, Chuck, and I glide into the softest chairs and revel in the fact that we now have the fantail to ourselves—at least until midnight when the night gang is again called to action.

Another advantage arises when we arrive in Montreal and one of the ship's pursers asks me if I'd like to make another $15 serving as a tour guide to some of the ship's ubiquitous senior passengers at Expo 67. Because I have no daytime responsibilities, this is too perfect and I readily and groggily agree. The opportunity to supplement my meager weekly income of $65 is a great incentive as is the opportunity to see the Expo from a different perspective. The fact that I have only been to the site once in my life seems to be no impediment as I am provided a sheet of directions and a time and place to meet the group.

Once there, I find that my few hours of experience and the map have indeed thrust me into a superior position. The group is too busy gaping to be concerned about my map-reading and the fact that I'm able to distinguish the German pavilion from the Russian vouchsafes my qualifications. I also discover that our formal status as a group allows us access to special queues that bypass the hour-long lines that last week prevented me from seeing more. And thus we glide through the big-ticket places like the "Man and His World" exhibition and the Russian pavilion. We are even able to get into the U.S. Bucky Fuller Dome, considered by many to be the highlight of the expo.

As the tour ends and I bid my guests a professional adieu, I discover that I still have many hours to spend at Expo 67 before my midnight shift. And so I explore places like the British bookstore full of Penguin classics and, feeling flush, actually purchase the collected writings of John Lennon in one thin volume. I go into the German restaurant and order some sauerbraten and beer, both of which

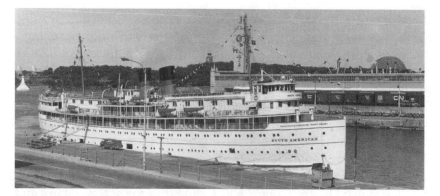

The *South American* at Quai 57, Victoria Pier, Montreal, with
Buckminster Fuller's geodesic dome and the U.S. Pavilion at Expo 67 in
the background. (Dossin Great Lakes Museum)

disappoint and leave me longing for the union hall bar near the ship.
I wander by the shows like Hellzapoppin' that require an extra admis-
sion fee and wind up at a free stage show watching a variation of the
Motown Review.

As the expo closes its gates, I wander back to Le Metro and
whoosh my way back to Quai 57 and its distinctive clock tower. I navigate the last few dangerous steps that separate the union hall from
the ship and think about how much more fun I seem to be having than
the wealthy old passengers who are paying me to be here.

Before I go on duty at midnight, I join some of my companions
on the fantail to witness the nightly fireworks spectacular from Expo
67 which is situated just across the river from our dock. As I watch the
soft colors explode over the dark water, I reflect that we are not merely
voyeurs but part of the beauty cascading all around us. If we don't see
it all this time around, we'll be back next week for another go at it.

The next night finds a few of us walking around Ste. Catherine's
Street past the boutiques and night clubs. The fact that we don't have
enough money to pay a cover charge is accompanied by the shared
feeling that we don't really need to get away to a night club. Our youth
and just being a part of this experience seems to be all we need. Being
a part of the *South* in this summer of '67 means that we work pretty
hard for six days and have a different Great Lakes scene from the fan-

tail every night. And then we have Montreal for two-and-a-half days before we are back in the seaway.

We arrive in Detroit on a quiet Sunday morning. After a lifeboat drill that actually sends a boatload of crew rowing around in the river, I take advantage of the timing to head home for a pleasant afternoon with the folks. But there is too little time to do more than say hello and cadge a ride back down to the dock at the foot of Bates Street. I need to be back at least a full hour before the five o'clock sailing time to report to my newest job—that of tea room porter. This position is regarded by many as the premier low-paying position on the ship. While the pay does not come anywhere near competing with that of deckhand or even waiter, the tea room porter, formerly held by a popular crew member known by all as "Tea Room Johnny," is seen by all as downright sweet.

The fact that the job has been offered to me has come via an unorthodox route—Tea Room Johnny himself. As one of the crew's most notable bon vivants, Johnny's desire to be in the midst of life has been somewhat constrained by his tea room duties. He has seen in my position on the night gang an opportunity to have more free time during the daylight hours. Coupled with the fact that the work hours are relatively short and coincide with the hours that the ongoing card game in the Flicker is in low gear if running at all, the night gang and Johnny could be a marriage made in heaven. And thus it was last night as the ship exited the Welland Canal and entered Lake Erie that Johnny approached me with the proposition for a job swap. He assured me that it was a done deal if I agreed, that he had already gotten Beauregard's okay. Once I was assured that I wouldn't be losing any money on the deal, I decided that going back to days was preferable to the all night grunting of lugging hoses around the decks of the sleeping ship. Even more important was the fact that I didn't like the hours. I couldn't figure out which way was up whatever strange hour it was that I awoke, feeling simultaneously that I had lost a precious part of the day and that I had nothing to look forward to except work followed by more fitful, unfulfilling moments of sleep. And so the deal was sealed on the fantail as we looked onto the black night enveloping Lake Erie.

The tea room itself is situated at the stern of the second deck immediately below the ballroom and two decks below the poopdeck.

It is a tiny spot tucked cosily into the curvature of the ship. On one side there is a tiny counter complete with soda fountain and candy counter. On the other side, a couple of small round tables and chairs separated by a book rack and a magazine rack tucked behind a shelf sharing space with caps and suntan lotions. Best of all, the room is windowed on three sides so that it is possible to see the world while working, a luxury afforded by few other nondeck positions on this ship.

As I report for duty I meet Marge and Violet, the other staff for the room. Marge is a spinsterish-looking woman, tall and thin with a peanut brittle frame. She is in charge of the tea room and therefore my boss. She greets me and explains to me my duties which sound a lot like just being around to help her and Violet serve the people who walk in the door. I am also supposed to be on call to deliver beverages to cabin parties that may occur at various parts of the ship. Not too tough, I figure. Violet is an Andalusian-looking plump young beauty, a few years too old for my young blond tastes but something to look at nevertheless. She is quiet and demure and Marge seems protective of her when introducing us. My new outfit is designed for public show and is a lot cleaner and fresher than the outfits I've worn the past couple of jobs on the *South*. I take my place behind the counter as the first few customers enter in search of a Coke or candy bar. Learning the cash register is a minor challenge and before long I'm ringing up sales as the traffic grows. From my post I can hear the ship's orchestra serenading the dock with songs like "Sailing Down the River (on a Sunday Afternoon)," "Mame" and "Hello Dolly" as the lines are thrown off and we swing around into the river for another voyage to Montreal. Tea room sales are not so brisk as to prevent me from stealing long glimpses as the ship makes its way under the Ambassador Bridge past familiar landmarks along the Detroit and Windsor shorelines. This Sunday has lived up to its name, I think as I gaze contentedly on. From my vantage point, I can look over the tops of the decaying riverfront warehouses and see the immense hulk of the Michigan Central Railroad station and the light towers surrounding Tiger Stadium as well as the spires of Ste. Anne's church. Appropriate to a Sunday afternoon, the city looks full of calm and tranquility.

The tea room is open most of the day and into the evening so our hours are split. For this first day, Marge has me work until ten o'clock so she can show me how to close up the shop, a not very time-consuming task that includes such exciting features as turning out lights and locking the French doors that open onto the stern deck. Because the tea room doesn't open until 8 AM for those wishing to forego breakfast and just have coffee, I head down to the Flicker thinking to change before heading up to the fantail for a glimpse at the lake to catch the breeze before rest. I look forward to seeing my shipmates either getting off their jobs or getting ready to go to work. I am surprised to discover that the tea room work has left me untired compared to the dishwashing and night gang chores. But as I get down to the Flicker, I begin to hear alarming words: "riot" coupled with "Detroit." I check into information central at the card table and can only learn that someone has heard the radio talking about my hometown under siege. The game goes on, regardless. In shock, I make my way up to the fantail and try to reconcile the visions of tranquility I had witnessed a few hours before with the idea of men running wild in the streets. I discover that most of the crew is not even from Detroit and has little empathy for me. Even those who live in the city seem unaffected and accept the reality of rioting as a fact of life in the sixties. I toss and turn in my bunk, unable to sleep, my prayers discounted by the haunting fears at what might be happening to my family and my city.

I manage to carry on through the next day, although I find my thoughts consumed with worry about my family and friends. I consider the possibility of having to request permission to get off the ship so that I can return by bus or rail. Yet those around me are content to shrug it off as another fact of life that goes with growing up in these crazy times of ours. I'm told by one of the crew that the situation is not even considered severe enough to warrant my placing a call over the ship-to-shore radio. As the *South* works its way through the locks of the Welland Canal, someone tries to comfort me by saying, "If someone really needs to find you, you'll know. And then you won't wanna know." I take no comfort in those words.

By the afternoon of Tuesday, our second day out, the ship stops at Ogdensburg and I race up the street in search of news. I find it in the form of a paper's headline that screams "Carnival in Detroit." The headline oddly comforts me and my images of the riot are transformed from those of maniacs running with machetes through blood-

Twelfth and Clairmount Streets, the epicenter of the 1967 Detroit riot, early in the uprising (Walter P. Reuther Library, Wayne State University)

drenched streets to jovial crowds peacefully looting and burning stores with goodwill and fun in their hearts. I keep coming back to a picture of a man exiting through a store's broken plate glass window with a television in his arms. He is smiling as are those who are running past him to the next place. I hold that picture as evidence against the other visions of anarchy and mob violence that torture me as the *South* continues her placid run through the St. Lawrence Seaway.

I manage to carry that carnival image with me into Montreal where I lose myself once again in the magic of the city. The "no news is good news" mantra is something I now take to heart. Tea room duty is very light while the ship is in port and I have plenty of time to explore Montreal. I rent a motorbike and visit Habitat 67 and the Labyrinth and Mount Royal Park, discovering more than a bit of Europe at the heart of the city. But my discomfort is rekindled at the news of these foreign papers now focused less on the looting and more on the burning and the fact that the death toll is mounting. To further my sense of depression I have my first encounter with what the ship's doc calls the "Flicker Flu," a good case that keeps me trotting to the distant bank of toilets in the very bowels of the ship.

On the voyage back home, I am beset with visions of what I will find when we get back. As the ship ties up in Detroit on a sullen, warm Monday morning, I sense the quiet. A very different sort of quiet than that of the tranquil city I left behind. This quiet is that ominous absence of sound in the vicinity of a smoldering ruin days after the echoes of terror have gone.

I am met by my mother who drives me home for a brief visit. She is silent during the drive, allowing me to absorb the aftermath of the riot on the east side of the city. I can only look on in awe at the burned-out buildings along Gratiot Avenue, looking for all the world like pictures I have seen of bombed-out European towns during World War II. After a while, she gives me bits of news of what has happened in this and other parts of the city: the families we know living in the riot zone that have survived, the former St. Bernard's classmate killed by a National Guardsman, the firefighters killed by snipers, the drives to food banks to deliver food and clothing to help the newly homeless, the acts of heroism and simple neighborliness in the face of madness. But the images tell the story of a city and a people that have had too much of what it could not endure. Although I am reassured at the sight of my parent's untouched neighborhood and the large parts of the city totally unscathed by these days of rage, I know that Detroit will never be the same for me again.

As the *South* departs that Monday afternoon for yet another run to Montreal, the glimpses I catch through the tea room windows are of another world and the feelings that weigh on my heart are unlike any I have ever known. I feel like I am looking out upon the smoldering ruins of a dead city.

On this, my fourth trip out from Detroit, my shock is somewhat abated by the realization that I am attaining seniority among my peers. Not only have I secured a lower bunk, I have been granted my own locker. This gives me a place not only to store my battered suitcase but also to consider making use of some insider information. A fact of life aboard the *South* is that shipboard life reflects the two-tiered society that I have grown up in—the same structure that is currently being debated and fought over in our entire nation. On the ship, this means that blacks have no place on board where passengers might be able to see them. In addition to the ship's deck crew, this means that everyone who serves passengers, from waiters to cabin girls to pursers to the musicians that play the evening dances in the ballroom are not "colored." These crew are restricted to jobs like dishwashing, laundry, and similar menial tasks that keep them safely out of sight from the white passengers.

In many ways this is similar to my experiences as a caddy at the country club where blacks were relegated to the invisible parts of the club to perform their tasks with one or two being given the very visible jobs of doormen or "shines." But on the *South*, for many of the young white college-aged crew, this is their first real encounter with blacks. The Flicker forces us to share bunks, lockers, showers, toilets and food with people like Clarence, Freddie, Leroy, and Kelsey. And we find that we are all comfortable in the substandard living conditions in that dungeon because we are all treated equally in that hole at the bottom of those stairs. Under these conditions, everyone practices Beauregard's strong admonition to get along or get off.

For all his bluster and his southern name, Beauregard doesn't seem to give any of the crew special treatment. Some have even said that he has been overheard arguing with the captain for more rights and better treatment for the crew under his charge. He is rumored to also be at odds with the SIU—for their unwillingness to recognize blacks as members and to represent them in bargaining. The white crew under Beauregard's charge are also affected by this under-representation issue. The company has successfully argued to place the nonessential crew in a special category. Therefore we are not paid anything approaching the union scale that the deck and engine crew receives. This also keeps us at par with the blacks and helps to reinforce the fact that we are all being equally mistreated.

All of that notwithstanding, there is a pecking order in the Flicker and it seems to be based as much on seniority as anything else. In my case, this means that, in addition to attaining the lower bunk and locker recently vacated by a departed crew member, I am provided the insider status that lets me know, among other things, that Kelsey, a genial dude, can provide me with bottles of liquor at a special price. How he can get it or why the price is so reasonable is none of my business. Do I want it or not and, if so, what kind? It only takes me a moment to decide on a fifth of Dewars at the special Flicker rate of $5. The transaction is completed with appropriate stealth at my bunk in the late evening. I secure the bottle in my new locker and silently exult in my new status in the Flicker aboard the *South*.

As the ship makes the by now familiar trip through the Welland Canal, Chuck points to the dozens of ships at anchor around the canal entrance at Port Colborne. "Lockworkers are on strike," he announces with pride in being someone in the know. "Deckhands told me at breakfast." I am duly impressed. To be acknowledged by a deckhand is high praise. To actually have one of them convey information of value is truly cool. What Chuck hasn't learned is that the *South* is being granted a right of passage. That the lockworkers have agreed to allow us to proceed because of the nature of our business. But, as the day wears on, I discover that there must be a fly somewhere in the ointment. It becomes apparent that we are tying up for long periods of time before being allowed into and even out of the eight locks that separate Lake Erie from Lake Ontario.

Later, toward noon, I hear one of the pursers telling Beauregard that the slowdown is the lockworkers way of letting us know that the favor has been bestowed begrudgingly and we will not be allowed to pretend that it's business as usual on this trip. As the *South* crawls in fits and starts through the thirty- seven-mile-long system, the sullen heat of the day begins to take its toll. I imagine that this is what the Panama Canal must feel like as we creep through the still muck that passes for a humid day in July in the lower Great Lakes. Of course, our slow progress, coupled with a lack of breeze, makes us ideal targets for flies and all manner of flying insects that invade the ship.

As the long day edges toward twilight, the message comes down that, due to the fact that we will not be able to take on fresh water until we hit Lake Ontario, the crew's showers will be turned off to conserve water. This comes with a best-guess ETA for Lake Ontario of early morning. Because the mosquitoes are drawn to our perspiring bodies, the crew stays away from the fantail and confine themselves to the fetid Flicker for the duration of our canal transit. The stench of the stagnant canal water permeates our quarters. Throughout the night we learn the meaning of the phrase "to stew in our own juices" as we feel the bump and tug of the ship making its painfully slow progress through the remainder of the locks. It is safe to say that the crew and passengers of this trip aboard the *South* will not soon forget the cause of the lockworkers, whatever their plight might be.

My seniority status transcends the Flicker and carries up to the fantail where the evenings among the waitresses and cabin girls become more interesting. I am finally being accepted into their circle as well as the fraternity of men aboard the *South*. I am making a lot of new friends among the crew and am finding the already good life becoming even better. Add to this camaraderie the bustling streets of Montreal and the atmosphere of Expo 67 and it is not difficult to admit to myself that I am smack dab in the midst of everything.

But at night, lying in my bunk, listening to the squeak of a single broken piston that sounds through the steel walls of the nearby engine room, I confront myself with the truth that I have not yet arrived at my goal of working on a Great Lakes freighter. This, coupled with the realization that, at the present rate, I will not make enough money to pay my way through college for the coming year, forces me to face the fact that I need to keep my goals in front of me.

The tea room job has to be one of the softest ever made. Hours pass where we get only one or two customers. I spend this time browsing through the book rack, reading in one afternoon George Plimpton's account of what it feels like to get three pitches from some major league pitcher. Another afternoon, Violet's boyfriend from Tennessee comes in to visit. He is a lean deckhand, somewhere in his late twenties, and exudes a silent proprietary right to his plump conchita. All I can think of is how great it would be—not to be him— but to be a deckhand. I have watched in the locks as the deckhands dressed in khaki casually handle the heavy manila lines around the bollards, tying up the ship while a lock ahead clears. In the wait time, they keep busy painting the white sides of the ship that have scraped down against the many pilings we have come up against in our passage. The more artistic will actually paint the ship's name on the side walls of the dock itself. That, along with the fact that deckhands have special seating privileges in the galley, are automatically given immediate service when we are locking through (which is often), and actually get paid way more than the rest of us for a job that seems to be way more fun, continues to stoke my desire to become one of their brotherhood.

I step out of the French doors that separate the tea room from the fantail deck to allow the beauty of the summer day into my soul.

As the narrated tour of the Thousand Islands plays over the PA, I take note of the small cruiser that joins us for the tour. It has mimicked the *South* in its white exterior and even has its stack painted the black, red and amber colors of the Georgian Bay Line. This causes me to reflect on my limited conversation with John the dishwasher about the fleets of passenger ships that once plied the Lakes. I remember relatives on those Sunday afternoons back on Pennsylvania Avenue talking about how it was possible to catch a ship to Cleveland, Chicago, or Buffalo just about any day of the week. And now there is just the *South* remaining. I was recently told by one of the crew that the *North American*, sister ship to the *South*, was sold to the Maritime Union in Maryland and was towed out there only to sink in the ocean en route. I sense that I am standing on history.

Our weekly stop in Ogdensburg is punctuated for me when I am told by Anita, one of the cabin girls, that she is leaving the *South American* with Joe, an older black man. She tells me she's not sure where they're heading, probably out of fear that her parents will interrogate the entire ship's crew when they find out. The only thing I can tell for sure is that she is determined to do this. I am sad to see her go. Anita is the only crew member who has been to Wayne State where I am enrolled to go in a few weeks. She has assured me that Monteith is a cool college and that I will like it. Then she is off and down the gangplank going to meet her man somewhere in the city.

In the blackness of that night, as the *South* traverses Lake St. Francis in the seaway, a group of us on the fantail are treated to a great running battle between a speedboat and our galley crew. From what we can discern and hear, the speedboat people have thrown beer bottles through the open gangway at crew hanging out on the first deck. We hear the shouting and roar of the boat motor punctuated by a loud clang as a barrel full of garbage is dumped directly onto the boat as it pulls alongside the *South*. The hooting from down below coupled with the departure of the speedboat tells us that our guys have scored a direct hit. The Flicker is full of tales of individual heroism as we settle down for the night in our floating barracks.

The female crew inhabits a similar lair, called the Harem. The Harem, though, is located above the water line in the bow of the ship and is difficult for me to describe because it is accessible only through the forbidden first deck. I do recall that my work on the night gang brought me by the entrance to that sanctum. As I drift off, I wonder

61

if my predecessor, Tea Room Johnny, saw that as a possible extra perk. If he did, he's not saying.

This time around in Montreal, my curiosity takes me and a couple of crewmates around Quai 57 to a dock where a foreign ship is moored. It turns out that a ladder invites us to climb onto the deck where we are greeted by some crew who manage to convey an invitation to visit their quarters. Turns out that they and their ship are from Bombay. The trip on this foreign monster is a first for me and I am overwhelmed by the sense of strange newness heightened by the language and manner of our hosts. We manage to interpret their fractured English and they come to learn a little about where we have come from. Perhaps most interesting is to learn that they earn the equivalent of $20 per month. I am reluctant to tell them of the whopping $65 per week that we earn. One of the crew tries to sell us carved ivory elephants that he works on in his spare time. We depart knowing that we have seen something and spend the rest of the night at the union tavern sipping heavy ale and trying to figure out just what.

The next afternoon, I am approached by a passenger offering me ten dollars to take his teenage daughter out on the town. While I consider the offer, I am reminded again of the fact that being a crew on the *South* is infinitely more fun than being a passenger. I decline, electing instead to just ramble around the town with some of the waiters and waitresses.

That evening, as we return to the *South*, I notice a small pleasure yacht bedecked with pennants on the adjacent quai. Having nothing better to do and not especially tired, I wander over and find a young man not much older than myself tending the vessel. We strike up a conversation and I learn that he is the deckhand of a three-man crew. They will be cruising the Great Lakes all summer before heading down to Florida. This brief discussion, coupled with the previous evening's encounter with Asia, only reinforces my desire to head for even greater adventure. Yet as I head back toward the *South*, I am mesmerized by the latticed curve of her fantail that beckons to me like a girl in tight jeans.

Late the next afternoon, a few hours behind schedule, the *South American* swings once again into the upbound channel of the St. Lawrence Seaway. I am at my post in the tea room, serving the occasional Coke and making the rare malt while stealing glimpses at the passing scene. I take special notice of everything we're passing on this voyage as I have made up my mind that this will be my last trip aboard the *South*. As the geodesic dome slips by and the skyline diminishes, I wonder if I am making the right decision to leave what has become one of the highlights of my young life. As the illuminated cross atop Mount Royal fades from sight, I vow that I will return to this beautiful city but probably not aboard this ship. I have convinced myself that there is an even larger world out there and that I want to be a part of it. That, coupled with the fact that I could really use the money of a real job, has cemented my decision.

Although the decision is made, it is difficult for me to execute. I have become attached to the ways of this ship and her crew over these mostly idyllic weeks of warm summer travail. I will miss the life of the Flicker, the squeaking cylinder, and the aroma of the hot, sweet oil from the engine room where the quadruple-expansion engine keeps plugging away. I will not miss the Hobart machine but will miss the tea room that no longer serves tea. I will miss the crew's mess and the fare they serve little but will greatly miss the nights on the fantail. I will especially miss the melodious chimes of the ship's whistle as it salutes everything in sight on trips through the Thousand Islands. My close shipmates, Chris and Al, with whom I have shared many adventures in a short time, will be difficult for me to leave—as well as many of the good-looking girls who have become part of our Montreal explorations over these past few weeks. I will miss the dishwashers, Freddie and John; the crazed potmaster, Leroy; Clarence, the Flicker keeper; and Kelsey (let's have a toast to Kelsey!). In all, I will miss the blend of people that I have come to know who have made the *South American* become much more than a ship for me.

As the *South* makes her way through the now reopened Welland Canal, Marge invites me to take the afternoon off and fill one of the vacant seats on a passenger tour bus to Niagara Falls. As I slip into the paid tourist thing, I reflect on how crazy I must be to give up a job that offers so many perks. Life aboard the *South* has become comfortable to me. Perhaps too much so as I think about some of my shipmates who have accepted this way of life as permanent. I find myself impatient to get on with my life. And so I am able to resist the entreaties of my shipmates as they try to convince me to stay on for just one more trip.

There is a fine mist late in the evening when I carry the remainder of the Dewar's to the fantail for what will be my last night aboard the *South*. I literally drink in the darkness with Chris and Al. The blackness surrounding the ship seems impenetrable. After the bottle is empty, my shipmates leave me to man my post alone. As the stiff breeze embraces me, I feel entirely in my element. The moist breeze and swaying ship are what I most desire at this moment.

I wander back to the emergency steering wheel that connects directly to the ship's rudder. I take my position behind the wheel and place my hands on the large metal spokes. I am where I have always wanted to be from the moment I caught my first glimpse of the pilot house of the *Columbia*. I sail into the black night, wheelsman of the *South American*.

There are no passengers on deck on this misty night. And so, after a while, I take the liberty of walking the decks that were declared off limits to me on my very first day. I end up on the bow facing into the breeze in the absolute darkness. Directly above me is the pilot house and in its faint illumination I make out the silhouette of a man peering into the radar screen. Now that is where I truly want to be.

And so it is with more than a few misgivings that I pack my suitcase and prepare to depart the following afternoon. I spend the morning washing the tea room windows as we traverse the Pelee Passage and approach the Detroit River light. The song "White Rabbit" by Jefferson Airplane accompanies me on my little transistor, tuned to CKLW. As the ship gracefully moves into the Detroit River and past Bob-Lo Island and the burg named after General Amherst, I spend time bidding farewell to my Flicker friends while harboring more than a few anxieties about what I will find remaining of the riot-scarred city. As the *South* slowly cruises into her Bates Street berth in the late morning, I anticipate contacting my high school buddies who will bring me up to date on what really happened. I lug my old grey suitcase over the gangway and toward my future. I look forward to sharing with my buddies tales of my adventures aboard the *South* and in Montreal.

As my parents' car swings around to greet me at the dock, I am surprised at a full-flung, good-bye kiss from Brooke, who says she'll miss me. I climb blushing into the car, feeling sad and great, full of proof that I am ready for the world. I look back on the *South*, gleaming white with a wisp of steam escaping from the amber, red, and black stack. She is too busy preparing for her next adventure to notice me, a young man in search of his next adventure. But I can't help noticing her there at the dock, resplendent and proud in the knowledge that she can still stop a young man's heart by being just the way she is. As the car curves around Atwater Street and the *South* slips from my sight, I sigh, my heart feeling weighted with the knowledge that a part of me will always be with her.

CHAPTER 2

Steamboat II

The Detroit, Belle Isle and Windsor Ferry Company: The SS *Columbia*

Time was when the water from the river could be drunk safely from any point along its cliff-lined shores. Game and wildlife were so abundant that the early explorer's report that "the whitefish parted to allow passage of our canoe" was more fact than fiction.

Tribes of Indians roamed these shores and lived a relatively peaceful existence of hunting and fishing even after the exploring parties were replaced by settlers and an army outpost.

Louis Jolliet in 1669 was the first known white to travel the waters of what became known as the Detroit River. In 1701 Antoine de la Mothe Cadillac founded the site of what became known as the city of Detroit.

Today, Cadillac Boulevard stretches for a little over three miles from Gratiot Avenue to the riverfront. In spite of its imposing name, it is simply a slightly wider residential street with a few more brick homes and apartments than are found on surrounding streets. Cadillac Boulevard ends at Jefferson Avenue and yields to the broad expanse of Waterworks Park that extends to the river. Although off-limits to the public since World War II because of its proximity to the adjacent water treatment plant, Waterworks Park is one of many east side riverfront parks. These parks extend east for several miles along the shoreline from Belle Isle to Grosse Pointe, occasionally interrupted by places like the Whittier Hotel, the Edison Plant on Connor Creek, and a handful of marinas. The parks range in size from pocket parks no larger than a football field to areas that extend for more than half-a-mile. These parks are almost all passive in that there is grass to merely walk along—no ball diamonds, monkey bars, beaches, or swings. I have used these parks all my life in one way or another. Memorial Park features a hill probably all of fifteen feet high that served as our winter sledding headquarters. I remember too well standing shivering in the cruel February wind waiting for my father to drive up and rescue us from certain frostbite, if not outright death. In balmier weather, we would construct a makeshift diamond to play softball at Owen Park, tucked between two apartment buildings. Although we were too young to experience Waterworks Park, my uncle never tired of telling the story of how he and my mother fell into the river while ice skating as kids and were rescued by Boy Scouts. On fall days in high school, the guys would meet up at one of the wider parks to play football. On days when Belle Isle's beaches, zoo, and golf course were packed with pleasure seekers, these riverfront parks were havens of refuge for people simply wanting to get away from the madness of the city.

And in this summer of 1967, the people who have come through the riots need all the escape they can get. Realizing that a return to normalcy will help residents through their state of trauma, city officials have tried to get things back to where they were before that fateful raid on the blind pig that started the riot.

My return from the *South American* to the natal city is less celebratory than I expect. Family and friends are consumed with stories about the riots and how it has affected their lives. My parents, instead of hailing my wisdom to return home to seek a better-paying job, wonder aloud why I would give up a secure job in a safe place for no job in Detroit.

The next several days are filled with a smoldering angst. I have very quickly caught up on the aftermath of the riots and have discovered that my friends are basically doing nothing beyond the usual assembling in search of beer and places to drink it without being bothered.

As far as drinking goes, we teens are at the apex of practicing nondiscrimination and tolerance. We will accept any label and will drink virtually anywhere that provides a relatively safe environment. But, after all, part of the thrill of underage drinking is the fact that it is against the law—the law created and enforced by the same people who invented the assembly lines where most of our fathers have worked most of their lives. The same men who will, after a beer or two, look upon their sons with a wistful gleam in their eye and softly suggest that they not be too eager to follow in their footsteps, that there is a world out there waiting to be discovered and, if they're wise, they will take the time now to do so. Although I have never actually heard my father say these words to me, there are days when I see him straggle home from his job on the line at Dodge Truck and feel him saying them. And, to his credit, he does nothing to discourage me from thinking that I can hear him just fine.

Angel Park is located on the river just below Windmill Pointe and the beginning of what once were the marshlands of Grosse Pointe. The park itself is located on an island created by Fox Creek and a canal dug back to one of the declining auto mansions. Angel Park is where we gather at night to stand outside our cars. Young people, most of them high school graduates from nearby St. Martin's and Finney with associates thrown in from places like Osborn and the now-closed St. Bernard's. We stand outside our cars and listen to music from someone's radio and watch the evening go by. Occasionally someone has some beer or a bottle of wine to pass around. But mostly we just stand around and talk and throw a frisbee back and forth.

Although the summer is at its peak, I am having a difficult time enjoying the warmth of the nights. Just standing around with my friends hearing tales from the riots becomes something that doesn't interest me, especially because I basically missed them. And there's only so much they want to hear about my fascinating nights in Montreal and at Expo 67. The most difficult part for me is that we are standing within a couple hundred feet of the river, within a stone's throw of the freighters as they ply their way up and down to ports that I'm still dreaming of.

I don't need a whole lot more encouragement to drive my rusty blue '56 Plymouth west down Jefferson past the Ambassador Bridge to the hall in River Rouge that houses the Seafarers International Union. This is the union hall that Chris, Al, and I visited a few weeks before and where we were treated as less than worthy of attention. The fact that dues were deducted from my pay makes me a current member and makes this my call of first resort.

Because it is the middle of the shipping season, there is a fair amount of activity in the hall and I am thrilled to see several postings on the chalkboard. A review, however, puts things in perspective. There is a posting for the *Sylvania*, the tub that sank under my friend's friend. But it is for oiler in the engine room, a position that requires a license. My Coast Guard-issued "Z" card states that I am qualified for only unlicensed positions on the deck (deckhand), in the galley (porter), and engine room (wiper). All other positions generally require some sort of certification. Therefore I'm not eligible to apply for the listed positions for AB (able bodied seaman) on the *H. Lee White* and *Joseph Young*. Nor can I apply for the fireman position on the *Richard Reiss*. But there, at the bottom, smudged so that I'm not sure what it actually reads until I can get right up to it: *porter on the Columbia*. I gaze, not sure if what I'm reading is correct. "Z" card in hand, I make my way to the window and ask the clerk if that porter position is open. He checks my union book and "Z" card without looking at me and says nonchalantly, "Yeah. You want it?"

I manage a "Yeah" and he makes an entry in his book and says, "Okay. Report to the dock, foot of Woodward at five o'clock." He shoves the paperwork back and dismisses me with a flick of his hand.

But I can't go yet. "Foot of Woodward?" I ask.

"Yeah," he snarls back. "That's the *Columbia*. The Bob-Lo boat. You know where it is, don't you?"

"Sure," I stammer. "I just didn't know if it was the same one." And I walk away.

My ride home is full of emotion. While I am elated at the fact I've actually got a job, I'm disappointed that I'm not going on a real freighter and will spend the rest of the summer right here in Detroit. On the other hand, I'm going to be working on the boat that I have grown up with and spent at least one day of each of my summers on since I was born.

By the time I pull up in front of my house, I am genuinely excited at the thought that I'm packing my suitcase and heading downtown to work for the Browning Line.

It takes no time to throw some clothes in the suitcase, announce my destiny, and cadge a ride to the boat dock, located a stone's throw away from that of the *South American*. I arrive at the old stone build-ing that has probably stood here since the turn of the century and am not especially surprised to find no boat present. The Browning Line

The Bob-Lo docks at the foot of Woodward, Detroit (Dossin Great Lakes Museum)

consists of two ships, the *Ste. Claire* and the *Columbia*. They spend most of their time on the river and can be found only for brief moments at one dock or another. That is, until after the moonlight cruises when they get an eight-hour rest. Presently, the *Columbia* comes into sight, four decks above the water, looking like a white swan.

I wait while she disembarks her passengers and then lug my suitcase through a gate I have never been—a special gate for crew members only. Over the gangway, I announce to the watchman, who is busy coiling line, that I'm the new porter. He barely breaks stride in his coiling to point me down the alleyway to a screen door marked "galley." Although I have been a lifelong habitue of these ships and cannot count a summer when I have not been on one, these next steps mark a new world of experience for me. As a passenger, I have seen every inch of allowable space on both the *Columbia* and *Ste. Claire*, from the gateway from which you can see the huge cylinders of the triple expansion moving up and down, to the gateway that enters onto the pilot house on the top deck.

I push open the wooden-framed screen door and am surprised to see a curving stairway. I clunk down the few steps until I am standing in the midst of a small dining room. The room is occupied by only a few diners at this point and I am at once spotted by a man who resembles Steve Allen gone to seed and is just about to set a tray of dishes filled with pie out on a table. He looks up, gives me a brief smile and says with a twang, "You must be the new porter. We're sure glad to see you. Hey, Johnny," he calls into the room from which he has just come, "Here's the new guy."

In a jiffy a squat figure sweeps out of the room that I see is full of a stove, steam tables, and a lot of hanging pots, pans, and utensils. "Hi, I'm Johnny," he says. I see a short, rotund man with glasses and a round flushed face giving me the quick once over. "Gimme a minute to get this stuff put away and I'll show you where to throw that."

He reemerges in an instant and leads me to the back of the dining area where there is a narrow hallway. The hallway has two doors on either side. He thrusts open the one on the right and reveals a dark cave-like dwelling. As I struggle to adjust my vision to determine what's inside, Johnny points to a shape just inside the door. "Looks like that's the vacant bunk. Just throw your suitcase underneath." By this time my eyes make out three sets of bunks in the tiny space, no more than eight-by-twelve feet. There may or may not be someone in one of the top bunks on the far wall. The close air is the next thing I notice as I move into the room to stow my bag as directed. As I am trying to make my suitcase fit into the tight space, Johnny grabs my elbow and says, "Hold on a second. Why don't you come over here before you do that."

Somewhat puzzled I follow him out of the room and across the hall to the second door. He opens this one to reveal a comparably sized room. But in this one, the lamp illuminates only two beds and a couple of chairs and even a couple of dressers. Johnny invites me to sit in one of the chairs, occupies the other and says, "I've only got a couple of minutes. I want to get off before we sail and get home for the night. Here's the deal. I'm really okay for porters right now. What I've really got is an opening for a second cook. If you want that job, I can teach you. It pays about two hundred forty a week. And this room goes with it," he says with an expansive flourish. So, you want this job or the porter job?"

It takes me all of two seconds to do the math and realize the living situation. "Yeah. I'll do the second cook job," I answer.

"Great. I'll tell Bruce to wake you around 4:00 to start training you." And with that, he sweeps out of the room to let me adjust to the idea that I will be second cook and that he will be back to wake me in about ten hours.

It only takes me a few minutes to stow my few clothes and, rather than sit alone in the bare room, I wander back into the dining room. There I once again encounter the Steve Allen lookalike who says with a chuckle and a smile, "Hey there. Johnny says you're the new second cook. Hell, that's even better news than I first thought. That means I can go back to my job being the night cook." I smile back, not knowing what to say. So he calls back into the galley area, "Hey Brian, Phil. C'mon out here." And from the galley two guys emerge who are closer to my age. The first wastes no time in shaking my hand and welcoming me aboard the *Columbia*. He has an Irish face and black curly hair and introduces himself as Brian, the waiter. The second guy is slighter, wears glasses, has a buzz cut, and walks with a limp. He says his name is Phil and he's the dishwasher.

"So Johnny talked you into being second cook?" Brian asks with a smile.

"Yeah. He just asked me if I wanted it."

"So do you know how to cook anything?" asks Phil.

"A little. I learned some on the *South American*."

"Yeah? You worked over there?" says Brian, interested.

"Yeah. But they don't pay so well."

"Yeah, well, we think we've got the best of the ships on the Great Lakes right here on the *Columbia*," continues Brian with nods of assent from the other two. "Johnny's probably one of the best cooks on the lakes and we've got fresh food everyday."

"And the crew's good too," adds Phil.

"Well, since I'm goin' back to night cook, I better catch some beauty sleep," says Bruce beginning to traipse to the back hallway. "I'll see you all later."

"Yeah, you can bet on that," responds Brian. "I live for food and the night lunch before I turn in." He turns back to us and says, "Let's head up and catch a seat on the bow. Catch some breeze."

So we climb the winding staircase through the screen door and back onto the main deck. We walk up toward the bow and slide magically under the line that has been strung across the deck to keep the passengers away from the crew work area. There are two green park-style benches in this area on the port side near the gangway. The rest of the area up to the bow is taken by the quietly-hissing anchor apparatus.

"This is the only place on deck we're allowed," explains Brian as we take a seat, adding, "even when there aren't any passengers on board like tonight."

I'm immediately thrilled at the fact that the six o'clock sailing to Bob-Lo is underway and we are already passing the Morton Salt terminals on the Canadian side. The late afternoon is still full of the day's heat and there are several other crew on deck enjoying the breeze created by the ship as she steams into the brightness of the slowly-waning day. Brian explains that, except for the mates and engineers, everyone has quarters somewhere below decks and the room I'll be sharing with Johnny is the best among them.

Brian introduces me to several of the crew who are either sitting on the benches idly chatting or standing at the railing staring into the water. On the bench I meet Tex, the wheelsman, and Tilly, the shiny bald watchman. Over there horsing around are a couple of guys my age, Skip and Larry who work on the night gang. There is Walter, the chief engineer talking to Frenchy, the fireman. They all say "Hi" in their own ways and soon we are all back to being on the river as the *Columbia* makes quick time on her rendezvous with the island.

As the boat makes her swing in the river to line up her port side with the island dock, Skip and Larry are talking excitedly with Brian about a game of miniature golf they'll play during the ship's ninety-minute layover. This is something I hadn't even imagined. "You mean that we actually get to go ashore?" I ask, my excitement joining theirs.

"Sure enough," answers Skip. "Whenever we have this layover—usually every other night—we get to go on the island and do whatever we want."

I gaze at the dock rapidly closing with the ship as the deckhands prepare to pass the thick manila lines to their waiting counterparts.

Since I was nine years old, I'd always wondered what it was I'd have to do to get the run of Bob-Lo Island to myself—to have an infinite amount of time to simply be here and enjoy the fun of being in what I have always considered to be one of life's perfect places. When the nuns at St. Bernard's would become enraptured with their talk of heaven, my mind would drift—not to some celestial nunnery full of harp-playing angels—but to this place on the river on a perfect summer day. Over time Bob-Lo has epitomized to me a place where all that is right with the world has come together. I have been coming here with my family every year since I was a baby. And thus, even in

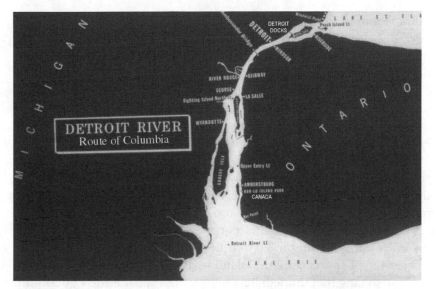

The route followed by the Bob-Lo boats from downtown Detroit to the island (Brendan Livingston)

The *Columbia* passing downtown Detroit (Author's collection)

years where nothing else seemed to be going right, I would always have Bob-Lo as my place of refuge. Because it seemed that, no matter what else may be going wrong with my world, the spirit of being on this island with my friends and family overshadowed everything else. And this is a feeling that all members of my family entered into. On the day we went to Bob-Lo, feuds were suspended and we all entered into the pearly—actually the wooden—gates of the dock to Nirvana on the river.

As the *Columbia* makes fast to the long dock and I gaze at the rides at the other end, I realize that, in a very real sense, I grew up on this island. Beyond the early experiences on the Brownie Coaster, my memory goes back to the not-too-recent times when there were only a handful of rides,—the merry-go-round, the Whip, and the Aeroplanes that swung in lazy circles around a tower in the middle. At that time I appreciated the island with all my senses, especially the vinegarish tang that immediately hit my nose the minute I got off the dock and started heading for the family picnic area. From my perch on the green bench, I can still catch a whiff of that distinctly Canadian-American smell that I have come to associate with the slightly off taste of vinegar-laced catsup used to compliment the French fries sold in the park cafeteria where we were rarely allowed to eat. When the family went to Bob-Lo, we never went without a large bag of sandwiches, chips, and fruit with perhaps some Cracker Jacks tossed in.

But the picnic was always secondary to the rides. By the time I graduated from the Brownie Coaster and the merry-go-round, the ferris wheel was waiting, followed by the Whip, the Caterpillar, the Moon Rocket, the Tilt-a Whirl, the Dodgems and then the Bug. The Bug gained notoriety the night it flew off the track and killed three people. Once repaired, it became a personal challenge to all Detroit teens. And about the time that those rides were becoming sort of lame, the management wisely decided to invest in a new wave of rides including the Rotor, the Scrambler, the Jet Planes, and the state-of-the-art Wilde Maus. Without a real roller coaster, Bob-Lo could not compete with Jefferson Beach, Walled Lake, or Edgewater Park. So the Wilde Maus with its sharp twists and European turns was a *coup d'egalité* for Bob-Lo.

For the Bob-Lo experience was much more than just a trip to another amusement park. Although all of the other parks offered unique thrills and atmospheres—Jefferson Beach with its marvelous

Big Dipper, Walled Lake with the Flying Dragon (tallest coaster in the state) and Edgewater with its mysterious silver- covered ride that also harbored dark secrets—none could compare to a day on Bob-Lo. The Bob-Lo experience, because of the hour-and-a-half boat ride, was much more encompassing. In the first place, if the weather got bad, you couldn't just trudge out to the parking lot and leave. There was only one way out. That Bob-Lo was a large island with loads of space beyond the midway meant there was always a great deal more to do than simply ride the rides all day. Bob-Lo provided a real sense of space for the rides were laid out over a broad area, not clustered together, broken up by groves of trees and large buildings of fieldstone that housed the dance hall, skating rink, power house, and restrooms. This space provided for a built-in sense of civility, a link to Queen Victoria and the island's owners who never let the park become overdeveloped. From any part of the park, one could always see the broad river glistening and filled with traffic. And, finally, Bob-Lo has been a family tradition for many Detroiters since it opened in 1898, and provided for our family a ready link to our Detroit heritage and a frame of reference. I never tired of hearing my mother and her brothers talk about walking home to the house on Pennsylvania after a moonlight cruise in the wee hours of the morning—something that I could never imagine doing in this postriot era.

Knowing that I have an early wake-up call facing me and that I haven't even unpacked my clothes, I decline the offer to play miniature golf tonight and, as the crew wanders down the gangway to enjoy the island, I head back down to the galley area to organize my gear. Since Johnny has gone home to Wyandotte for the night, I spend time simply becoming accustomed to all the space at my disposal. The two beds are single twins, not bunk. The lamp casts a nice soft reading light over the room. The light is necessary because someone has welded the portholes at the top of the wall shut. Since we are almost below the water line where I'm standing, I can understand why. I empty my suitcase of clothes and still have two drawers of my dresser staring back emptily at me. This is luxury.

Not feeling tired and with some time on my hands, I wander back into the galley and up the stairs to the main deck. Although there's plenty of daylight left, the deck lights have been turned on to accommodate the trickle of passengers who have tired of the island and want to make sure they get good seats for the ride home. I wander back up to the crew area to find Tilly and another deckhand monitoring the gangway. I gaze at the rides for a few minutes. Their lights are turned on also as the sky darkens to twilight. The air is warm and humid. Although I really don't feel tired, I force myself back down to my room where I get ready for bed. I wander out into the galley in search of a shower. I haven't seen any sign of one near the commode located just astern of the sleeping quarters. Tex the wheelsman is making himself a sandwich from the night lunch and I ask him if he knows. He turns to me with a smile and says:

"Shower? Not back here. You've got to go down the forward stairs to get to one. When this ship was built, I don't think the builders worried too much about those things."

He's still chuckling as I head back up to the main deck and walk to the doorway that leads down to the forward quarters. At the bottom of the stairs are four doors, three of which are closed and I deduce to be sleeping quarters. The fourth opens into a bathroom that contains two shower stalls and a couple toilets and sinks. This makes the accommodations on the *South American* look luxurious by comparison. I take a quick shower and am out of there. I make my way through the now-swelling crowd of boarding passengers and am back in my cozy room and reading a magazine in bed in no time. I feel the deck vibrate beneath me as the whistle blasts its fifteen minute warning. And then I know no more.

Until I am shaken awake by Bruce, the night cook. "Four o'clock, time to get moving," he says, pausing only long enough to make sure I'm awake before closing the door. I crawl out of the surprisingly comfortable bed, pull on the galley whites that have been provided and make my way back out to the galley. There I find Bruce bustling around. He says, "First thing is to get the stores. Here's the list. Take it to the stores room on the dock. You'll see it. They'll get you a cart to truck everything back here with. Make sure you get all the ice. With this hot weather, we need every bag."

With the note in hand, I make my way to the stores room, dutifully hand my note to the fellow on the other side, let him know the importance of the ice and wait as the materials are brought out for loading onto the four-wheeled hand cart. I check to make sure I've received everything on the list, sign where he tells me to and trundle the cart over the gangway and past the silent cabins that house the engineers and mates on the first deck. I truck the cargo down the winding stairs one package at a time where Bruce is waiting to direct me to an appropriate pantry or walk-in cooler for storage.

Once the goods are stored, Bruce walks me through the tiny galley to familiarize me with the work space, stove, and steam table. "Your job is to make breakfast. Today I'll show you how. Tomorrow it's all yours." I watch this chunky Steve Allen as he deftly cranks up the stove and throws a couple of rows of sausages in to bake. A couple of pots appear on top, filled with water. "Smaller one's for poaching eggs. Larger one's for oatmeal."

He leads me over to a corner and says, "And this one's the most important. The coffeemaker. You make sure you got fresh hot coffee ready by the time your first customer hits the door."

I watch and try to remember the recipe for coffee in my head as Bruce whips through the steps: empty and clean the pot, empty filters from basket, clean basket, refill with coffee, fill the pot, flip the switches, and stand back. Not too difficult for a coffee drinker to remember. Problem is, I'm not. But before I have too much time to think about it, Bruce has me over to the walk-in cooler where he's pulled out a gallon of milk and some eggs. Then he's grabbed some flour and baking powder from somewhere and he's demonstrating how to make pancakes from scratch. While my eyes race to follow his hands, my ears are full of listening to him talking about the breakfast regimen: "We basically alternate pancakes and French toast every other day. Same with sausages and bacon except Sunday when we have ham. Eggs any way they want 'em. Waiters take care of the toast out there. Every few days throw on some hash browns. Just keep 'em coming. You don't wanna waste food but you never wanna get caught short. These guys can get fussy."

The time passes quickly and, before I know it, Phil, Brian, and a second waiter, named Walter, have appeared and are busy preparing the dining room for the crew due to arrive at seven. They glide around clearing tables and setting out fresh silverware and glasses, pulling juice from the cooler, and slicing bread for toast.

The galley is humming and the dining room ready for crew when Johnny arrives from his night in Wyandotte. He gives the place a quick once over on his way to the room. He notes that Bruce has me under his wing and says only, "Pay attention to him—tomorrow it's all yours."

The night gang, Skip, Larry, and Bill are the first three customers. They are early because as Skip explains, "We want to catch some sleep."

Brian banters with them while Bruce quietly curses their lame excuse while he starts three orders of pancakes and eggs sunny side up. He doesn't say much when he flips the cakes and covers the eggs with a saucepan top. The stove is a large dark industrial type and has a cooking space at least three-by-four feet not counting the area devoted to the water heating for other things. Bruce deftly flips the finished cakes onto three plates, adds the eggs and three sausages each and places them on the counter where Brian glides by for the pick-up and delivery to the table and the three hungry lads.

By this time Johnny has emerged from the room dressed in his whites. He scoots around to check on the stores and, satisfied that the order is in, turns his attention to me. "Basically, Bruce has shown you everything you need to do to get the breakfast ready. By this time you also need to be thinking about the dinner menu and what you're gonna be serving. We always serve soup and two or three entrées along with a salad. And you gotta have some desserts too. Soon's you get caught up with the orders, I'll show you around for the next steps."

And then he is gone and I am back watching Bruce put together another order, this one involving some scrambled eggs along with the sausage. It takes him less than two minutes to fill the order, slowed somewhat by an order for a bowl of oatmeal in the midst of things.

At Bruce's invitation, I try my hand at a couple of easy overs and am pleased that they've come out pretty good. Bruce corrects my plate appearance by going around the edges and wiping off spots of grease. Thus approved, Walter carries my first order away to its customer. I feel pretty good.

Then a challenge: two poached. I know absolutely nothing about poaching eggs and watch as Bruce carefully breaks the eggs into a small pot of boiling water. He cautions me on the timing and then carefully extracts them to be dried before being placed on the plate with the toast Brian has already prepared. And so the early morning goes as one order after the other rolls in with careful attention paid to those of the captain and the chief engineer.

By eight o'clock, Bruce is showing me how to clean the grill and the frying pans ("Always use salt and then oil them, never water—it gets them rusty"). As I absorb that information, Johnny has zipped back around the corner and is showing me the dinner menu. He quickly shows me the vegetables for the salad, the knives and bowls, and gives me a quick orientation to the steam table. Brian pops in to pick up the menu so that he can transfer it to the blackboard in the dining room. He and Walter have just about cleaned up the room and transferred the last of the dishes to Phil who has also finished washing most of the breakfast utensils. As they wrap up their work and prepare to leave the area, I am comforted at the thought that my break time is also approaching. But Johnny ignores them and takes me on a more detailed tour of the galley to make sure I know where everything is. He makes sure that I know where the soup is located and the proper pot to cook it in. Then he leaves me to work on the salad, returning to check every few minutes and to add a tip or two on preparing fresh vegetables. By this time Bruce has disappeared to his room and it's just Johnny and me and the menu.

He comes by to find me finishing up the salad and takes the bowl and places it in the cooler. Then he says, "Make sure you've got plenty of time to help me get the dinner on. You can take a break now, but make sure you're back here by ten. We start feeding by eleven-thirty." The alarm clock in my room says 9:10. I've been up and running over five hours and I get less than an hour break before my next immersion. Too exhausted to rest, I wander up the stairs to the main deck and the crew area. There's no one sitting there now. Not too much activity. At the main dock directly behind us, however, the *Ste. Claire* is humming with life as passengers for the ten o'clock sailing are already boarding. I watch the show unfold as the band assembles on the third deck and begins playing for the boarding passengers. Then the company mascot, a short-statured person known as Captain Bob-Lo, emerges from the ticket office waiting room and takes his place at the gangway, greeting people as they come on board with his familiar "Hawaya."

Then the *Ste. Claire* blows her fifteen-minute whistles—three long—and the countdown begins. It is amazing to sit and watch this unfold from this perspective. The only other times I've seen this is from the passenger standpoint, racing to get from the parking lot to the ticket window and then onboard, usually with only a few minutes to spare.

Finally, several minutes after ten, when there is some certainty that the last person from the parking lot has made it onboard, the ship gives its ten-second long blast and the lines are finally thrown off.

Captain Bob-Lo (Joe Short) with a fan at the dock (Harry Oliver and Alice Hall Pace; donated by Frank Ripley)

Two crew members in the *Columbia*'s galley with stove in the background (Harry Oliver and Alice Hall Pace; donated by Frank Ripley)

Then it's a matter of less than a minute from the time the *Claire* has cleared her berth to the time that the *Columbia* slowly backs into the space she has just vacated. By the time the *Columbia* has relocated and the gangway is in place, the first passengers for the eleven o'clock sailing are in the waiting room, ready to board. By this time, I'm aware that I'm overdue in the galley and head back down.

Johnny appears in full stride, as though he has never even taken a break. The work counters are full of dishes and meats in production. He takes enough of a break to point me to a large can of green beans and says, "Get these into a pan," and disappears into the cooler.

Left to my own devices, I find a large pan and search for the can opener. Johnny reappears to check my progress, clucks, and steers me by the elbow to the steam table. "This needs to be started every day by this time. Here's how you do it." And he proceeds to turn a number of valves beneath the trays that release water throughout the system. There is a final brass valve at the end of the system that he points toward while gripping my arm. He makes sure he has my attention as he walks through this step. "That's the gas. When everything else is on, light a match, give it a turn, put it near the ring and stand back." I watch as the orange flame flies under the length of the steam table, bringing it hissing to life. Johnny continues, "If it doesn't light right away, blow out the match, turn it off, and come get me. Remember every day at ten-thirty to have it lit."

By this time, he has moved over to the oven where he is taking out a huge piece of beef and placing it on the counter. He explains, "I'll cut this and put it in a pan on the steam table, cover it with some au jus so it stays moist and warm for serving. Now you've gotta get those potatoes boiling on the stove and mash 'em." In an instant, I have found thick gloves and am pouring the spuds into a strainer and then into a large mixing bowl where I follow Johnny's directions for adding butter and milk. He continues to carve the roast as he monitors my progress. When I have achieved a consistency that he approves of, I transfer the mash to the steam table. Before I have time to turn around, Johnny is next to me ladling some kielbasa and sauerkraut into another tray on the table. "Time to get some vegetables in here. Open that can over there," he says, motioning with his head to another table where a couple of institutional sized cans of lima beans rest under a large opener. I follow directions until they are nestled in the steamer next to a tray where corn on the cob have magically appeared.

Now we are joined by Brian and Walter who once again size up the situation and pitch in to make sure we are on time for the eleven-thirty onslaught. Brian plunges in to put the finishing touch on the salad while Walter slices bread for the tables. They walk into the cooler and emerge with salad dressings and Brian then makes a large pitcher of lemonade while I make an equal amount of iced tea and Walter makes another vat of coffee. Somewhere along the line, Johnny yells out "Desserts" and flies into the cooler from where he emerges with a tray full of pies needing to be sliced and placed on plates and sliced peaches needing to be ladled into bowls. While we busy ourselves with that, Johnny returns to the steam tables to make sure that nothing is being overheated and to stir the gravy. I notice him as he places another dish into the steam table that turns out to be stuffed green peppers. By the time that Brian has finished writing the menu on the blackboards in the dining room, I have come to the understanding that the galley on the *Columbia* makes that of the *South American* look like a high school cafeteria.

Even before the appointed time, crew begin filtering down the stairs to the dining room for the dinner meal. I am forewarned that there will be more than at breakfast, for we are expected to feed the band as well as two security officers who have been added since the riots. I take my station at the steam table next to Johnny. As Brian and Walter bring the orders to the counter, it is my job to take a plate and then begin to fill it accordingly. Johnny is at the end of the line, handling the prime rib or sausage orders. His meticulousness ensures that no plate will leave the galley bearing any trace of misplaced gravy or any disproportionate amount. He has memorized the whims of every crew member and personalizes every departing dish.

As the orders fly in, I can only concentrate on the next item to get onto the dish in my hand. Johnny's experience sees us easily through the rush and, before I know it, Walter and Brian are doing their clean-up routine. Once again I'm left in the middle of a busy galley not knowing what I should do next. Johnny patiently directs me from task to task, taking care to explain the steps I need to take to accomplish them. There is a need for him to start thinking about supper and he asks me to shut off the steam table. After five minutes, he discovers me staring at a valve with a puzzled look on my face. He goes through the routine for me again but I can sense exasperation in his tone this time. He dismisses me for an afternoon break and this time

I simply collapse on my bed for an all too brief nap. My rest is occasionally broken by the blast of the steam whistle as the *Columbia* continues her run back to Detroit for the four o'clock sailing.

I am up and back at it by three o'clock once again cutting vegetables for the evening salad. The pace is slightly slower this time around only because Johnny doesn't provide quite as elaborate a spread at supper as he does at the midday meal. There is no soup on the menu this time around and he leaves the kielbasa and kraut on from the dinner. However, this is the meal that he tends to bring out the big desserts. Brian asks me if I've ever made pies. When I answer in the negative, he tells me he has and that it's part of the second cook's responsibilities. Fortunately, Bruce had spent time last night preparing pies for today so there are fresh lemon meringue and chocolate pies to lay on the sideboard for this evening. I haven't the foggiest what I will do beyond that. But I have no time to think about it because Johnny is asking me if I've turned on the steam table yet and then if I've mashed the potatoes. Once again I find myself in the midst of a maelstrom without any clue as to what I'll be doing next. But when the crew begins filing in at 4:30, I'm at my station at the steam table filling orders as quickly and carefully as I can under his watchful gaze.

When at last the steam table is turned off and the last of the crew has departed (with a lot of compliments to Johnny), I'm left to put things back in the cooler and prepare for the morning. Johnny walks me through the tasks to be done after I awaken at 4:00 AM on the morrow. I nod obediently and he dismisses me. I wander up onto the deck and discover the *Columbia* just departing the island and full of people heading home to the city. I find a seat on the green bench and fall into discussion with Phil, the dishwasher, Brian, Skip and Larry from the night gang. Phil and Brian are talking about catching a movie downtown. Skip says, "Naw, we can't go. We've got the nine o'clock moonlight tonight and we've got to start work at 11:30. The boat won't get back to the dock until midnight so we've got to stay on."

"Too bad," says Phil. "You guys hardly ever get a chance to get off at night."

"That's true," agrees Larry. "If we're not on a moonlight, we're probably just getting back from the nine o'clock from the island and there isn't enough time then either."

"You poor babies," mocks Brian.

"How about you, second cook?" says Phil to me. "You don't have to get back for anything special."

"What time does the boat get back here?" I ask.

"Around midnight," answers Brian.

"Yeah," laughs Larry. "That'll give you about four hours to sleep before breakfast call."

Brian turns to Larry and says, "Depends on how runny you like your eggs."

"Or even if he's awake enough to start cookin' 'em," adds Phil.

So, as the *Columbia* makes her berth at the foot of Woodward, I watch Brian and Phil head up the hill toward Jefferson. Larry, Skip, I, and the third member of the night gang—a slightly older fellow named Bill—sit and watch the twilight descend as people begin massing at the dock for boarding the nine o'clock moonlight.

As we sit, Skip and Larry recount what it was like to be sitting in the midst of the riots as they spread through the city a few weeks earlier. Skip recalls how the rumors that there was a mob descending on the Bob-Lo boats with the intent of burning them were convincing enough that the owners ordered them moved to a downriver anchorage for several nights.

This makes me recall the fact that, in all the years that I've been going to Bob-Lo, I've seen relatively few blacks on the boats or the island. The only blacks I've ever seen employed on the island have been maintenance or cafeteria workers hired from Amherstburg, a final stop on the underground railroad prior to the U.S. Civil War. As far as the boats are concerned, I struggle to recall ever having seen a black employee even around the docks.

I sit absorbing this as hundreds of white youth from a Lutheran group board the *Columbia* for a night of fun on the river, while on other nights we have hosted parties from Motown and black church groups. It is no wonder that the rumors to burn the boats were taken so seriously. I retire to my cabin as the *Columbia* is in the river, all too aware that four AM is not far away.

I leap from my bed with Bruce's wake-up call and wash and dress quickly. I find the order list for the stores and take care of that piece of business with dispatch. As I wheel the cart back on board, I am overwhelmed by the absolute silence of the ship. It is as though she too is asleep. With the stores brought below, I settle to the task of breakfast.

Yesterday was pancakes and sausages so today is French toast and bacon. I prepare the bacon the same way as the sausages, baking the strips in the oven. Then I break a bunch of eggs in a bowl, add some milk and cinnamon and find the bread. By this time I realize I've forgotten to turn on the burners and am fortunate to find that Johnny has arisen early to keep an eye on me this morning. I get the water heating and then am free to talk with Johnny about his menu for the rest of the day.

The crew, led by the night gang, comes marching in before I know it and I am in over my head. Somehow, with the help of Walter and Brian, I manage to keep pace and am amazed at how quickly I can get an order of French toast into their hands for delivery.

Johnny has to step in only once when an order for poached eggs comes in. I notice it's the same as yesterday's. But just as soon as I'm congratulating myself on successfully negotiating breakfast, I realize it's time to begin preparing desserts for the dinner and supper parades to follow. I spend the next hour trying to put a cake together and am embarrassed when Johnny finally takes the bowl from my hand to finish the project so that I can begin preparing the salad and vegetables.

I only have time for a quick break today and spend it watching passengers board the *Columbia* as she prepares to make the ten o'clock sailing. As the whistle roars and the band plays "Anchors Aweigh" and thousands of people turn their minds to fun, I am back down in the galley trying to remember how to turn on the steam table before Johnny has to show me how again.

While the workday is similar to yesterday's, I realize just how much there is to the job of being second cook. Johnny's idea is that I will be able to take on an increasing amount of the work load and he is not interested in waiting until the season ends three weeks from now for that to happen. Try as I might, I struggle to remember all the details of the tasks he has taught me to date. I work into the afternoon after dinner and come back early to prepare for supper so that I've had barely any break this day at all. By the time I have cleaned up after supper, it is all I can do to drag myself onto the first deck to see what else happened today. Johnny has jumped off the ship before it sailed from Detroit at six. He will return before breakfast tomorrow.

The *Columbia* is already steaming toward Bob-Lo when I join the group on the green benches. I am quickly energized by the familiar sights and the pleasant warm night. By the time we hit the island,

I am ready to go with Skip, Brian, and Larry for a tour of the midway. What is amazing to discover is the ultimate Bob-Lo perk—that simply by waving the "Z" card of the U.S. Merchant Marine, we are able to hop on any ride on the island. I have arrived at heaven. We spend the hour and a half allotted us going from one ride to another, my ride-weary compatriots tolerating my lust to go on as many as possible before I wake up from this dream.

"The only one we can't do is the miniature golf," complains Skip."

"Yeah—he makes us pay fifty cents," adds Brian.

"Got time for a game tonight?" asks Larry.

"Naw, we've gotta get back. Sailing in fifteen minutes and they're gonna need the night gang tonight," says Skip.

"Yeah," agrees Larry. Look at the crowd trying to get on."

"Probably a full boat going back," observes Brian.

But I never wait up with them to count heads or enjoy the trip back. I am sound asleep in my bunk ten minutes after boarding.

The next morning arrives before the dawn. This is the day that Johnny won't be coming until close to breakfast time so I am on my own. I go through the routine as quickly as possible and am feeling confident when the first orders begin to be delivered by Brian and Walter. I have prepared the pancakes and sausages and have the water ready for the poached eggs, oatmeal, or whatever else someone orders. However, it isn't too far into the meal when Brian brings a plate of half-eaten pancakes back from the dining room with the message that they are not fully cooked. Within seconds Johnny has emerged from nowhere to dissect the plate and confirm the presence of uncooked batter. His offer to recook the breakfast is declined by the wheelsman who brought the complaint. He has to get to work. Johnny quickly examines the batter and proclaims it too thick. He hastily puts another one together with me drifting helplessly at his side. While he is focused on the food, I can tell that his tolerance level is dangerously low.

"Should never have allowed this to happen," is all I can pick up from him as we finish up the breakfast together.

Shortly after the meal is complete and preparations for dinner are underway, Johnny comes up to me and says, "Listen, kid, I just got word that the hall's sending over the second cook that used to work on here. So I guess that today is it for you."

I have been half expecting this news ever since the pancakes came back.

"So I just get off today?" I ask to confirm my worst fears.

"Yeah, you just get off when we're done with supper. That way you get paid for today."

Dispirited, I halfheartedly continue making the salad until news comes down that there will be a fire and boat drill in fifteen minutes. I find my vest and begin making my way up to my station on the port side of the third deck. The deck crew handles the fire hose drill and I stand by and watch. When we move up to the boat deck, however, the crew insist that I handle the winch that lowers the lifeboat down almost to the river before the order comes to end the drill.

As we walk back down the stairs to the lower deck, Tex, the wheelsman walks beside me and says, "I hear that Johnny's letting you go."

Amazed that the word has spread so quickly, I grunt a "Yeah" response.

Tex says, "You know that's a union position and we can fight it if you want us to."

"Naw. That's okay," I answer. I realize that it would take me more time to learn that job to Johnny's satisfaction than I have. So it's better to cut my losses, collect my check, and go home.

So I go through the motions of preparing and helping serve dinner and am amazed at the number of crew who come up to say nice things about my cooking. And do so within obvious earshot of Johnny. But it's all to no avail as I pack my suitcase in anticipation of getting off when the *Columbia* arrives in Detroit at 7:30 tonight.

But then, in midafternoon, Brian approaches me with strange news: A deckhand is leaving the *Columbia* to go back home to be with his sick father. Bill the third night gang member is moving to take his place. Brian is moving to the night gang. Would I want to take Brian's waiter job?

Within minutes, we are on the phone to the union and have received their okay to make the switch. When I help Johnny dish out the food at supper, it is understood that I will be staying on not as second cook but as a waiter starting tomorrow.

After supper I transfer my gear from the cook's room to the quarters across the hall. They are as dark and dingy as I remember from

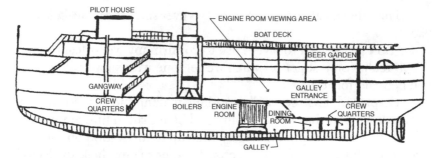

The *Columbia*'s deck profile (Brendan Livingston)

my first encounter. I find a bunk, stash my suitcase, and go up on deck feeling good about still being a member of the *Columbia*.

Although the pay won't be quite as good, I'm still being paid about three times what I was getting on the *South American*. And although we work a seven-day week on this ship, I will immediately begin to work the reduced work schedule of the waiter. I will get to sleep in until five o'clock and have longer breaks during the day. I go to bed content with the way things have worked out.

The next morning I am awakened by Bruce who will assume the second cook responsibilities until the new one comes aboard. I throw on my clothes, refreshed by the extra hour of sleep and ready for a job I know I can handle. I am somewhat taken aback when Johnny asks me to help Bruce unload the groceries from the cart. But I find that even with the time that consumes, I've got so little to do in helping Walter clean up the dining room and setting the tables that I feel like I'm on vacation. My four days of experience as second cook have prepared me for the crew as they file into the room and make their orders. Brian joins Skip and Larry from the night gang in ordering a large breakfast through bleary eyes. But he's smiling at the fact that he's now a part of the deck department and also at the fact that he can go hit the hay in a few moments, leaving the work of running the galley up to the rest of us.

I find my groove between taking and filling orders and discover my sense of relief contagious. Even Louie, the quiet fireman, gives me a pat on the arm as I deliver his two poached and rye toast.

"Looks like you like your job there," says Bruce as he pats dabs of grease from a plate on its way out.

SS *Columbia*

Built	1902
Builder	Detroit Ship Building Company, Wyandotte, Michigan
Owner	Detroit, Belle Isle and Windsor Ferry Company
Length	216'
Beam	60'
Draft	13'6"
Capacity	2,566 passengers; 30 crew
Engine	triple expansion steam
Boilers	Two Scotch oil-fired

"The kid's a natural," exclaims Walter, my new partner. "You should see him slice the bread—like he's been doing it all his life."

I notice even Johnny casting a friendly smile my way as he throws a roast into the oven.

The sitting goes faster than ever and I even have a chance to serve Captain Beattie and to joke with Joe Short—the man behind Captain Bob-Lo—who says "Hawaya" to me as he sits down to order a small breakfast. Before I know it, we're sweeping the floor and on our break—one that will extend until ten-thirty. I wander up on deck refreshed and even have plenty of time to accompany Phil, the dishwasher, up to Woodward to a drug store. The day is warm and humid, full of clouds and impending thunder. We dawdle along the way, mostly because Phil has the crippled gait, which I guess is due to polio. Phil is from California, in his early twenties and is pretty quiet, so I don't find out the cause on this walk.

The *Columbia* has the eleven o'clock sailing today so I'm back in the dining room setting up as the ship departs the dock. By the time we've swept and mopped up and I make my way back up to the first deck, we have been docked at the island for over half an hour. The thundershowers have kept the crowds down today and the sky is still full of sullen threats. This is the slowest time of day on the boat, after the crowd has been released to the midway and we await our two o'clock departure time in growing stickiness. A few hundred yards

91

away the partially filled Jet Planes drone up and down on blasts of compressed air and the screams from the Wilde Maus ripple across the small lagoon. We sit on the benches and suffer the damp hint of bug-laden air off Lake Erie as the deckhands coil and recoil the thick manila lines into hieroglyphic circles just to keep busy. I enjoy every second of my new-found freedom knowing full well that down below Johnny and Bruce are laboring in the very warm galley as they prepare another meal to knock the crew's socks off.

Tex, the wheelsman, is my new buddy and pleased that I have figured out a way to thwart Johnny's attempts to remove me from the ship. But he is the first to praise the work of the galley on the *Columbia*. "Damn finest mess on the lakes," he drawls.

"Hell," chimes in the first mate, "I'll bet it's the best on the water anywhere."

"That Johnny knows how to keep a crew happy," adds the deck-hand Herb between coils.

"He demands a lot of the galley crew," says Brian knowingly.

"I'll tell you one thing," adds Skip. "From what I hear, we're in a lot better shape than those guys on the *Claire*."

Claire is the crew's nickname for the *Columbia*'s younger sister, the *Ste. Claire*.

This brings a chorus of snorts, chortles, and guffaws from the gang surrounding the gangway.

"The *Claire*," giggles Frenchy, the oiler. "Now there's some shit of a boat."

"Second class all the way," adds Louie, the otherwise complacent fireman.

These disparaging references are the way the *Columbia*'s crew asserts superiority over the younger of the two vessels that sail for the Browning Line. The *Ste. Claire* is ten years younger than our ship, and its design has accommodated for crew needs in the new century. Where the *Columbia*'s captain and mates are housed in cabins on the first deck, the *Claire*'s have a Texas behind the pilot house on the top deck. This frees up valuable space on the first deck and allows their galley crew to berth with the other crew in the forward end of the ship in an area that has real showers and port holes that can open. In a word, luxuries.

Art, another fireman, mutters, "And I can't believe they've got all those camel jockeys as crew."

Now here is an issue that I find difficult to fathom. I have heard similar disparaging remarks on the *South* regarding the fact that the Seafarers International Union (SIU) allows Arabs to work their ships on the Great Lakes. I am bemused but not surprised that these comments come from men who have also expressed total disregard and animosity toward sailing with blacks. The other international union, the National Maritime Union, hires blacks as well as Arabs on the Great Lakes.

The SIU is closed to blacks. The only exception is the passenger cruise ships of which the *South American* is the only remaining vessel on all the Great Lakes. On the *South*, blacks are given restricted union membership with the understanding that they are not given a vote and limited to specific low-wage jobs. This basically ensures a labor force for the company, especially in the spring and fall when the college crew are still in school.

On the *South*, blacks and whites learned to work together and avoid the flash points of words or actions that could easily have thrown the ship into turmoil. And I observed a mutual agreement by all crew to ignore the fact that Detroit was burning while we sailed to Montreal. Although I knew that many of my black shipmates came from affected parts of the same city I inhabited, there was no way for me to share my fears and talk with them about it.

But this thing about Arabs is new to me. I have been vaguely aware that there is an Arab population somewhere on the west side near the Ford Rouge plant, but I have never knowingly come into contact with any. So I really don't have much to offer in response to the comment made by the fireman. Except to know that I have heard people say the same things about blacks without anything real to say except that they hated them, sight unseen.

The rest of the *Columbia* crew evidently feels the same way as no one challenges the slur. Instead, one of the engineers gestures back toward the *Claire* and says, "I worked over on that boat last year. Jesus, I lost weight."

"Looks like you got it back and then some with Johnny".

"He sure as hell don't skimp on the food like other cooks I've known," says the chief engineer. "Now you young guys'll be spoiled. You'll come to expect this food wherever you sail. And you'll be disappointed every time."

"Wonder what he's got goin' for supper," says the purser, which quiets everyone down for a few moments of thinking.

"Hell, look at the time," says the mate. "Okay, you guys, get ready to cast off. Rest of you clear the area so they can get the line."

And, with only the fanfare of approaching thunder, the mate signals up to the pilot house, the lines are cast off, the telegraph rings three gongs to the engine room, the whistle gives a short blast and the *Columbia* is underway to downtown Detroit. I enjoy the motion of the ship without passengers, the quiet way it glides through these waters, somehow swifter than usual. The breeze generated by the ship cuts the oppressive heat of the day and I luxuriate in the knowledge that I don't have to return to work until three-thirty—a whole ninety minutes away! As the ship prepares to make the Detroit dock, I will be cued to get back down to the dining room. And so I have the time to enjoy the entire ride back along the river, not as a passenger but as a paid crew member.

The supper hour goes just as quickly and the good news is that we will again have the evening to spend on the island, from six until nine o'clock when we are the last boat back to Detroit. The daylong storms have taken their toll and the four o'clock boat has taken most of the small crowd back home. However, as often happens on days like this, the storm has blown over and we are greeted by a blast of cool, fresh air from Lake Erie as we arrive and the sun is breaking through. Although it's too late for Detroiters to get to the island on the big boats, we notice that the small ferry from Canada, the *C. E. Park*, is almost overflowing with folks from Amherstburg—which indicates that the island will be populated this evening. We are the first ones over the gangway and hit the midway in full flight. This time we follow Skip's lead and promise to play a game of miniature golf first. But we find that the soggy course has closed earlier in the day so we head to the rides where the magic "Z" card ensures us immediate access. In the dizzying fresh breeze of the Scrambler, I feel like I have landed in paradise.

To my amazement, I discover that this isn't all. I watch as Skip moves in and successfully separates a Canadian honey from her friends with promises of free rides. The magic "Z" card works for female friends of the crew as well! Paradise expands as Brian and I too find success with our cards. With Larry and Phil in tow, we waltz from ride to ride until the lights come on and the haunting whistle of the *Columbia* calls us back for the return cruise to the city.

The *Columbia* at the Bob-Lo Island dock (Walter P. Reuther Library, Wayne State University)

We are now approaching the middle of August and the long days of early summer are beginning to wane a trifle earlier with each passing night. Although we are confined to our space on the first deck, it is still thrilling to watch the lights along the shore as full twilight descends. The gas burn-offs near Great Lakes Steel in Wyandotte are now sharply visible against the black-grey background of the complex and it takes no imagination to capture the sweet smell of the fuel as it mingles with the sharp tang of the smelters on the evening air.

As the *Columbia* docks, it is past ten-thirty and full evening has descended. Within minutes, before the last passenger has straggled across the gangway, my night gang buddies are impressed into early service and are going full tilt at restacking the hundreds of wooden chairs that are strewn about the top three decks of the ship. There being not much to do except sit on the wooden benches and watch the quiet darkened dock, the only option is to turn in. En route to the squalid quarters, I take a quick break to catch a piece of pie in the galley. As I sink my teeth into the chocolate goo, I reflect that it's good to know that Bruce and Johnny are on the job and that the reputation of the *Columbia* galley has been saved.

Finding my bunk in the tiny room is not especially difficult. But getting undressed in the dark leaves a lot to be desired when it comes to locating my toothbrush and some clothes to throw on tomorrow. Even though the night air is warm, the below-decks room is clammy and I scrunch up under the wool blanket. As I drift off to sleep, I am aware of the exhalations and farts of my four or five bunkmates that mingle with the dank smell of the river that seeps in through the welded portholes. Fortunately, my training in the Flicker of the *South* has prepared me for this and I fall asleep without much difficulty.

The following days are filled with much the same routine: Breakfast, dinner, and supper conducted by Johnny with the able assistance of Bruce who has somehow managed to continue peeling spuds at night so that he can mash them the next morning. I am more than content to shuttle their preparations from the galley to the dining room. The pace of the waiter job is such that I have time to banter with the customers from time to time. But when the captain is in the dining room, it's all business. Johnny will always make a point to drop whatever he's doing and personally prepare the captain's plate, making sure that he dabs up errant gravy before it runs into the vegetables.

One particularly hot afternoon I follow Skip and Brian up to the forbidden third deck that houses the beer garden. But our intent is entirely legal and sanctioned by the captain, or so they tell me. We walk along the deck until we come to a ladder that stops at the ceiling. Further inspection reveals a trap door and, in an instant, we have clambered up and arrive on the top deck of the ship, well behind the pilot house near the life boats. Now I understand why my shipmates have urged me to bring along my woolen blanket as we spread them on the hot tar of the deck. The day is blazing full of summer sun as we stretch out and let the rays blast and fry our white bodies. I have brought along my tiny transistor and have it tuned to the new underground station—Detroit's first—WABX. The music of *Sgt. Pepper's* has yielded to "All You Need Is Love" and "Baby You're a Rich Man" as well as the music of groups like Jefferson Airplane, Jimi Hendrix, and the Peanut Butter Conspiracy. Our conversation somehow turns to what we're going to do with our lives. Brian takes the lead when he says, "My plan is to get a job on a real freighter on the lakes. I'll work ten or fifteen years and save all my money. By that time I should have enough to buy a bar and kick back. Hell, you live out here on the lakes, you got nowhere to spend your money and no responsibilities except to your job. I'll probably have enough money to quit in ten years."

The rest of us, wise in the ways of the world, nod our heads in agreement. For my part, I am amazed that anyone eighteen years old—the same age as myself—would be able to come up with a life plan just like that. It is all I can do to contemplate the school year to come when I will be entering college.

After a while, when Larry and Skip have retreated below for a snack, Brian confides, "I really want to work as a wheelsman. I've been up here before and once, a few weeks back, Tex even let me handle the wheel. Course it was an empty run back from the island. What a blast," he says smiling. "Man, that wheel pulled this way then that in the current. Look at the river. Doesn't even look like it's moving. But then you feel the wheel in your hands and it's taking you all over the place. Tex grabbed it back from me before the old man came back up from the can."

"That must've been cool, even to be in there," I say.

"Never been in there?" he asks. "Well, let's go check it out."

"Won't the captain get mad?"

"Naw, as long as we're quiet and don't get in the way we're okay."

And before I can register any more resistance, I am following Brian along the top deck and through a small gate that separates us from the pilot house itself. The pilot house on the *Columbia* is about fifteen feet wide and twenty feet deep. It is full of dark wood and rounded windows that have pull down sashes to allow for breeze or shut out rain as needed. As we enter, the first thing that captures my attention is the wooden wheel, a full three feet in diameter. Standing astride the wheel, jaw set and eyes focused on the river ahead is Tex himself. He acknowledges our presence with a glance and grins at Brian. "Up here for another lesson, huh? Guess the river didn't teach you enough last time."

Brian nervously laughs and responds with a glance at the captain who is sitting on a brown leather couch in the rear of the room. He is intently reading a newspaper and listening to what sounds like CKLW on a small radio next to him. He barely glances up to mark us and disappears immediately back into his world. I glance at the Old Man, as

The *Columbia*'s pilot house as it appeared in the 1980s (Dossin Great
Lakes Museum)

they refer to him, and wonder if it's true that he can be paid one hundred dollars a day to sit on that couch and run the show.

Tex, with eyes in back of his head, says softly, "The reports from
the first races at Hazel Park are just coming in. Not a real good time
for conversation, but you're welcome to stick around."

That's enough for an invitation for us and we assume silent positions on opposite sides of the wheel watching the river unfold before
us. From out of nowhere, a voice croaks, "Put her over on those
smokestacks, the far one."

Tex is already moving the wheel to port as he responds, "Aye,
Cap."

It is then that I notice what appears to be a white swan approaching us from the middle of the river. A very large white swan. My first
thought is that it is the *Ste. Claire*, sister of the *Columbia*, on her two
o'clock run to the island. But something about it isn't right. Too large
a profile. Too sleek. Too white. With a thrill I realize that we are about
to pass my former ship, the *South American*. Time is suspended as the
two ships draw together and there's our Old Man Beattie out on the

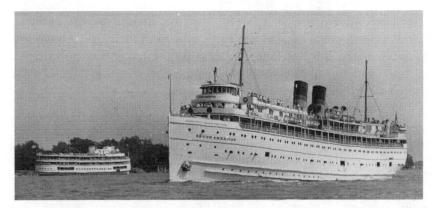

The *South American* passing the *Ste. Claire* (Dossin Great Lakes Museum)

tiny bridge waving up at the figure of Captain Testyon high up on the bridge of the *South*. And of course they both get deeper into the act saluting each other with throaty full blasts of the *Columbia* versus the more melodious chimes of the *South*. I watch and listen with Brian, both of us transported into the river magic that has enveloped us. And then, just as quickly, the sleek, sexy stern of the *South* is presenting as she zooms once again toward Montreal with Chris, Al, Brooke, Freddy, John, and all my old shipmates from just a couple weeks ago. I don't stop to realize that I have made it to heaven still breathing, but every bone in my body knows it.

As the *Columbia* approaches the Ambassador Bridge, the captain communicates telepathically to Tex who shrugs his head toward the door while making eye contact to give us the message that it's time to retreat back to the sundeck next to the lifeboats. As the ship approaches the silent dock, we clamber back down the ladder and pad along the near empty decks to our still life at the water's edge. It is time for me to return to the galley to help get supper on. After which the *Columbia*'s engine will once again churn us down the river to the island some eighteen miles and a full world away.

That evening, after the tables have been cleared and the night lunch set out for the midnight snackers, we are again sitting on the green benches near the gangway as the *Columbia* ferries a handful of passengers on the six o'clock run to the island. The day has been a scorcher and we are all grateful for the breeze, warm as it is. Conversation drifts back to the riots, still too much an open wound in my memory. But Bob, one of the assistant engineers, is pointing to an open expanse of river near the Rouge River saying, "Yeah, right there's where we were just four weeks ago."

"Not long enough," opines Tex.

"Too long for me," says Phil. "I was going crazy with nowhere to go at night."

"You could've swum and been in downtown Ecorse," laughs Johnny.

"Oh, and they weren't shooting each other there too?" asks Brian.

I ask, "How long was the ship here?"

"Four or five nights, wasn't it?" responds Phil.

"Yeah," explains Larry. "They heard a rumor that a mob of blacks was coming downtown to burn the Bob-Lo boats so they figured the best thing was to get them out of there."

"The business was closed because of the riots," adds Tex, "so there wasn't anything to stick around for anyway."

"And I sure as hell wasn't about to go walking around in downtown Detroit, no matter what," adds Phil.

It is funny to me to hear them relate their tales of the riot because I realize that they were as removed as I was seven hundred miles away in Montreal. And yet, after the boat was taken downriver, the crew might as well have been in Siberia. But the full horrors of that recent period are still too fresh in my mind for comfortable dwelling and I am glad when the conversation moves in another direction.

What happens, actually, is that Skip, bored with all the talk, has decided to act like a chimpanzee and is swinging from a water pipe that runs along the ceiling of the lower deck. One long hand clings to the pipe and in the other, to complete the picture, is a banana. Various crew give the wannabe ape the attention he is clamoring for while others choose to ignore him. But, just as Skip releases himself to the hard iron deck, down the grand staircase comes bandleader, Joe Vitale. Joe is one of those guys who always seems to be "on," and he doesn't disappoint the audience at his disposal.

"What the hell we got here?" he enters with a big smile on his unshaven Mediterranean face. "Some kind of hippy love-in?" And that is enough to get the crew out of their rut and into another frame of mind altogether. This Vitale cat has the kind of presence that makes everyone come out of their dark self and into the new day. Joe is a drummer for the ship's band and he's been around for a long time and knows his way around both the boat, the river, and the city. And, when he gets those buddies of his to play "Watermelon Man," you'd think he was drumming for Herbie Hancock himself.

Aside from the boats themselves, there are two humans who go back as far as my Bob-Lo consciousness allows. Joe Vitale is one and Captain Bob-Lo the other. On bright and sunny mornings as I tugged my mother's hand from the old brick building that served as a waiting room toward the gangplank, two images would seize my attention. The first would be Joe and his band perched along the railing of the third deck playing "Sailing, Sailing over the Bounding Main." The second would be on the dock directly below the band where Captain Bob-Lo would prance along to the music, wearing a pink lei that clashed with the one yellow sock he would daintily display. Once safely aboard, we would climb up to that same deck to watch the band play "Anchors Aweigh" as the whistle roared, the lines were released, and the *Columbia* would begin another voyage to the true magic kingdom.

And now, in the dining room of the *Columbia*, many years later, I am serving lamb chops and mashed potatoes to Joe Vitale and Captain Bob-Lo as they enjoy each other's company. Joe sits like a king at his table in the dining room and spreads cheer to everyone around. And, outside of the dining room, he takes special notice of my being a part of the happiest place on the *Columbia* by making sure I am included in his special audience. This includes being a part of the crew watching him descend the grand staircase during another moonlight charter, this one for a Greek Orthodox group. Joe, caught up in the music (and possibly heading for a nip of the red wine he's reputed to keep hidden in the tiny band room) swings into a Zorba the Greek dance with his arms waving in the air. He accompanies the dance with a litany of pseudo-Greek that he finishes with a high "Wock you" delivered cheerily to all of us sitting on the green benches. He is a born showman.

Even the shrimplike watchman, Tilly, is taken by Joe Vitale and they spend a couple of minutes trying to figure out where Tilly bought his ears to the delight of everyone there. The banter helps make the river ride fly by and, before we know it, the *Columbia* is swinging around to the dock that juts out into the river.

The *Columbia*'s band-
leader, Joe Vitale
(Dossin Great Lakes
Museum)

Without much discussion, Skip, Larry, Brian, and I head down
the long dock to the island. With an hour-and-a-half to kill on a beautiful warm summer night, you couldn't pay money to be anywhere
better than here. I check out the CKLW trailer at the dock entrance
to see if a DJ is doing a live broadcast this night. I think back to a few
years before, when Beatlemania was in full flower and a guy by the
name of Clay—Tom Clay—made his rep off of Beatle Booster Balls
and how he would collect hundreds of screaming teens around this
same trailer booth to listen to the current Beatle hit of the moment.
And he was shameless, playing a good song like "Love Me Do" and
following it with the weak "Till There Was You." And getting away

with it every time with his honey-dripping voice that oozed sincerity and empathy with the zit-filled teens wallowing around the tiny trailer.

On this night there is someone sitting in there with a face and name I don't recognize. The proven format of CKLW—a mix of British beat and Motown—is being challenged by the psychedelic music from San Francisco.

But our gang walks past the trailer without comment, focused on the miniature golf course and the game that Skip has arranged for us with the fixed determination of a badger. We take time and care in selecting our putters and ensuring that the colors of our balls are different so we won't be confused at a critical moment. He doesn't even tolerate our grumbling at having to put down fifty cents each to play the game on an island where we are used to having everything covered with a flash of our "Z" cards.

He guides us out onto the course, nothing special, just your run of the mill miniature golf course with a million-dollar view of the Detroit River and the Amherstburg shoreline on the far side, perhaps a third of a mile across. And the game itself is nothing special except for the dead serious approach that the otherwise manic leader takes to it. Skip is a stickler for rules and when a ball becomes lodged in a tree root he insists that Larry play it where it lays. When it becomes obvious that Skip will win the game at the fifteenth hole, the rest of us relax and, after conceding the game, have some fun knocking balls here and there. Our main concern is getting the game over with so we can head onto the midway and start going on some rides and perhaps meet some sweet young things that will help ease the loneliness of the long, dark ride back to the city.

Skip does not resist this initiative. Assured of his mastery of the golf course, he leads the way to the killer Bug, a big friendly ride where it is often possible to share a car with other people. The day has been warm and, in spite of the riots or even because of them, the island has been crowded these past weeks—perhaps partly because people want to restore a sense of normalcy to their lives—to prove that nothing has taken place. And perhaps folks are saying to themselves, "I'll be damned if the riots are going to cheat me out of my right to enjoy what has been the one of the key experiences of Detroit summer for going on seventy years."

Whatever the reasons, we navigate a medium-long line and flash our magic cards and find ourselves in a big round car with three giggling girls just like that. But their giggling is a bit too much for even lonely sailors to bear and we de-Bug without them in tow as we head for the Tilt-a-Whirl, another good girl-meeter.

By the time we have tried five or six rides, the sun has set and the sky is drawing a purple curtain around itself. We realize that it's only a matter of minutes before we hear the ship's whistle announcing the boarding of the nine o'clock return to Detroit. But we are occupied with a rendezvous with the Dodgem cars. The ride is located in a dimly-lit fieldstone building constructed to last for centuries. It complements many of the other buildings erected on the island around the turn of the century. Preeminent among them is the dance hall designed by John Scott. The building stands a full eighty feet tall and is reputed to have been the largest of its type in the world. And this at a time when people took their dancing very seriously. Even the bathrooms on the island are made of fieldstone as are the power house and the large roller rink. These buildings, graced by large oaks and elms and open spaces, give Bob-Lo an air of permanence and stability.

The Dodgem building, along with these other attributes, contains some of the fastest and slickest cars of their type found anywhere. And we have run into a crew of girls from the west side of the city who we think might definitely enjoy the idea of hanging with the sailors from the big boat.

The Dodgems are run by Canadian rules—fast and loose. The ride operator mumbles the rules over the PA and then sits back and lets the good times roll. And we blissfully ignore whatever he said and go whichever way our hearts desire in the sturdy machines. The floor is warm and slick at this hour so the cars slide a good five feet with every tight turn around the tire barrier in the middle. But the goal, instead of not being hit, is twofold. First, to smack as many of your buddies as you can. Head on is okay, but broadside is definitely where the points are. And a broadside when the driver is in the midst of trying to nail someone else and don't notice you is best of all. The second goal is to meet new people. If the new person is a guy, the best way is a blind broadside. The only reason you'll waste your time doing this is if there are no attractive females on the floor. In the company of females, the important thing is to get them to notice you successfully bashing someone else and having fun doing it. If you have singled out the girl of your Dodgem dreams, the ultimate experience is to slam another guy as he's trying to get her attention by bashing someone directly in her field of vision. This not only makes the other guy look foolish, it also exposes his vain intentions for the girl to see and judge for herself who she'd rather have approach her after the ride is over. Dodgem can be cutthroat and requires much strategy. It is not a sport for the faint of heart.

Luck rides with us as the operator has decided to take an extended break while we are on the floor. Our cars roll round and round in endless variations on the circle and, by the time he has emerged from his break to cut the electricity that connects the metal grid on the ceiling to the rods extending above the cars, we feel that we have successfully bonded with the west siders. As we march through the tiny wooden exit door, the silver-throated whistle of the *Columbia* can be heard echoing throughout the island calling her errant children of all ages to the return ride home. This gives us perfect timing to introduce ourselves to the girls and to invite them to share in our world on what might be an otherwise lonely ride home for all. While the girls are initially thrilled at the idea of hanging with us in the crew-only area of the first deck, it is difficult to expect them to give up the freedom of the rest of the ship that they have paid for and is denied to us. In particular, they are free to go and explore the dance floor and listen and dance to the Joe Vitale orchestra. Or they can climb the stairs all the way to the top deck and watch the lights of the passing freighters and shoreline as we slowly make our way back to the city dock at the foot of Woodward. We crew members are denied that privilege and suffer every sailing day of our lives for the loss.

And so it is that, on many an occasion, a successful evening is ruined when the girls of our dreams, their curiosity of what it's like to work on the Bob-Lo boat sated, decide to take a stroll to the upper realms of the *Columbia*. If the boat is crowded, like it is tonight, that may well be the last we'll see of them. Or, on other nights, they might wave to us as they are going over the gangplank, sometimes in the hand of a guy who, less than two hours before, was rammed by one of us on the Dogdem floor. But on those rare evenings when the gods sail with us, it is possible to catch some necking and even a kiss or two from a willing lass while standing at the railing of the crew's tiny area.

105

At those magic moments, silence reigns as we watch the ship's hull push the river into a wall of black water sent to crash up against the shore of passing islands.

On less propitious evenings, such as tonight, the options are limited to doing the same thing with fellow crew, with the petting mercifully excluded. Or there is always a visit to the night lunch in the galley. Bruce and Johnny always strive to have some fresh pies or cakes out to complement the lunch meats for those who didn't stuff themselves sufficiently earlier. So we check that out and find ourselves back on deck five minutes later, a little fuller for the experience.

Our honeys have still not returned and we fear the worst. But instead of moaning at the river, I decide to accept an offer made earlier in the week by the chief engineer. The chief was down visiting the galley making his hunting-camp recipe of pepper steak for the crew. Johnny assigned me to work with him hoping that his amateur love for cooking might rub off on me. Although the pepper steak was a hit, it didn't light my fire as second cook. But in the course of cooking, the chief invited me to come down to the engine room and take a look around.

The stairway down to the engine room is located right next to that of the galley. I open the metal gate and climb down the stairs to explore another enclave previously restricted to passengers like me—the engine room. For those who grew up on the Bob-Lo boat, as I did, there are probably two memories that will remain long after the boats have been reduced to scrap in some sad ship breaker's yard. The sound of the whistle will forever haunt my inner ear with the escaping hiss of steam signaling the full-throated roar of the beast unleashed from its cave in the netherworld of iron. And then there is the vision and sound of the triple expansion engine that feeds the whistle its diet of steam. This engine is on full display from the first deck and it's not unusual to have a crowd of people standing around the railing midships just gazing down, mesmerized by the sight of the churning pistons as they glide up and down, up and down, at a steady rhythm around the shaft that turns the ship's propellor. I have come of age within that vision and have spent many an evening when sleep would not come simply imaging the flow of the huge machine as it carried me to the island. In those cases, I would never arrive before I myself glided into the port of a deeper coma.

The iron stairs of the engine room are secured from the public by a metal gate that children too small to peer over the railing look through to see the engine at work. So it's necessary to clear them out of the way to begin the short flight down past the sign that reads "Engine Room—No Visitors." At the bottom of the stairs, reality sets in. What was an uncomfortably warm day on the first deck suddenly becomes a tropical day in the hot season. The smell of oil is everywhere as is the motion of the engine and a variety of smaller machines that perform all manner of auxiliary functions. Right at the bottom is a worn green leather chair that is normally where the engineer on watch will sit to better monitor both the engine and the stairway. Next to the chair is a large fan used to provide the illusion of air in this stifling area. A drinking fountain and a small porcelain sink round out the cramped amenities. The engineer's chair is located only a few feet away from the telegraph that is used to communicate the intent of the mate in the pilot house to the engine room. On it are written in bold letters words like "Dead Astern," "Full Astern," "Slow Ahead," and "Full Ahead." There is a large bell located just above the stairs that gongs to alert the engineer that the telegraph has been changed in the pilot house. One gong will indicate "finished with engines," the signal used when the *Columbia* is tied up at dock. Next to the bell is a brass plaque that reads simply *Columbia—Built at Detroit Drydock Company—1902.*

The engineer is normally glad for some company at any time. I look around and consider how watching these engines day in and day out could effect one's outlook on life and probably not for the better. In addition to the engineer, there is an oiler who's job it is to ensure that the engine is properly lubricated and not overheating. This involves squeezing his body along narrow catwalks that allow him access to the swiftly-moving cylinders and throbbing pistons to periodically add drops of oil from his can and to feel the bobbing pistons to check for excessive heat. This is a job that requires strict concentration. It is akin to walking inside a huge car engine with the moving parts exposed.

The third member of the engine gang is the fireman. He is secreted in a tiny dark room behind a bulkhead that shields the rest of the engine room from the ship's two large Scotch boilers. Here is where the heat is most concentrated and intense. The fireman's job is to sit on a chair and monitor the flow of oil to the boilers and to ensure that the boilers are capable of producing enough heat to generate steam to power the pistons that rotate the shaft to the *Columbia*'s propellor. On freighters that ply the Great Lakes and require a constant flow of steam for full ahead, the job can be quite boring. However, here on the river run, with speed limits, narrow passing lanes, and docking every hour-and-a-half, the firemen is kept busy. When the bell gongs, he'd better be ready to respond in a hurry. Louie, the fireman on duty on the run back from the island, sits very still in the room that is illuminated only by the glow of the flames that escape through the small slit that allows him to see inside the boiler. The only air that comes to him on this night is a faint whisper that is directed down a shaft connected to a funnel on the top deck.

I escape this hellhole and clamber back into the relatively wide-open spaces of the engine room. It is possible to walk around down here and marvel at the smaller engines that perform such functions as filtering the potable water and assisting the steering gear. These little gems are beyond the view of the paying customers one deck above us. But after a couple of meanders in this mechanical jungle, it is time to escape back to the first deck that now seems commodious by comparison.

The *Columbia* has made some progress toward Detroit and we are cruising under the Ambassador Bridge. The ship begins its approach to the dock by angling toward the U.S. shoreline. This puts us into a position that is the sailor's equivalent of driving on the wrong side of the street. Approaching ships are accustomed to passing each other port to port (or left side to left side) just as drivers do in this part of the world. But Captain Beattie has claimed special privilege and the *Columbia* regularly breaks this rule to make this dock. And so we cruise along the Detroit shoreline, angling ever closer to the warehouses that crowd the river. At some point, we actually leave the shipping channel and hug the shoreline. This sets the *Columbia* apart from other ships that cannot afford to leave the channel, dug by the Army Corps of Engineers to a uniform depth of twenty-nine feet. The thirteen-foot draft of the *Columbia* puts her in no danger of the shallower bottom out of the channel that would quickly capture and ground the bottoms of freighters.

The engines are checked down to allow the *Columbia* to ease up to the dock where a couple of workers handle the lines tossed to them by the deck crew. Within seconds we are tied fast to the dock and I watch with the others as our might-have-been girlfriends walk over the gangway and out of our lives. Since it is a weeknight, there is only a single moonlight at nine o'clock. The *Ste. Claire* has taken that run for this evening and will probably return in an hour or so. The night gang goes to work stacking the wooden chairs and I take this as my signal to head down below to my dismal and lonely bunk where my dreams will be steeped in the dark waters of the river.

And thus the whirr of the cicadas on the island and blue flowers of the wild chicory poking up through cracks in the asphalt near the Detroit dock mark our passage through the summer. Within a couple of weeks, I have bonded with this crew as though we all went through grade school together. Even the captain greets me by name and Captain Bob-Lo recognizes me and occasionally holds my hand in his arthritic grip greeting me with a "Hawaya" as his clouded eyes meet mine. I discover that one of the big differences between this crew and the one I left on the *South* is that no one else is talking about going to college in the fall. My peer group—the night gang—are more focused on heading for the union hall after Labor Day when the *Columbia* is laid up for nine long months. Brian plans to catch a freighter and sail all the way through to lay up, the end of the Great Lakes shipping season, at Christmas. Skip and Larry echo their "me too's" when they hear of this long-term strategy. Brian has even thought about the possibility that he will be drafted and get called off to Vietnam. Yet he doesn't seem all that concerned whether he goes or not. The other two don't seem to have given the subject too much thought one way or the other. Phil, the dishwasher, is in his early twenties and, because of his afflicted leg, is not at all worried. However, he comes to us all the way from California and tells us stories of punk kids on college campuses staging marches and burning draft cards. While this sounds perfectly logical to me, the others can't fathom why anyone would question the fact that when your country's at war, everyone should be expected to help.

I find my simple arguments against the war in Vietnam receiving no sympathetic hearing from this group. As a matter of fact, they seem more in tune with the older members of the crew, their attitudes formed by experiences in the world of work rather than the world of play that so clearly envelops me. And it is this sense of play and dreams of golden California that drive my conflict with the emerging reality of the war in Vietnam. One of my older brothers has even done the unthinkable and left the University of Michigan to join the army. With all of the good life before me, as presaged by the love-in on Belle Isle earlier this spring and the music and pictures of California flooding the radio and TV waves, I am absolutely unable to begin to understand why the U.S. should be fighting in Vietnam. And the standard answers that the crew of the *Columbia* give me are not at all reassuring. On the *South*, even amid all the frat and sorority types, I encountered few who expressed serious opposition to U.S. involvement in Asia.

But now I am beginning to grasp that there is something happening here, as the Buffalo Springfield put it. While I am secure in going to Wayne State and benefitting from the draft deferment for college students, one of my high school buddies, Rick, has just been drafted and is going through basic training in Georgia. The letters he has sent back so far are full of army jargon and facts of life in hell which clash terribly with my visions of the promise of freewheeling times offered by California.

And so the days and nights of *Columbia* play themselves out in the decline of the summer of '67. August is full of beautiful warm sunshiny days that already are losing the stickiness of full summer. After the sun sets, the nights are cooling down and it's not uncommon to see passengers coming down to stand near the engine room for warmth toward the end of a moonlight cruise. As a crew member, I take advantage of one of the perks offered when I invite my parents and brothers for a cruise to Bob-Lo, courtesy of Mr. Browning, the owner. The man himself arranges to meet me and my family at the gate before the four o'clock sailing and graciously ushers them aboard through the crew's gate. The only thing that spoils the event is that, because of regulations, I am not allowed to sit with them above the first deck and am embarrassed when Brian, in his new role as deckhand, informs me of this when we are visiting on the second deck in front of the bandstand.

Unlike California, all is not golden aboard the *Columbia*. As a member of the crew, I join in the general gripe sessions about the cramped quarters and ancient washrooms. Yet, so far as I'm concerned, this is small stuff compared to the fact that I am actually being paid to go to Bob-Lo. There is not a day that goes by that I don't exult in just about every trip on the Detroit River, still thrilled at the fact that I get to be out on the water day in and day out. And my job as waiter has become a downright pleasure. It is a great feeling to be able to find something that you can do well in this world. I discovered, along with the rest of the crew, that cooking is not my forte. But waiting tables is a different story and the *South* has prepared me well for this role. I am working less strenuously and getting paid twice as much. And I have all kinds of free time to hang around on the first deck and watch the life of the river. It is amazing simply to watch the endless parade of ships of all shapes and sizes as they move their cargoes through the heart of America. Or to just sit on the deck and watch the lights of the rides come on as they dart and swoop through the oncoming dusk against the backdrop of the massive dance hall and tall trees that make this place unlike any other amusement park I have ever seen. And then there are the moonlights where parties seem to break out on each deck and the *Columbia* feels more like California than the Golden State could ever be.

However, the morning comes when I discover the tug of the land and the thought crosses my mind to leave the *Columbia* for some time on my own. I have managed to make enough money to see me through the school year and my high school buddies are leaving messages with my parents about the good times I'm missing. And so, a week before the season ends on Labor Day, I give Johnny the news that he'll have to find another waiter to finish out the season. He takes it in stride and says, "Well, you did a good job as waiter. Maybe by next year, if you practice, you can come back and cook." While I am happy to hear that he likes me, if not my performance, I know deep in my heart that I want more of this sailing life than this milk run on the Detroit River can offer. I am ready for the real steamboats that cover all these Great Lakes and can't be held back by something as basic as my love for Bob-Lo. And besides, I can come back and enjoy the pleasures of Bob-Lo anytime I want and even sit anywhere on the boat I please.

And so it is that the following morning I perform my final waiter duties in the dining room. As usual, Captain Beattie is eating breakfast at the large table reserved for himself and the ship's officers. Somehow this includes the diminutive Captain Bob-Lo. Captain Beattie beckons me over and says, "Leaving us so soon?" I explain that it's time to get ready for college and where I am going. He seems satisfied with my stock explanation and says, "I can always use good crew aboard this ship. You come back next summer. We can use you on the *Columbia*." I take that praise and head back to my room. It only takes me a few minutes to throw my few clothes into the cardboard suitcase.

The *Columbia*'s last trip from Bob-Lo Island to Detroit, Labor Day, 1991 (William A. Hoey)

Then I am on my way back out through the now empty dining room where the galley crew—Johnny, Bruce, Phil, and Walter are busy cleaning up and preparing for the dinner to come. Johnny takes a few moments to shake my hand and wish me well as does Walter. Bruce is less available and calls out a twangy "So long" from the walk-in icebox. Phil takes time from the dishes to come out and shake my hand and tells me to come back and visit. On the first deck, my night gang buddies, Skip, Larry, and Brian are lounging on the green bench, having foregone sleep to bid their farewells. I cross the gangplank in the warm early morning sunlight. The tang of fermenting mash from the Hiram Walker distillery across the river is heavy on the air as I walk up the hill to catch the Woodward bus for a long ride home.

The waning days of summer are less exciting than I hoped they would be. I spend evenings with my friends driving to various city parks and socializing with a lot of other people who also have no place better to be and nothing better to do than stand around in the parking lot listening to car radios or tape decks. Invariably, the police will show up to clear the park and so we are obliged to drive to another one nearby. Among the most popular east side gathering spots is Angel Park. It is my favorite because you can watch freighters glide by more closely than anywhere else in the city, including Belle Isle. The park is located at a point where the Bob-Lo boats generally make their turns on moonlight cruises. And so it is that I am able to catch up on the non-events of that summer while seeing my old ship. While my friends are duly impressed, they really don't share in my enthusiasm about ships and so I often leave the social scene and wander to the river to watch alone. As I watch the lights of one freighter after another fill my vision and float away, I feel slight pangs that, although I did manage to sail this summer, it was only after a fashion. I still find myself yearning for a real Great Lakes experience aboard a flesh and blood freighter, particularly one that sails to the upper lakes. Ever since I was a kid, I have thrived on stories about shipwrecks and ghost ships of the Great Lakes. While Lake Erie played host to a few strange and tragic occurrences, it is Superior, Michigan, and Huron that captivate my imagination and set themselves apart in my mind as the real lakes.

Over the Labor Day weekend, a couple of friends and I take a drive into Michigan's "thumb" and end up spending the night on the beach of an the otherwise closed camp on Lake Huron. We light a campfire near the water and stretch our sleeping bags out on the sand. I am sure to place mine as close to the water as possible so that I can look out over the lake and see the strings of lights that are the only visible part of the freighters sailing through the blackness of the big water. Whenever I watch a ship heading up into Lake Huron in the autumn, the thought that I may be one of the last persons from the shore to see it afloat is never far from my consciousness.

Only nine autumns ago (1957), the *Carl Bradley* of the U.S. Steel Limestone fleet went down near Beaver Island in Lake Michigan in 100 mile-an-hour winds with only two survivors. And just last November (1964), the *Daniel J. Morrell* went down in a fierce storm on her last trip of the season off Harbor Beach in Lake Huron. The single survivor of that wreck floated around in a life raft for thirty hours covered by the bodies of his shipmates. When rescued, he claimed that he was visited on the raft by an apparition that advised him not to eat ice and thus was saved from freezing to death.

Stories like these only serve to feed my hunger for adventure. I was weaned on stories of the storm of 1913 when eight ships and over 200 sailors were lost in a single twenty-four hour period on Lake Huron and winds were so fierce that bells rang unchecked on their davits from schools across the city of Detroit all night long. The Armistice Day storm of 1940 wreaked similar havoc upon ships and sailors on Lake Michigan.

The rest of summer glides effortlessly into fall and I dutifully begin my college life at Wayne State. What is unique about the experience is that I have been accepted as one of 800 students in Monteith, a college within the university focusing on interdisciplinary studies among the arts and sciences. Coming from a rigid Catholic school and then a massive high school, I have a difficult time adjusting to small tutorial settings in which I am encouraged to offer my own opinion or even to hold an opinion. In the transition from one high school to another, I missed biology entirely, which doesn't help in my first natural science class or with the theory of evolution with a stickler of a prof named Joe Armstrong. He is one of those dedicated guys with a beard and an intellectual attitude that is disgusted with the noninquisitive attitudes of young punks like me. Armstrong gives me bad grades for my papers and tests where I fail to describe the declination of the axis and other such stuff. He makes freshman year hard on my personal solar system.

Another Monteith prof is reputed to give A's whether or not you bother to show up for his tutorials and colloquia. More importantly, he lets it be known that he is interested in trying any sort of psychedelic drug available on the underground market. No one in the faculty or student body seems taken aback by this. The remainder of the staff fall somewhere between those two extremes, making the college one of the hipper places to be on campus at a time when hipness seems to be equated increasingly with the essence of being.

Discussions begun in those tutorials and seminars often carry over into adjacent cafeterias where I learn to drink coffee and actually make new friends. One fellow, Horst, is an émigré from god knows where. He has arrived in Detroit by way of the Vista program where he married, at the age of nineteen, a covolunteer. He has stories of life in San Francisco and proclaims the summer of love over. Horst has come to Wayne State specifically because its president, William Ray Keast, has publicly vowed to protect his students from the draft through deferments. Horst is very impressed at the fact that I possess a "Z" card and can't believe how easily I was able to attain it. One night I am visiting him at his large semi-communal house off campus in the middle of a rough working-class neighborhood not far from Tiger Stadium. As I am about to take my leave, one of his housemates, Bob, brings in a rolled up newspaper and begins to shred something I've never seen before—a dried marijuana plant. Shortly after, a TV show I have never seen, named *Star Trek*, comes on, making for a very confusing hour as I struggle to figure out why everyone is hanging on every word of the guy with the pointed ears. When I have difficulty finding the door on the way out, I hear Bob laughing in the background saying, "Man. And those were only the seeds and stems!"

I find Wayne State to be a hotbed of protest and rage over the war in Vietnam. While our studies are grounded in the classics and scholarly research, every lamp post is alive with posters screaming to overthrow the system that is turning the world upside down. The student paper has been renamed the South End and has taken on the tone of an underground paper. Its writings are full of condemnation of our political and social systems with an occasional swipe at academic discourse thrown in as an afterthought. It seems like there is a teach-in or protest scheduled daily somewhere on or near campus. And, of course, while there are large numbers of kids dressing in the prep fashion of high school (most greasers, true to form, have gone to work somewhere), I am exposed to the world of long hair styles and ragged blue jeans for both sexes.

In mid-October, I take a break from campus life and hop in my '56 Plymouth for the short ride to the foot of Bates Street—the Georgian Bay Line dock on the river. While the Bob-Lo boats have been covered in their canvas shrouds for weeks, this day marks the last sailing date of the season for the *South American*. This event alone would not have attracted me out on this rainy afternoon. But I find myself standing at the dock with a gathering of people who have also heard the news that this will be the last sailing date for the *South* ever. The Georgian Bay Line has announced the sale of the *South American* to the Seafarers International Union. The SIU had, earlier this year, bought the *North American* to be used as a training ship in Maryland.

The *South American* receives a salute from the fireboat *John Kendall* on her final voyage from Detroit, October 1967 (Dossin Great Lakes Museum)

But, on the trip there, she parted lines with her tow in a storm and sank mysteriously in the Atlantic. Now the union has come for her sister to have her perform the same function.

As I watch the white beauty at the dock hissing against the grey gloom, I think back to the rumor come true of the *South*'s demise heard in her sultry Flicker during the summer. The word then was that the U.S. Coast Guard had condemned the *South* because of her wooden superstructure. At that time, sweat-soaked and sick of shoving piles of greasy dishes through the Hobart, I'm sure my reaction was close to "Why wait? Let's close down this firetrap now." A ship's oiler corroborated the rumor by pointing out the source of the perpetual noise that penetrated my dreams whenever the ship was underway and the pistons were at work in the engine room. "That sound's gonna be with us all summer," he predicted. "Bad cylinder they're not gonna fix because it's not gonna be needed anymore."

With these thoughts as background, I stand in the light rain at the dock, watching as the crew goes about their usual slow preparations for another sail. There might be another forty or fifty people around like me to say goodbye to the old girl. Every few minutes, a few passengers are dropped off by taxi to embark on the last cruise that will be only one way to Montreal. I spot Clarence, the black laundry man, standing under shelter near the brick office building and join him for some commiseration. He says, "Why don't you come on board and go for the trip? I can get you a job, no problem." I ponder this offer as the deep melodious whistle sweeps above and through us and makes the *South*'s presence known to everyone in a two-mile radius. I think of one more run to fantastic Montreal and the life of that cosmopolitan city. But the rain sobers my emotions and I end up responding, "No thanks, man, I've got classes I can't miss." Clarence nods a mute understanding, bids me so long and walks back aboard the ship where the crew are already casting off the lines.

With one more long blast, the *South* is slipping away from the Bates Street dock, her home for decades. This time with no round trip scheduled. As she slips into the mist, the Detroit fireboat, *John Kendall*, meets her and sends a shower of water into the air from her water cannons in salute. The *South* answers with three longs and two shorts and continues to do so until she has completed her turn and is on her course toward the Ambassador Bridge and Lake Erie. I watch until her white body becomes enshrouded by the mist. Then I get back in my rusty blue Plymouth and head back to campus for a late afternoon anthropology class. A week later the *South* is formally decommissioned in Montreal. Her colors are taken down, ship's personnel dismissed by Captain Testyon and she begins her tow toward the East Coast.

The remainder of the school year settles into a routine of classes and parties punctuated by long evening discussions in various coffeehouses or apartments. I slip into the world of free thinking with remarkable ease and have no problem letting my hair grow. I watch classmates expand their minds to the point where they simply cease to be part of the Monteith experience and choose instead to become part of the burgeoning campus fringe scene. Psychedelic music is all around us, supplied by the Grande Ballroom on Grand River that regularly hosts the hottest British and U.S. groups and supported by local bands. For my part, I enjoy the spirit of liberation but prefer to maintain my draft-deferred status as a full-time college student.

I also get a firsthand feel of the war in Vietnam via correspondence with my high school buddy Rick, who has been there as a medic since the start of the year. He writes on U.S. Armed Forces stationery that features a map of Vietnam in the corner that identifies all the principal geographical sites. He has drawn a small circle around a place called Pleiku about halfway between Saigon and the border with North Vietnam where he is stationed:

> Here I am finally and still alive. I'm in an engineering unit now so that'll keep me out of the jungles for a while.
>
> I'm in a room with one other guy and a stereo tape recorder. We pay a woman to keep our room clean, wash our clothes, and shine our boots.
>
> I'll be going to the field mostly on reconstruction sites. I've got a 45 pistol but I may buy a rifle. I'm not sure yet.
>
> My roommate is the bouncer at the club so I get my beer free. Almost everybody around here smokes pot or pops pills—some of the guys stay messed up.
>
> We treat about 10 cases of v.d. a week with about 8 cc's of penicillin in the rump.
>
> Does your brother think he'll make it over here or what?
>
> See you soon
>
> Ten Months
>
> Ps. Write sooner than soon.
>
> Rick

Somehow, by spring break, I find myself on a plane with my high school buddy Sammy cruising for L.A. Late that evening, we are walking down the streets of Glendale, having hitched that far from LAX, in search of his cousin's house. The cops naturally stop two kids walking down the street carrying duffel bags and we discover that one of the officers is originally from Detroit's east side. His warning to watch our step around here is disregarded and we find cousin Joe's place without much difficulty. Cousin Joe and his family welcome us in and he plies us with Coors. Then we ride to the beaches where I make my first serious encounter with body surfing and find it good. But the good life in LA can't stop me from the pilgrimage to Mecca and so early one morning Cousin Joe takes Sammy and me to the northern outskirts of Santa Monica and deposits us on Highway 101, El Camino Real, where we stick out our thumbs. The trip down the coast is eventful and we meet many of our ilk along the trail. The car radios around L.A. are playing a lot of George Harrison's "The Inner Light." When it is getting dark and we are only halfway to our destination, we accompany one fellow traveler to a small police station where he is able to reclaim his car, towed the past Sunday from the site of a concert in a canyon off the Big Sur. The remainder of the drive along the dark coast is haunted by the blackness of the ocean, our only companion. By the time he drops us in Oakland, it is approaching midnight and we find a motel willing to take our money.

By early morning we are back on the road and catch a ride from some guy dressed in pin stripes, chauffeured in his Mercedes limo in style into the city. We walk the streets of Frisco, eyes wide open, carrying our duffel bags, seeing everything and ignored by all. When we reach what quickly become the nadir of our trek, Haight-Ashbury, love is not in the air. Instead, we discover an intersection full of traffic and people with tourist buses crawling by to allow everyone on them to get a good look at us. We continue on to Golden Gate Park where the hippies hang out. The day is warm and full of spring beauty so we sit on the grass and watch the world of love unfold around us. "Sort of like the Belle Isle love-in, but all the time," Sammy observes. He is from more conservative stock and has been reluctant to take this trip up the coast, preferring the comforts of L.A. to this scene.

Tiring of watching a fair amount of nothing—a girl introduces us to her mutt named Roach—we wander the city and hop the cable cars down to the piers where we watch a group of conga players perform for each other and the sea lions. As evening falls, we realize that we are not funded to secure another motel, even if we could find one. So I take the lead and approach a mission that someone on the street says gives out free rooms. At ten o'clock, with two room passes in hand, we are admitted to a genuine fleabag hotel in the heart of the city where we spend the rest of the night staring at the ceiling and fearing attack.

Bleary-eyed, we catch an early ride out of the city the next morning and begin the long hike back to L.A. Our rides take us to all the great tourist spots but we are unable to do anything but offer thanks and get back on the road. When night falls and we are still fifty miles outside L.A., we break down and hop a bus into the city where Cousin Joe meets us and informs Sam that "Grandpa has died" and the entire family is Detroit bound. With Sammy gone, I spend the remaining

119

days of my vacation living with a Detroit family that had been my closest friends ten years before they moved out here. They are all busy in school or working, leaving me a couple of days to wander the city and the beaches. Then it's time for me to catch my own flight back to the Motor City and the school thing. I return knowing that I have seen a part of the world that has intrigued me for the past year since I first heard *Kooler World* on my bedside radio.

Another letter from Rick in Nam:

Greetings,

I'm truly glad you found time to write. It's too bad all the rest of the pricks have broken hands to where they can't write.

So you and the number one prick really made it to California. I thought for awhile you wouldn't make it.

From what I hear, Frisco is the place we've got some so-called hippies.

You're right about those parties. I've been to a few here and mostly they use a water pipe to blow, or should I say a home made water pipe.

I'll give you a diagram if you want to try it. The majority of the guys just pop pills—it's easier and less chance to get caught. For ten bucks you can get a bag about the size of a potato chip bag.

Maybe we shouldn't be here. I've asked several people, kids and a whore and none of them even know why we're here.

Little girls come around selling cake for 60 cents and the dumb GI's buy them. The price of a shot of leg is about $5 depending on how much business they had. If they like you, you can get it for free.

This pimp brings his girls to our work site. He drives a Honda. It seems the girls have a strong constitution. They don't blow.

How's my boy Lou? Doing good I hope? Do you see much of Bob? He's getting to be pretty cool. Remember when he wouldn't let me drive his car if he knew we'd be drinking.

There's two kinds of people here—Vietnamese and Montagnards. The Montagnards are dark but don't have slanty eyes and they hate the Viet Cong and the Vietnamese. The Vietnamese hate the Montagnards and are also afraid of them and you can't tell if a Vietnamese is a Viet Cong or not.

The Vietnamese Army are called Arvans—They ain't shit. The Montagnards also have one and kick ass.

If we wanted to we could end this war in a couple of months—if we could just kick ass.

Hey, watch the wise cracks about my school. The two main religions here are Buddhist and Catholic. The Buddhist sign is just the opposite of the Nazis.

My design of the pipe. [drawing of a water pipe]

If you can make it work, beer is better than water or any type of alcoholic beverage, scotch, whiskey, or whatever, but is harder to keep lit.

9 more months

Me

During the late spring, we spend a lot of time hanging out at Rick's girlfriend's house on Euclid near Woodward, not far from the New Center area. Due to a live-in invalid crazy grandmother, our parties are confined to the tiny second-floor bedroom of her brother Raymond. Raymond, another St. Bernard expatriate, is preparing to graduate from St. Philips, and because he is not planning to go to college, is apprehensive of the draft. He writes often to Rick, asking him about what to expect and hoping that Rick will be home before he is drafted.

Mostly we spend our Friday nights sprawled around the floor of this room, listening to Ray's Motown collection and trying to put the make on the girls who share our candlelit space with little success.

One late evening, as a thunderstorm splits above the downtown skyline, he shows me a letter he is preparing to send to Rick.

Hi Brother,

I finally kicked myself in the ass and decided to write you. I saw that picture of you with the machine gun so I figured I better write or else.

I am in perfect condition as far as health goes. I finally decided that all young girls are all bitches who don't know when they got a good thing. Sandy, Toni, Linda, and Sharon are all doing fine in their own stupid silly ways. I can't wait till you get back so we can hit the real women.

What the hell is happening over there with those whores? Do they have pimps in Vietnam? I went to the president the other day and I said, "Dammit, Lyndon, what the fuck are you doing over there?" He said he was going to end the war. Fuck Vietnam.

Well, Richard, I'm afraid it won't be long. As of now, I haven't had my physical, so I have at least another thirty days.

Before this week is up, I am going to apply for a driver's license. The old man said he would loan the car to me if I had a license.

Guess what? I called Gail and talked to her for about two hours. I told her I was digging her from a long way back. She thinks I like her. Do you think she is a bad girl or will I have to train her?

Well, I'll see you. Stay sharp, brother. Don't get VD or I'll kick your ass. I graduate in four days. Then I might get drafted. I hope I can stay out till you come back.

I'm out of school now and got plenty of time. Write soon.

Bernard Boys Forever.

Ray

Two weeks later, Raymond is called for his physical.

CHAPTER 3

1968

Welcome to My Nightmare

Wayne State's classes are not out until early June, long after University of Michigan and Michigan State University students have been released to find summer jobs. With the *South American* at rest somewhere on the East Coast and Bob-Lo not a real option for my wanderlust, I clutch my even more valuable "Z" card and make the trek to the union halls on the west side. The SIU hall on Jefferson offers little help, even though they had no problem accepting my dues just last summer. While the blackboard shows a smattering of openings for galley, engine, and deck, the hall master, or whatever they call him, demands $500 for permanent membership before they'll ship me out. That serves only to reinforce the negative feelings I have been cultivating about this place since last year. And then he has the nerve to tell me that, once the dues are paid, there is no guarantee when he will be able to ship me out. While it's true that the SIU doesn't represent all that many ships on the lakes, I know that they ship for Boland and Cornelius and the Reiss boats, as well as Tomlinson and, of course, the Bob-Lo boats. Throw in a few cement boats and you've got a couple dozen ships at least. With no encouragement except to pay most of what I could hope to earn in a summer and then wait and hope, I decide to try the competition. I leave the place with a sense of relief. The stories I heard about these union people last summer, coupled with the fact that they won't hire blacks, makes me glad to be rid of them.

It is a short ride from the SIU to the National Maritime Union (NMU) hall on Fort Street. This is the same place in the shadow of the bridge I wandered into a few years ago with my buddy Roger. As I climb the stairs and enter the dark room, I note that the cigarette-laden air, the chrome-and-leather furniture, and the face of the guy who kicked me out back then is still the same. Louis Streho. I will not forget his name as he asks me what I want. This time I'm able to flash my card and have him regard me seriously. While the hall is strangely quiet and virtually empty, he gives me some hope and encourages me to stick around—something will probably come up soon. With the Ford fleet and the Cleveland tankers as well as a couple other companies, the NMU probably represents the same number of lakers as the SIU. So I hang around the near-empty hall, counting dust motes through the late morning and into the afternoon. The blackboard located near the broken TV lists a number of jobs that read:

Benson Ford	AB watchman
Meteor	wheelsman
Polaris	oiler

The rating on my card still qualifies me only for entry-level positions in the engine room, deck, and galley departments. Although my goal is to work on deck, Streho notes that not everyone has a galley rating—something I had to have to get my job on the *South* last year. So I wait and watch as the occasional shorebound sailor enters the room and finds a friend in a similar situation. They come in, check the board, smoke a cigarette or two, chew shipping news with a buddy or pump Streho for information, and are on their way. I sit and observe this for the remainder of this day and all the next. It is not until my third visit to the hall that I notice Louis take a call from his glassed-in cubicle. By the time he has finished scrawling something on the blackboard, I am at the window, card in hand, pointing at his writing that reads "*Mercury*—porter."

"Do I qualify for that?" I ask, pointing.

He stares at his own writing as if he's trying to decipher what he's just written. Then he turns back to me and says, "Yeah. But I can't tell you for how long. That's just a replacement position. You could get bumped any time."

When he sees me still standing there, he goes back to his desk, pulls a card, and says, "Okay, I'll give you a shot. You've got to report to the Sun Oil dock in Toledo by six tonight."

I waltz out of the hall into a dazzling world full of blue sky and goodness even though I am actually in the midst of one of the world's

The *Mercury* (Thomas Manse Collection)

darkest and most heavily industrialized areas. I gaze at the blackened spans of the Ambassador Bridge stretching south to Windsor and revel in my great fortune. At last. A job on a real freighter!

The celebration quickly turns to action as I return home to pack a suitcase, make my goodbyes to my parents, and cadge a ride from my mom down to the Greyhound station. The bus ride to Toledo takes me over endless stretches of flattened land, most of it covered by factories and railroad tracks. As the bus lopes into the emptiness of downtown Toledo after five, I begin to consider the next leg of my journey. Fortunately, a cabbie knows the way and takes me across the Maumee River through a maze of docklands until we emerge at a tank farm identified by the name Sun Oil. I pay the man, all the while focusing on the ship tied up a short distance away with the name *Mercury* on her bow. I walk the short distance from the parking lot to the dock, taking in the features of the ship.

CHAPTER 4

Steamboat III

Lost at Sea on the Tanker SS *Mercury*

The *Mercury* is shorter than most freighters I've seen on the Detroit River but certainly fits my description of a lake freighter. I walk alongside the black hull, noting the large rivets that hold the plates together as well as the occasional scrape caused, I imagine, by coming too close to docks. Near the stern, I climb a short ladder onto the deck, where I am greeted by a bearded man who introduces himself as Sully. He is wearing an olive field hat of the type made popular by Fidel Castro. He directs me to a cabin on the starboard side and leaves me standing in the tiny space, surrounded by a bunk bed, a dresser, a sink, and a chair. Other than the brief time I enjoyed in the spacious steward's cabin on the *Columbia*, this is my first real cabin. I revel in the fact that I have to share this space with only one other person.

I unfix myself long enough to unpack my suitcase and throw my clothes into the two empty drawers of the dresser. Then I head back onto the deck in search of someone who can provide me with bedding for my upper bunk. I find Sully still near the ladder, talking with another guy in his late forties who introduces himself as Jerry. Jerry is dressed in dark green coveralls and also wears a friendly smile in greeting me aboard. He and Sully, the two men apparently on watch, are discussing an approaching storm and whether they need to use another four-inch manila line to better secure the ship to the dock. They allow me to participate as an observer in their debate, which broadens into a discussion of the relative merits of manila versus cable. Jerry takes a break to tell me that most of the crew has gone "up the street" and probably won't be back until the town shuts down.

Taking the cue, Sully leads me back to a door on the port side that enters into the galley. Just off the galley is a cabin where he shows me to a bald-headed older man sitting in a chair who appears intent on watching his socks, or perhaps something growing on his socks. Broken from his reverie, the man introduces himself as Ray, the second cook, and welcomes me aboard in a drawl that I associate with Kentucky. He finds some bedding for me and tells me what time to report to the galley in the morning. He also relates that Russ, my roommate, has gone to Illinois to pick up a car and probably won't be back until late in the night, and that the *Mercury* won't sail until noon tomorrow anyway. As I make up my upper bunk I think about the fact that, based on my first three encounters, the crew of the *Mercury* is going to be a friendly bunch of guys to work and sail with.

My first night in the hot little cabin passes uneventfully and I am awakened around six by an unknown voice telling me to report to the galley. Noting that my roommate hasn't yet arrived, I pull on my clothes and head through a passageway that cuts across the width of the ship to the washroom just off the galley. I accept this without complaint, having yet to be spoiled by such modern conveniences as in-room toilets and showers and the like. Like a good sailor, I heed the metal sign above the sink that reads WASH HANDS BEFORE RETURNING TO GALLEY and head in.

I immediately recognize Ray, who is talking with another man dressed in galley whites whom he introduces to me as Bill Giddings, the steward and first cook of the *Mercury*. Bill is a tall, lean fellow who reminds me of Jeff, of Mutt and Jeff, without the moustache. He welcomes me to the galley, a small, square room about the size of the galley on the *Columbia* and dominated by a large black stove and oven. Bill wastes no time in turning the breakfast over to Ray and initiating me in my duties. He first walks me to the forward end of the ship and up a flight of stairs to a deck that houses the first mate's and captain's quarters. My responsibility will be to daily straighten out these rooms and make the beds, and weekly clean the bathrooms. Bill talks as he demonstrates the procedure on the first mate's bed and cabin. He tells me that I will also need to perform these duties for the second and third mates' room, as well as those of the chief engineer and his three assistants. "The tricky part is knowing when you can get in their rooms," Bill counsels. "For example, the first mate's watch is four to eight, which means you've got to get to it before eight, when he gets off. The best time to catch the second and third's room is just before noon, when both are up and having dinner in the galley—they share the same room. Same with the engineers, who have the same watches as the mates." Bill slows down enough to allow my college education to absorb this information overload, then he hits me with, "And the captain and chief engineer have to be caught whenever they aren't in their rooms. And that could be anytime or no time."

On the way back aft, Bill points out the engineers' quarters, all located on the starboard side, on either side of my room. As we enter the galley, I am preoccupied with trying to memorize the locations of the cabins and the timetable for getting to them. Bill breaks my reverie by giving me a quick introduction to the sink and my other responsibilities as dishwasher. I watch as he demonstrates the proper amount of soap and water I need to put into the sink, and try on the rubber gloves he thrusts at me. By this time, there is a pretty good pile of dishes to start washing that Ray has trucked in from the crew's mess and the officers' dining room. These two rooms are located off separate sides of the galley. A quick glimpse into the crew's mess reveals a couple of old-fashioned lunch counters and round stools to seat the sailors. The officers' room has wood-paneled walls that surround a large oaken table, around which real chairs are drawn. It reminds me of rooms I've seen at the country club at caddie banquets.

I am soon up to my ears in suds and scrubbing as the clean dishes slowly assemble in the rack next to the sink. As the morning meal comes to an end, Ray shows me the mop, bucket, and soap used to wash down the floor and leaves me to it. By the time I drag myself back to my room, it is pushing ten o'clock and I'm thinking about a little nap. But as I push open the screen door, I encounter a guy who's trying to stuff some shirts from a duffel bag into the drawers. He quickly introduces himself as Russ, the waiter, and just as quickly asks why it was necessary for me to get his sheets dirty as he points to the edge of the bunk. I apologize, explaining that it must have happened as I was making my own upper bunk. Russ accepts the apology and then we fall into small talk. He tells me he is from Chicago and is not normally a sailor but has taken this job to help get him through a divorce. Russ is probably twenty-five or so and an alright sort although we don't have a whole lot in common. He wears flannel shirts and sports a Buddy Holly haircut with black frame glasses, a look that is definitely out. He is not interested in the college life and doesn't seem to me to be a part of my generation at all. But he is friendly enough for a cabin mate and is decent enough to remind me when the time approaches for me to get the mates' room up forward.

And so I spend my first day aboard the *Mercury* learning the tricks of my new trade in seafaring. Nothing dramatic or romantic, save for the fact that I am aboard a genuine freighter on the Maumee River in the port of Toledo. I am bothered a little by the fact that the ship has not budged an inch as my second night aboard descends. But the rest of the crew, captain included, seem to take it in stride and I retire to my hot cabin and the upper bunk next to the ceiling for the rest that has eluded me all day.

I am roused out of that same bunk eight hours later and emerge from the cabin to encounter a brand new scene in the grey morning light. I know from remarks offered by some of the crew last night that we were destined for the Rouge River near Detroit and spend a few fleeting seconds trying to orient myself to the wider-than-expected body of water that the *Mercury* is docked perpendicular to. I go through my morning routines with some reminders from the galley crew and then, around ten-thirty, am amazed to witness the *Columbia* come sailing past my vision as I walk forward to catch the captain's room. It takes me a few moments to realize that what I have been looking at is the Detroit River, and the *Mercury* is not in the Rouge, as I had led myself to believe. I ask Smoky, the first mate, where we are and he explains that we are tied up in a slip at the Nicholson docks off the Detroit River. I point to the old ship we are tied up to and he answers, "That's the *Panoil*. God knows how she got here." The *Panoil* is a rusting tanker that looks like it's been here forever. Most tantalizing is the lettering under the ship's name on the stern that reads "Mexico City" as her last port of registration. I go about my room cleaning, intrigued and hoping to have a chance to find out more.

These Nicholson docks, located about a mile from the Rouge, are at the heart of what was a major shipbuilding industry until recently. Now the slips, once alive with welding, serve as havens for rust buckets like the *Panoil* that allow ships like the *Mercury* to slip in and unload fuels like the Bunker C that is flowing from our holds and over the *Panoil* to a tank onshore.

After the dinner dishes are done, I decide to cross over from the deck of the *Mercury* to that of the *Panoil*. I discover a wreck of a ship that has been stripped and left to rot. At the entrance to the dark engine room, the doorway allows me enough light to see a plate that tells me the ship was built in 1920. She is younger than the *Mercury*. As I clamber around the decks of the hulk, I notice Clark, the second mate, observing me from the deck of the *Mercury*. He asks me if I've found the treasure in the hold yet and I am reminded that I should be attending to the sheets and garbage cans of the engineers instead of meandering around on the blackened ghost of the *Panoil*.

Yet the *Panoil* continues to intrigue me as we while away the afternoon hours. Her faded wooden crew quarters perched above decks, her worn portholes and coal box, the vanished engines that brought her to this end as a dock over which thousands of gallons of oil, once her lifeblood, are pumped. It is inevitable to compare the *Mercury*, a steamboat, yet vital and thriving, to the hapless *Panoil*. The *Mercury*, born less than ten years earlier in Lorain, Ohio, is still sporting fresh paint with gleaming brass, pumping engines that emit a scent of fresh oil, and a warm galley full of food and human life. The comparison is life to death. Totally unfair to the *Panoil*. Watching her wallow in her own remorse, I wonder what twenty years will bring to the fate of the *Mercury* and the *Columbia*.

Even though the late June day is warm and muggy, a light chill courses from my shoulder blades up the back of my skull and down my spine until I feel the pain at the fate of the *South American* stirring in my gut. She is gone before her time for sure. I saw her go into that gloom. From the bits and pieces I heard over the winter, she made it through the seaway to the ocean to some dock on the East Coast. Yet I don't know if I would have felt better had I heard that she sank like her sister, refusing the fate of survival in a strange, uncaring place.

With my first voyage on the *Mercury* having taken place while I dreamt, I stand steadfastly at the ship's railing the next morning as the lines are cast off and I witness the *Mercury* gain headway under her own power. Actually, I am able to witness the entire voyage, for the ship lopes down the Detroit River to the Rouge, where she twists and turns with the river under lift bridges, past sludge dumps and rusted jungles of car carcasses and even past the Ford Rouge Plant itself before coming to rest at an oil dock in the heart of nowhere to take on a load of jet fuel. After two hours, we are about two miles from where we started. I find myself melting at the railing, thinking of all the ugly water that the *Mercury* has slithered through, and wonder if this is all there is to Great Lakes steamboating.

With nothing better to do, I decide to disembark for a stroll in the small field behind the dock. My natural science classes with Joe Armstrong have helped me to appreciate life even in the remotest urban jungles. I think this will be a real test of that appreciation. Several minutes later, I wander back to the ship, having identified some plantain, Queen Anne's lace, stinging nettles, and Belladonna. I also discover a family of field mice nestled in a tire surrounded by last year's yellowed grass, as well as several sparrows flitting from tree to scrawny tree in some undergrowth.

As I make my way back to the ladder, I come across John, an oiler distinguished by his blue cap with polka dots, and the third mate. They are engaged in an animated conversation that ends abruptly as John walks up the ladder and onto the deck. As I begin to ascend, the mate motions me over, where he confides in a low tone, "Whatever you do, watch out for that guy. He's nuts and could be a psycho." I thank him for his advice and make my way back to the galley wondering if I haven't uncovered more on this field trip than I'd bargained for.

Late that night, tanks full, the *Mercury* emerges from the heart of darkness and steams for the open reaches of Lake Erie. I awaken to a warm breeze laced with bugs and the lone skyscraper—the Terminal Tower—of Cleveland beckoning on the horizon. We crawl past the stone break wall and into the mouth of the Cuyahoga, only recently made famous for becoming the first river in the world since biblical times to catch fire. The Cuyahoga is similar to the Rouge, and we twist for hours as we wend our way up, with the Terminal Tower always close by. The only real difference is that there are several freighters tied up to each bank. Clark, the second mate, who is standing watch on the stern with a walkie-talkie that connects him to the pilothouse, tells me that this is because the local 5000 steelworkers, who are the union for these sailors, has called a strike and refuses to man these ships. I stand at the rail, thrilled at seeing so many ships in one place, as the *Mercury* parades past.

The ship finally ties up near another tank farm. As the crew prepares to connect the hoses, I note the captain leading the third mate with a suitcase down the ladder to a waiting taxi. Ray, the second cook, who is watching with me, confides, "Thank God he got him off in one piece. That guy's gone stark-raving nuts." All I can wonder about during my afternoon siesta is John, the oiler, who wears the blue hat with white polka dots.

It is in Cleveland that some of the other *Mercury* crew begin to slip away. The captain, for one, has departed and been replaced by a grey-haired, trim guy named Charley Stanley. Captain Stanley is a cheerful sort who seems to laugh a lot. I think it will be fun to work around him, compared to the other captain, who, like many of the crew, hasn't had a real vacation for the better part of a year.

The following afternoon, as the triple-expansion engine thrusts the *Mercury* toward Buffalo, I am thrilled to be invited up to the pilot-house by the second mate. Clark is a small man in his forties who wears black frame glasses and has jet-black hair combed back. He shares the twelve-to-four watch with Jim, the wheelsman, who, in his early twenties, is the closest to my age of anyone aboard the ship. After a while of just sitting and talking, I realize that I have been invited up here to help break the monotony of life aboard the *Mercury*. Clark makes much of the fact that I am a college student and uses that as a pretext to grill me about the types of theories I have been exposed to in my first year. While on the *South American* college was considered the norm, on the *Mercury* I probably already have more formal education than the entire crew. And because of this, I am fair game for the crew to prove that life and experience is the greatest educator of all, something I am not equipped to argue with.

For his part, Jim is fully accepted as a sailor among sailors on the *Mercury* and acts closer to forty than twenty. Clark explains that Jim is protected by a U.S. Merchant Marine law that exempts sailors from being extradited for crimes against states. Therefore, he is free to sail the Great Lakes but cannot set foot in Michigan, where he has an outstanding warrant for his arrest on a drunk driving charge. Jim's status has shot up several points and he wears it like a pro while he wheels his life away on the *Mercury*. He is closer to an old salt than a college punk.

And so we talk about Freud and Jung and Darwin and even touch on Einstein, where we agree on sharing a profound lack of comprehension. At some point, while Jim looks straight ahead, Clark asks innocently, "You believe in flying saucers?"

"Well, I guess so. I mean, why not?"

"I don't believe in 'em. Know why?"

"Why?"

"Think about it, college boy. I've been standing this twelve-to-four watch for years. Middle of the night for twenty years. Out here in total darkness in the middle of these lakes. And there are millions of guys just like me all around the world who've been standing the same watch. How much of the world is water? Didn't learn that? Two-thirds. And ships have been sailing since the times of the Greeks, for over two thousand years. And in all that time out here I haven't seen anything that looks like a flying saucer and I have never heard of a sailor who reported seeing one."

Clark rests his case and I am no one to counter his argument, conceding that book learning can't compete with this world. Jim looks over from the wheel and laughs as he lights a cigarette. "I'll bet you could teach these college kids a thing or two more, Clark."

"You're damn right I could. All these kids running around these campuses think they know so much. Get 'em out here and we can teach 'em about the real world."

But Clark says it in a nonthreatening way that seems to say, "But you're okay, kid. You're not like them. You're one of us now and we'll teach you the world of steamboating."

At this point, our discussion is interrupted by the ship's radio, which is picking up a distress call from a ship that gives its position as sailing through another part of Lake Erie. The voice is thick and Germanic and is calling for help with the message, "One of our crewmen has fallen down into the hold and is unconscious. We need a doctor and to get him to hospital immediately."

The pilothouse of the *Mercury* falls silent as Clark mutters, "Salty from Germany." He waves his hand to hush us and stands next to the radio to catch the response.

"This is the U.S. Coast Guard in Cleveland responding. We have received your message and need to know your coordinates."

"We are in Lake Erie at latitude 42°20'N and longitude 81°10'W, heading upbound for Detroit."

We look at each other in the long silence that follows. Finally the Coast Guard voice returns with, "What are the injuries to the crewman, Captain?"

"The man has injuries to his back and head and may also have a broken leg. He is not conscious and there is a lot of bleeding."

"We copy that. We will be sending a vessel to evacuate your crewman but it must come from Cleveland and will not arrive for at least two hours."

A longer silence follows. The Coast Guard voice asks, "Did you copy that reply?

The thickly accented answer comes slowly and sadly, "Yes, we copied. Two hours will be too long. I think he is dying now."

"Copy that. The vessel is under way to meet you. Let us know if there is any change in status."

After another long pause, "The man has stopped breathing. We think he is dead."

Clark shakes his head and turns down the radio, and the three of us exchange glances.

"Hell of a way to go out here," he muses. "Guy doesn't stand much of a chance for help when something like that happens."

Jim lights another cigarette and nods his assent. I sit on the pilot's stool, stunned at what I've just heard. Here on Lake Erie on a beautiful summer's day, a sailor probably less than a hundred miles from where we are sailing has died. The fun has gone out of the pilothouse and I leave a somber Clark and Jim to ponder the truth of this other side of sailing.

We arrive in Buffalo late that afternoon, where I am mildly surprised to be invited to go "up the street" after supper with Clark and Jim. They quickly overcome my feeble objections and within a couple of minutes I am walking down the dock with them. We hop into a taxi that zips us to a bar in the old downtown area. Although I'm only nineteen, just like the summer before, I'm servable thanks to the New York State drinking laws. Finding the first place empty, we careen down Chippewa Street from one to another until we find a place with some jump to it. This bar is small and cavelike, with enough room on the back of the bar for three girls to perform topless for our "edification," as Clark puts it. We catch a taxi back toward the *Mercury* much later in the evening, and I part company with my shipmates to wander back alone while they go into a little dive near the dock for just one more.

The next morning is a waking nightmare for me. Time ticks forward in microseconds. Just when it seems that the second hand will reach the twelve, the device seems to reset itself a few painful seconds back for me to live through again. I am reminded of the myth of Sisyphus and am sick to death with a hangover. I struggle through the day pretending to perform my duties as the *Mercury* heads back out into the lake, bound for who cares where. The experience reaches a climax when I shake a box of detergent into the sink and the powder blows back into the galley and onto some steaks that Bill is setting out to cook, coating them with a fine layer of soap.

He turns on me with a vengeance, removing a cigar stump from his mouth. "What in the hell do you think you're doing?" he yells. "Coming back drunk to the ship like that. I oughta fire you for all the grief you're causing me."

After the supper dishes have been done, I discover that my sickness has been replaced with the dread prospect of actually being let go. I hunker down in my bunk and vow that I will never touch another drop if I'm allowed to continue. For the moment, the thought of the trade actually comforts me and I let it carry my mind away.

In the morning, feeling bad about yelling at me, Bill takes it upon himself to bring me back into shipboard life. "I've got a good story to tell you only I can't cause you're too easily amused." And I am thus welcomed back to the galley.

In my pursuit of my own selfish desires, I have never really paused to think about the lives of my fellow crew beyond the crazy stories they are capable of relating. I don't know if Bill has kids and, if he does, whether they are my age. But he does share with me his reality of the life of a sailor ashore. "You go home to the city you grew up in and people won't give you the time of day. You want to get a loan so you go to the same bank your neighbor goes to and they turn you down. They never say it to your face but it's because you're a sailor and they think you're gonna take their money and they'll never see you again." The same law that prevents the state police from coming and carting Jim the Wheelsman off the *Mercury* in handcuffs is responsible for Bill's being considered a high flight risk by the bank.

"And your neighbors don't really want to know you," Bill goes on. "Treat you like a stranger or worse." Even in my youth I am capable of seeing a burnt-out case in Bill the steward. When he tells me of the *Mercury* being trapped in ice in Lake Michigan for a week this past winter I begin to understand what too much time aboard ship can do to one.

One afternoon, the *Mercury*'s union reps host a meeting in the wood-paneled officers' dining room. The meeting cruises along until

The *Mercury* trapped in ice during the winter of 1967 (Newspaper clipping circa 1972, author's collection)

the subject of food is brought up. When someone suggests it might be good if there were more variety of food, Bill takes it to heart.

Back in the galley, I hear him muttering at the stove. "Monotonous food, huh? Look at where we were this winter, kid." And he thrusts a newspaper clipping that shows the *Mercury* stuck in the ice of Lake Michigan with tugs all around her hull." I fed them when we were stuck for eight solid days. Kept the spirits up when they thought we'd have to stay there till spring thaw. Eight solid feet of ice. After, the captain thanked me personally for the good job I'd done to help keep their spirits up. And now look at the thanks I get. I'll tell you what I'm gonna do now. I'll feed 'em until their goddamned eyes fall out." This is when I become fully aware that Bill is becoming burnt out from twenty straight months aboard the *Mercury*. As I mop the floor, I wonder if it's possible that Bill has been a part of this routine so long that he is incapable of making the decision to get off.

A couple of days later, there emerge a couple of factors that play into Bill's decision to take his long overdue vacation. The first is when my roommate, Russ, decides that he has had enough of the sailing life and packs his bags for a one-way trip to Chicago. I will miss his refrain sung throughout the day that goes "Happy, happy, happy horseshit." I will also miss the cigarette pack that he casually left around for occasional smokers like myself to pilfer. He announces his decision in the morning and is gone before supper, leaving me a couple of tattered flannel shirts in the dresser to remember him by.

Through the supper hour I notice that Bill is becoming increasingly upset with something that I can't see and so I blame it on the fact that we are understaffed in the galley. For my part I enjoy having to hustle a little more, knowing that Ray and I will split the departed Russ's pay until another porter is assigned.

But that evening as we relax around the rusted pop cooler on the fantail, Ray tells me the real reason for Bill's consternation. As we sip the ice-cold beverages provided gratis to the crew by the Cleveland Tankers Company, he says, "Looks like Gidding's going to take his vacation whether he wants to or not." I sip on my root beer and ask, "Why's that?"

"Cuz the union's sending a new waiter he can't stand. At least that's the word." Ray chuckles, his bald dome shiny with sweat "Yup, old Bughouse is heading our way. Crazy son of a bitch. And Gidding's getting out. Hee hee hee."

As the red sun breaks over the flat lake the next morning, there are more signs that this is the case. Bill Giddings is beside himself with worry and more than once I observe him unnecessarily flipping bacon and muttering things like, "Why's he have to come here?" and "Why can't he leave me alone?" Later in the day he breaks the news to me that he will be leaving for vacation soon. He makes it sound like he's telling me of his impending death. Bill is distraught at the thought of leaving the only home he's known for the better part of two years. The view of the rest of the crew is mostly unsympathetic. "Shoulda been off here a year ago," observes Clark.

The following days are filled with rumors of the impending arrival of Bughouse. I discover that many of the crew know him and soon men are gathered around the pop cooler in the stern, swapping their favorite stories about a man seemingly determined to point the wrong way. In the meantime Bill Giddings haunts the sweltering stove, muttering like a wet hen. He is first relieved when Bughouse fails to catch the ship in Cleveland and then disconsolate and resigned when he learns that tomorrow in Toledo, Bughouse will meet the ship.

The following morning before the crew has arrived for breakfast, Bill slides away from the inevitable by deserting the *Mercury*. His parting words to me are, "You're a good worker. You'll go far if you get by Bughouse."

By midafternoon I'm still pondering those words in my sauna/cabin when Ray raps on the door and ushers in an elfin figure in a shiny blue suit. "This here's Bughouse Schultz," says Ray with a chuckle. "They call him that because he's been in and out of the bughouse so many times."

Bughouse grins mushmouthily and steps into the cabin, clutching a battered cardboard suitcase that makes mine look like something from Hudson's. In his other hand is a grey fedora that looks as though it was once intended to complement the suit. Now its chief purpose is to cover the close-shaved head of white bristles and shade the stubble field of three-day growth that springs from his gaunt cheeks. The three-day growth probably accounts for the time that elapsed since he was supposed to catch the *Mercury* in Cleveland and the present moment in muggy Toledo. Still grinning, Bughouse gives the cabin a quick once-over as though he is recognizing an old friend. As he throws his hat on the upper bunk that was formerly mine, I note the face wizened well beyond the fifty years that Ray has told me Bughouse has attained.

He tucks the suitcase into a corner and turns to me. "So halonbenonhere?" he asks from a mouth that is full of mush.

Having anticipated the question, I answer, "About three weeks."

Bughouse cackles and points to the brown spittle dribbling down from his chin as he steps across to the sink, where he lets flow the tobacco juice in a small rivulet from his mouth.

Still wiping his chin, he turns back to me and says with a bit more clarity, "Ray tells me Giddings couldn' get offahere fast enough when he heard I was coming. He fired me from here back in the spring. Guess I missed the boat one time too many," he muses philosophically as he deposits another load of the brown liquid into the sink.

In spite of his tobacco problem, I find something likeable about this guy. His friendly, harmless manner allows me to relax and listen to his thoughts on being back aboard the *Mercury*. I am even more impressed to be in the presence of a man who has made a profession of being a steamboat waiter and of desiring nothing more from life. He arrives in the galley on time for supper and slides effortlessly into his role as though he has never left it. He is even more at ease with the crew, the vast majority of whom recognize him as a fellow traveler in the realm of the ships that sail through the National Maritime Union and the Cleveland Tankers fleet.

As the *Mercury* continues her monotonous forays back and forth through "Bug Lake," as Lake Erie is called for good reason, I have a chance to view the other ships that make up the rest of this motley fleet. The *Mercury* is the second-oldest in a family of seven. She was born in the shipyards of Lorain, Ohio, in 1912 and was soon joined by two siblings—now known as the *Rocket* and the *Comet*. All three were destined to be tankers from birth, sired by the monopolistic Standard Oil Company. Each of the ships are similar in length and range from 330 to 390 feet, around half the length of the newest ships of the day. The three ships are each powered by an old-fashioned triple-expansion engine, the same as I'd grown up with on the Bob-Lo boats. In appearance, the builders followed the traditional laker design, enhanced with a layer of pipes and a catwalk that runs from the forward to the after deckhouse. The picture is completed on each ship by two tall masts, one jutting up from the pilothouse and the other near the stern just before a tall, thin smokestack painted in amber with a black band around the top set off by the blue CT logo on a white shield. In keeping with their diminutive size, the quarters are uniformly cramped and unventilated, which makes traversing Lake Erie in the summertime at best an unpleasant experience.

The *Mercury* is in the midst of butterworthing one afternoon in Cleveland when another stepsister, the *Venus*, chugs by lakebound under full steam. Butterworthing is a tank-cleansing process that consists of filling the holds with hot steam and then pumping out the residue of more tarlike cargoes so that we can load cleaner fuels like rocket fuel without threat of contamination. The process takes four to six hours to complete and has to be done at the dock as need dictates. Because the *Mercury* carries a variety of cargoes, we find ourselves sitting around the deck while the noisy steam cleaner does its thing on an almost weekly basis. The *Venus* is a fourth Cleveland Tanker to come out of the Lorain shipyard. Around the same length as her sisters, she is distinguished by a short, squat smokestack that carries exhaust from her diesel engine that, judging by her sound, must make sleep a trying experience for those housed in the stern.

The remainder of the fleet is very dissimilar. First, we claim one of the oldest and most interesting ships still afloat—the *Meteor*. This is the last operating whaleback of forty-one that once plied the Great Lakes. Built in 1896 at Superior, Wisconsin, by Alexander Mac-Dougall, the ship was given the name *Frank Rockefeller* and was fitted as a bulk freighter to haul iron ore from Lake Superior. The genius of MacDougall's design is that the hull is curved to allow waves to run over the ship's decks and off again so that the ship is much more a part of the lake than the traditional design. Watching the *Meteor* steam into Cleveland one afternoon as the *Mercury* is departing, I am struck at the blunt, cigar-shaped appearance she presents. Although there are safety railings, I wonder how crew could walk around the decks in any kind of seas. Not only that, but the *Meteor* is designed unlike anything I've ever seen on the lakes. Instead of a forward cabin and pilothouse, the main cabins are in the stern with the pilothouse on top. On the bow is this tiny oblong cabin with a couple of portholes where, Bughouse tells me, four crew members reside. She is, at 380 feet, about the same length as the *Mercury*. Bughouse smiles mushily and says, "What a hellhole. They can't keep crew on that thing."

In addition to iron ore that she carried while wearing the colors of the U.S. Steel Trust, the ship was also known as the *South Park* and carried automobiles before being driven on the rocks near Manistique in 1942. The following year she was converted to a tanker in Manitowoc and given her present name.

In contrast to the *Meteor*, the newest ship in the fleet is the *Polaris*. She was launched as a Landing Ship-Tank (LST) ship in 1945 and converted to a tanker in 1949. The *Polaris* has more of an oceangoing appearance, with all accommodations located in the stern. Bughouse tells me she has the reputation beyond even that of the *Meteor* of being the most cramped and hottest ship in the fleet. Rounding out the aging fleet is another motor vessel, the *Taurus*. Built in 1924 in Pennsylvania, the *Taurus* is only 260 feet in length and looks more like a floating barge with a very low profile. In passing, I have to look closely to see that the pilothouse is located midships, with all crew quarters and cabins in the stern and no visible smokestack—nothing fun or even pleasant to look at. Part of the invisible convoy of ships that plod around the Great Lakes, unobserved messengers keeping alive some of the busiest ports in the world.

As we pass these vessels, Bughouse is often reminded of events that have shaped the lives of some of our current shipmates aboard the *Mercury* when they sailed on those ships. "The *Rocket*," he laughs as we pass in the Maumee. That's where the chief engineer lost it all." He goes on to relate how Wally, our current chief and then first engineer on the *Rocket*, was fast becoming a wealthy young man through his wise investments in the stock market. He invested all his steamboat savings while raising a model family on the path to Shaker Heights. "Couldn't pick a loser if he tried," says Bughouse. That was until one Friday morning when the *Mercury* left Buffalo bound for Detroit. The chief got the news on the radio that the market was falling but he was helpless to get a message to his broker until late afternoon via ship-to-shore radio. But it was too late. By the time the *Mercury* reached the Detroit River Light, Wally was a ruined man. His back broken by fate and the steamboating life, he began hitting the bottle. His marriage, difficult enough under the normal sailor's circumstances, soon fell apart. Now Wally is on the *Mercury* with a past he's trying to forget and no future save the next port.

Bughouse also has stories about Ray, who has been promoted to steward. These are prompted by the sighting of the *Venus* in a river passage. "I'll never forget that time we were on the *Orion* and old Ray he went on a toot and just disappeared. Everyone figured he went over the side until the second day the cook went to get some potatoes from the deck locker and found Ray under a burlap bag with his bottle." Bughouse expectorates a wad of brown goo into a dixie cup and continues. "But he could get crazy mean too. One time he was chasing us all around the galley with a meat cleaver."

I listen, amazed, to these stories, trying to imagine that he is talking about the genial man I have come to know. I figure that Bughouse is telling me what it was like in the old days and leave it go at that. Of course, I can't let go of the fact that I'm hearing all of this from a guy named Bughouse and I haven't figured out how he got his name yet either.

And before I know it, the crew of the *Mercury* is undergoing even more changes. The third mate who was sent away under custody in Cleveland has been replaced by a real straight-arrow-looking guy named Ed who will share the forward cabin with the second mate Clark. Most important to me is the arrival of the new second cook who will take Ray's responsibilities until Bill Giddings returns. His name is Mike. He is about thirty, has all of his black hair and a cheerful, outgoing personality. He arrives on board all ready to work in his own galley whites and gets right into it. Mike takes great delight in making special cakes and pies. The breath of fresh air he brings with him makes him instantly popular with the crew. I feel better about returning to my own duties now, knowing that we have a full galley.

Our new captain, Charley Stanley, slips into the void left by the old cap, a very quiet man who was suffering from the same overdose of steamboating that caused the departure of Bill Giddings. When I go to clean his stateroom, he invites me to have a seat in his small sitting room and tell him about my year at Wayne State and my plans, whatever they are. He tells me not to worry about the cabin, to hit it every other day and to enjoy my work on board. Aside from the sitting room, there is space for only a double bed and the bathroom with the only tub on board. This wood-paneled room, located directly beneath the pilothouse, represents the height of sumptuousness on the *Mercury*. Adjacent to this cabin is that of Joe Flores, the first mate. His bearlike appearance has earned him the nickname Smoky. Smoky's quarters are almost as big as the captain's and include space for an office and a shower. The new captain, like the new second cook and third mate, brings a burst of energy to the *Mercury* and I'm starting to feel like one of the old hands as I flit from cabin to cabin on my rounds.

With the new hands on board, the *Mercury* continues to load rocket fuel in Toledo on a muggy Thursday evening. I am up forward on the dock, talking with Sully, the watchman, and Jim, the wheelsman, when the steam whistle of the *Mercury* begins blasting. After several seconds, we look at one another and then up to the pilothouse to try and figure out what's going on. Jim sprints up the stairs to see who might be up there pressing on the lever and discovers no one. Then our eyes retreat back to the whistle itself and we see John, the oiler with the polka-dot hat, peeping out from behind the smokestack.

"Son of a bitch is operating it from there," says Sully as he and Jim begin to head back. By this time, a couple of minutes have passed and the whistle has drawn the attention of a couple more of the crew as well as the Coast Guard people from the station just down river from where we are docked. The whistle roars its flat, factory sound as the crew sets about finding exactly how John, who has now disappeared, has rigged it. Finally, a ladder is found and one of the engineers is dispatched to the valve of the whistle itself at the top of the smokestack to undo the knot that John has tied to keep the valve open. By the time that is accomplished, a full five minutes have passed and John is nowhere to be found.

As he is still missing the next morning when the *Mercury*'s whistle officially announces our departure from Toledo, another crew shift is in order. Another John, this one from Brooklyn, who signed on as a wiper a few weeks back, is promoted to oiler. This is the same man who only a week before was promoted from the lowliest job in the engine room—wiper—to that of fireman. Now, in his third week on the job, he is being bumped upward again to a job that is considered to be, along with the cook's, the busiest job on the ship.

Brooklyn John is an easygoing guy in his mid-twenties who wears his hair in a marine crew cut. The *Mercury* is his first ship ever, making him the only person on board with even less sailing experience than I have. Along with Jim the wheelsman, he is closest in age to me but tends to associate with the older crew. After the previous summer spent with crew my own age, it is different to discover that I'm more on the periphery of the *Mercury's* society. Fortunately, the crew is quite tolerant of all types of characters and has little trouble assimilating me at least to the point of including me in conversations. But the truth is, I lack experience in three areas—bars, sailing, and women (both married and unmarried)—and thus have little to contribute to the conversation that occupies most of the waking moments of the crew. Another thing that distinguishes the crew of the *Mercury* from that of the *South American* and *Columbia* is that, as members of the NMU, several *Mercury* crew have oceangoing experience and therefore a much broader frame of reference for their discussions. While I can relate to San Francisco from a flower-child perspective, they talk about shipping from there after an all-night bender in Oakland where the captain had to bail half the guys out of jail before they could set sail for Jakarta. I can only listen and hope that no one asks me how many Great Lakes I have sailed on (two and counting).

Because the second engineer has invited me to come down to the engine room anytime during his twelve-to-four watch, I have been able to observe Brooklyn John's progression through the ranks, from wiper, to fireman, to oiler. In the space of three weeks, John has been field promoted to a position that normally requires at least a few years of sailing experience. Although the job has been posted in the union halls, it may take a while for a qualified oiler to apply and make it to the *Mercury*. Thus the chief engineer has decided to give John a go at one of the most important positions on the ship.

While it was easy to visit Brooklyn John in the tiny room that housed the twin Scotch boilers where his primary responsibility was to watch the steam gauge and make sure the boilers were producing enough pressure to build and maintain steam, it is something else when I walk down the stairs to catch his first shift as oiler. The first thing I notice are the strips of colored rags that are draped around the entire room, hanging from valves attached to all sorts of pipes. As I watch John walk from one to another under the direction of the second engineer, I realize that the rag strips are there to help him learn the various steps of his job.

The second engineer is also easygoing and hails from one of the Carolinas. He reclines in a lawn chair that is very appropriate for the tropical heat down here and calls out to John in his drawl, "Okay, now go to the release valve—no, the one above the red rag. No, just a half turn at a time until you sort of feel it release. There you go. Now you've got to check the steering gear box to make sure it's got steam. No, that's the box on the port side. You want starboard for that. If it's not up to 600, you've got to open it some more. No. Go slow on that one." I watch, amazed, as John dashes from one rag to the next, always glancing nervously at the second to make sure that he is doing the right thing. After guiding him through what looks to me like a complicated dance from valve to valve, the second says, "Okay, now you've got us under way. The next steps are the routine." John, looking a little like a squirrel dazed by a close encounter with a moving car tire, nods his glistening head and turns to gather an oilcan and mounts the catwalk that threads through the churning pistons of the triple-expansion engine that drive the ship's screw. He moves slowly from one to the next, gingerly feeling the tops of the mounts for excessive heat and feeding oil to the moving parts as he goes. I am exhausted just watching him conduct a job that even his crazy predecessor made look like a day in the park.

The second, comfortable that John is momentarily okay, turns to me and says, "It'll take him a while, but he'll get it. Probably, just about the same time he does, a replacement will come aboard and he'll get bumped back to wiper."

To make up for the loss of a fireman, the remaining two are forced to work six and six, meaning two six-hour shifts a day. Having observed them in their cramped, dark firebox, I wonder aloud how anyone could do that job even four hours a day without going (my new term) bughouse? One of them responds, "This is nothing. All you gotta do is sit there and watch the pressure gauge. Before we went to oil we were coal fired. Now that kept you on your toes, watching that thing dance all around. Then you had to do some fancy twists with the feed. Now it's controlled. Piece of cake." Maybe for them, I think. But for a guy who feels hot and claustrophobic inside my tight cabin that at least has a porthole, I can't imagine doing their job day in and out.

When the ship is in port and at rest, the firemen can sneak into the engine room for little breaks. But when the engines are working, they are expected to be at their posts. Because there is no room for a fan in the firebox, the firemen are at the mercy of the ventilators that sit atop the ship next to the smokestack. More than once when visiting, I am asked to go up and shift the vents around so that they are facing the wind and it will be channeled down to their space.

At the other end of the ship, I take advantage of another open invitation—this by Clark, the second mate—and spend sweet afternoons in the pilothouse, passing time with him and Jim the wheelsman. Finally, one afternoon as the *Mercury* makes her way from Hamilton to Ste. Catherine's and the Welland Canal, Clark turns to me and says, "Okay, kid, your turn to relieve Jim. Take the wheel." Hardly believing my ears, I jump down from my stool and try to control my spinning head as I swagger over to the wheel. With a knowing smirk, Jim demonstrates his hands on the wheel and says, "She's at 98 degrees, a quarter right." Having seen this routine, I know enough to repeat, "Ninety-eight degrees, a quarter right," as I place my hands where his have been. Suddenly my world is connected and I am totally here. I am steering the *Mercury!*

It takes me a few minutes to get the feel of the large wooden wheel and I discover that it is difficult to keep the compass on the heading. Clark says that the basic rule is to try to keep her within three degrees either side of the heading. He guides me and tells me when the waves of the lake—that seem to have suddenly gotten larger—are pushing the ship off course. Over the vastness of Lake Ontario, I can make out the shadow of the shoreline we are heading for. But the smokestack that Clark wants me to head for keeps moving from side to side. After about ten minutes of this, the pilothouse phone rings. Clark picks it up and says "Yep. Uh huh. You got it. Okay." He hangs up with a chuckle and says, "That was the second engineer. Wants to know why the steering gear's racing back there. But he figured it out himself. Okay, Jim, break's over. Back to the wheel."

As I resume my position toward the rear of the room, Clark explains, "See, kid, the engineers are kind of nervous about the steer-

The *Mercury* after her collision with the *Ernest T. Weir* in Lake St. Clair, 1964 (Historical Collection of the Great Lakes/Bowling Green State University)

ing chains. They got hung up three or four seasons ago and stopped working and the *Mercury* hit another ship in the St. Clair River."

"I heard it tore a huge hole in the bow," adds Jim.

"Damn right it did," affirms Clark. Lucky it didn't hit midships. That kind of impact could've caused a pretty nice size explosion." And so ends my first experience at handling the ship's wheel.

By the time we have made a couple more runs in limpid, almost dead Lake Erie, Brooklyn John's luck has run out. He has gamely plugged away at the oiler job and has gotten the hang of it. But the union has found a replacement who is coming aboard in Toledo. To further complicate things, the fireman position has been filled. The final blow comes when word arrives that a wiper with more seniority will come aboard and bump John from his original position. Thus I am able to witness firsthand his meteoric rise and descent within a few short weeks. John is philosophic about all of this. "I'm going back to

Brooklyn. Maybe now I've got enough experience to ship out on the ocean from there. If I get out, at least it'll take them longer to bump me." And, overnight, he is gone.

While I am a little upset at losing John as a shipmate I could actually talk to occasionally, Bughouse is ecstatic about his replacement. "They're sending out Rodger D. Rodgers the Third," he gushes to Ray. Ray doesn't quite share his enthusiasm and gets back to his roast. His only comment is, "As long as he don't get you going crazy, I don't care who gets on. The both of you'll probably be back on the beach soon enough anyway."

But, later in the day, Bughouse introduces me to a man who looks around thirty. He has red curly hair, a wiry, athletic build, and a furrowed Irish face that looks as though it has mapped the world a couple times too many. Rodgers the Third sneers at me and snarls "College kid" by way of greeting. But Bughouse is obviously thrilled that his great friend is aboard and talks with me until I fall asleep about all the great times they have had together.

And so, with a complete crew, the *Mercury* turns her bow north and, for the first time, I sail into Lake St. Clair and past Port Huron into my third Great Lake. The *Mercury* has a consignment for Bay City. After too many trips on Lake Erie, the fresh breeze from the upper lakes awakens my sailing spirit. As the ship works her way against the current and passes beneath the Blue Water Bridge, I make sure I am on the bow, gazing at the azure-laced waves and allowing the almost cool breeze to wash over me. I go to my cabin that evening feeling the swell of the deep lake as it rocks me to the first sweat-free sleep I've had in what seems like ages but has been only a few weeks.

The *Mercury* spends the next morning and early afternoon winding her way up the Saginaw River, similar to the Rouge but with a lower concentration of industry. Between the piles of stone and refineries there are stretches of wetlands that move far inland but ultimately give way to walls of concrete that remind me of freeways. By the time the *Mercury* is tying up near downtown Bay City, Captain Stanley—Charley as he's known to the crew—barks over the ship's speaker system, "Alright. Tied up and it's only three o'clock. Who wants to go for some pizza, pizza, pizza?" The older crew I'm standing with laugh heartily at this strange invitation. The way they laugh lets me know that they know more than I do about Charley and pizza.

Because I am nowhere near drinking age in Michigan and appear even younger than my nineteen years, I opt out of the group that piles into a couple of taxis. Instead I decide to finish my cabins and then ask for the supper hour off so that I can go and find some toothpaste. With no taxis waiting at the dock, I walk up a gravel road that reeks heavily of oil until I get to town. I find my toothpaste and, as I'm walking back, I pass the bar where the crew are gathered. At the same time I see them, I am spotted and Jim is out on the sidewalk, hustling me inside before I know it. There are about ten of the crew sitting around a couple of tables filled with bottles and glasses. I am thrilled to be greeted like one of the crew. Charley himself, his face much reddened, commands me to take a seat, which I do. But before they can seize an empty glass and fill it with whatever's sitting there, a waitress is hovering over me protectively, glaring at the men, daring them to try something illegal on her watch. She goes through the embarrassing formality of asking for my ID and then asks if I'd like a soft drink. That kind of kills the fun for everyone, so after a few minutes I graciously excuse myself and let the crew get back to having their own good time, regaling each other with stories of ships and shipmates they all know.

I walk back to the *Mercury* in the twilight. Because we're miles from the open lake, the mug of Michigan summer descends once again upon the ship. But my boredom is somewhat relieved because Jerry and Sully have found a stray terrier that they have decided to adopt as a ship's mascot. I am assigned to take him down the ladder for a run before the ship sails. Although Jerry tells me the ship is ready to sail at nine, a call has to be made uptown to get the crew back to the ship. Eventually, around ten, two taxis pull up, disgorging a regular Barnum and Bailey crew who stumble out laughing and swearing up a storm. In the center of the mayhem I can still hear Charley's voice above the rest. I watch as he weaves his way up to the pilothouse, stopping for a few ominous moments in his room. He makes it up the stairs and talks with Smoky, who's on the eight-to-twelve watch. Soon, the command is given to cast off the lines and we are under way down the river toward Saginaw Bay. I have moved from the stern to the bow, where I'm standing with Sully, who's been pressed into lookout service. The concrete river channel is very narrow in spots, marked by flashing red and green buoys on either side. Sully's job is to make sure there's nothing in the water between the buoys like logs that could wreck the propellor and to look out for any traffic coming upriver.

From his location directly below the pilothouse, Sully can simply call up anything worth noting to the captain and mate who are standing at the open windows. From here it is also easy for us to hear the captain singing and laughing as the ship progresses. His occasional directives to the wheelsman are softly countermanded by Smoky, who is a straight arrow standing by the opposite pilothouse window, his gaze on the river and his emotions in check. To his credit, Charley, who is quite blotto and oblivious to everything else, knows enough to concede domain. We hear him say, "Okay, Smoky the Bear, I'm going back down below where it's safe. You steer the fucking boat."

Poor Smoky the Bear. Poor *Mercury*. Poor us. Back down in the muggy heat of the lower lakes, we plod from port to dirty port. And much of the time it is Smoky who gets to take responsibility for cleaning up after Captain Charley has gone back down below after another shore leave. Although he takes it in stride, the big guy has to be feeling something, I think. I get a hint of what that is on a Saturday afternoon when we are tied up in the Welland Canal waiting for a lock to open for our upbound transit. I am standing at the deck railing near the forward end, watching the scrub weeds grow and praying for a breeze. Smoky is standing at the railing of the wing that extends out from the port side of the pilothouse, waiting patiently for a signal to move ahead. Along the dock, a kid comes riding up on his bicycle. He stops to take a look at the *Mercury* and then calls up to Smoky, "Hey, mister. You taking this ship to the scrap yard?" The kid is referring to the shipbreakers at nearby Ramey's Bend where a lot of lake ships have ended their existence. Smoky remains motionless, expressionless. He stares straight ahead and responds, "That's right, kid."

Probably more than anyone else aboard, It is Smoky's stabilizing, tranquil presence that allows the *Mercury* to keep moving forward in the canal and on her rounds of the terminals in the lakes. With him standing there like a rock, everyone else, myself included, is free to do their thing, an increasingly popular thing to do in 1968 that I think most of the crew have been pursuing for a long time. It takes a man like Smoky to be there when the captain doesn't feel like taking responsibility for the ship—which is the responsibility of the position, after all. But, lock after lock, it is Smoky the Bear who is on top of things and keeps the *Mercury* and Cleveland Tankers afloat in more ways than one.

It is difficult to imagine a more inept and comic-stricken cast of characters than the crew of the *Mercury* in full sail. Later that same day, as the ship is sluggishly transiting an open stretch of the canal, Bughouse decides it is time to clean out the filthy cabin. Dressed in his galley off-whites, I watch as he becomes a mini whirling dervish, gathering up the many pop cans and transferring their tobacco juice to a three-pound coffee can. He even goes so far as to change the water in the container in which he soaks his false teeth for the first time in weeks. I have never seen Bughouse so animated as he scrubs the ancient sink with Spic and Span back to its original stained yellow. To give him more space, I exit the cabin and stand at the railing, watching the monotonous banks of the canal, listening to him clatter around behind me. After a while, Bughouse emerges from the door proudly bearing the coffee can, which is full to the brim with his hawked tobacco drippings and other unidentifiable slop. Aware of the laws prohibiting dumping in rivers and ports, he carefully examines the deck and shoreline before he upends the can's contents over the railing for a glutinous commingling with the equally suspect waters of the Welland. But, instead of the pure splash we are expecting to hear, there is a sound like water hitting a rock on its way down. How can this be, we wonder simultaneously as our eyes follow the sound. At this point, the sound of the water hitting rock has been replaced with a squawking noise that is coming not from a rock but from the bespattered, brown, domelike head of the first engineer, who has unfortunately stuck it out of an engine room porthole directly below us at a bad time. It takes Bughouse only an instant to drink in the situation before he thrusts the can into my hands and turns tail, yelping, into the passageway that will take him to the other side of the ship. Fortunate that we have been able to see him before he saw us, I quickly drop the offending can to the deck and head forward to take care of the first mate's cabin, which I figure can use a second once-over at this point in time.

The crew of the *Mercury* encounters another change in Tonawanda when Jerry, the deckhand, who is returning from a late night visit up the street, misses a step on the ship's ladder and breaks his arm. I will miss his good-natured smile, one of the ingredients that has helped the ship make it on her rounds through the debilitating heat of this summer. To make things more difficult, Smoky the Bear decides it's time for the ship's dog, which has gone nameless for the ten days he's been with us, to get back on land as well. The mutt has blended well with the veterans, who, accustomed as they are to the vagaries of this life, offer little resistance or hard feelings to the unpleasant edict. They have seen so many comings and goings on these ships that one more will not change their lives. And so the mutt joins Jerry and the third mate and John the oiler and Brooklyn John, Bill Giddings, Russ the waiter, and the captain in becoming part of my *Mercury*'s history in A.D. 1968.

Brooklyn John's replacement, Rodger D. Rodgers the Third, does what he can to ensure that the diverse broth that comprises the crew remains properly stirred. Although a good fifteen years younger than Bughouse, they resume their friendship from whenever the last time it was they found themselves together on one of the Cleveland Tankers. On a late Saturday afternoon they are ready to head up the street in Erie, Bughouse in his blue pinstripe and tie, wearing the WWII vet's pin in his lapel, and Rodgers in his best pressed blue jeans and cleanest blue work shirt. Several hours later, the voice of Rodgers can be heard singing in the galley accompanied by Bughouse on his stained harmonica, to the dismay of the engineers trying to get some sleep.

Rodger D. Rodgers the Third is another who is closer in age to me but miles away in the realm of experience. Like his predecessor, Rodger hails from the New York City area. But unlike John, who was a sailing novice, he has sailed on ships around the world for many years. In spite of those experiences and a native intelligence, Rodger has remained at the entry level in the engine department as a professional wiper. But instead of being ashamed at not having risen up the ladder, he wears this position as a badge of honor and a link of solidarity to men like his friend Bughouse who is still a professional waiter.

Rodger approaches his job professionally. He spends a great deal of time making sure that the brass railings leading down to the engine room are kept polished and shining. He keeps to his routine of an eight-hour, six-day week and is loathe to answer the call for any special cleanup schemes the engineers might be cooking up for him. He is proud to be his own man even though it may have made him slightly crazy. One evening as the *Mercury* is outbound passing the Toledo Light at the mouth of the Maumee we are standing on the deck near the stern, waiting for what we hope will be a cooling lake breeze. Rodger is relating to me the fact that, when saltwater veterans need a break from the rigors, dangers, and monotony of life at sea, they come to the "bathtub" of the Great Lakes for some "R and R." Then he asks me about some of the books I have read as part of my college education. I am surprised to discover that he is well read and can hold opinions on theories that I have thus far been unable to grasp. When he asks whether I "subscribe" to the theory of dialectic, all I can do is pretend to understand what he's talking about. He can sense this along with the wanderlust in my soul that makes me believe that a sailing life leads to adventure and enlightenment. He is quick to disabuse me of this notion as he says with a touch of genuine menace, "You know what I should do with you right now? I just oughta save you from becoming a goddamned sailor and pick you up and throw you over the side." He manages to say it casually enough to make me feel he just might do it to prevent me from finding myself here ten years from now as a professional wiper with naïve kids and stumblebum sailors as my only companions.

The *Mercury* resumes her humdrum routine of visiting the ports of Lakes Erie and Ontario exclusively. For me, like for the rest of the crew, I accept the monotony as part of the job. I manage to break the routine slightly when the ship makes a delivery to the Bethlehem Steel Mill in Lackawanna and I hitchhike down Highway 5 to visit my brother Jim living in Dunkirk. Other than that, I endure the bugs, the limpid water that even *looks* dead, and the endless tropical mug of America's Dead Sea along with the rest of the crew from day to day and from port to port. The *Mercury* chugs along on her faithful triple-expansion perhaps high on the memory that, as the *Renown*, she came out of the Lorain shipyards as the flagship of Rockefeller's American Oil Fleet. Whatever the memory, the reality is that she is now home to a collection of salty dogs who are building a collective yearning for some sort of respite from the drudgery of day-to-day life aboard what has become a tramp steamer.

BLACK SATURDAY

Although the *Mercury* is constantly arriving at ports, it is amazing how rare it is that the ship actually arrives when conditions are optimal for a real celebration that everyone can be a part of. Yet on a late Friday afternoon as the *Mercury* ducks past the swing bridge on the Maumee and docks at Sun Oil, it becomes clear to all aboard that we have sailed into such a serendipitous crack in time in Toledo.

Although the day is summer warm, the air has been dehumidified and recharged by the passing of a front. The crew, sensing the change in the air and a perfect night ahead, waste no time in getting over the side and heading up the street, ignoring en masse the cold supper laid out by Ray, who takes no offense.

With the galley cleared, work is over for me as well and, sensing the mood in the air, I accept an invitation to join Mike the second cook and one of the oilers in a walk to a nearby place they both know. We cover the distance along the asphalt road in a matter of minutes. At the end of the journey is a run-down grey-shingled flat with a neon light in a side window proclaiming "Rolling Rock." "Ah, Black Marie's," announces the oiler with a mad little twinkle in his eye as he pushes open the screen door. "It's been a long time."

The interior of the place reinforces the impression that this was once a house. The ceiling is low and the room still cramped, although a few walls were probably knocked out at some point. There is the typical bar along one wall; a few badly scarred, black-topped tables with matching chairs; a pool table, around which are clustered a honking gaggle of *Mercury* crew; and a pay phone, around which two or three others are huddled, counting coins.

Making myself as innocuous as possible, I sidle up to the crowded bar and croak out an order for a Pabst in a voice I hope will belie my boy scout looks. The black-haired woman behind the bar says, "Twenty-one, huh?" and gives me a quick once-over before producing my beer with a straight face corrupted by a wink. I am home.

This is the first time I've been in a bar setting with the crew since that afternoon in Bay City, and the first time I've actually been allowed to stay since being in Buffalo, where I'm legal.

As I sit with Mike, sipping my beer, I look around to discover that every department—engine, deck, and galley—is represented here tonight. From the next table, Captain Charley takes a break from regaling the second and third mates and Jim the wheelsman to wave a greeting to me with a big, friendly smile on his face. Captain Charley has treated me well on my days aboard the *Mercury*. He hasn't asked me to do anything more than my job and has taken time on a couple of occasions to simply stop and chat with me about my college experiences. I have long grown accustomed to being known as "college boy" aboard the *Mercury*, a role I have grown into as the only crew member with any real college experience, or so my shipmates tell me.

The fresh night air brings the crew together and there is a lot of joyful shouting and laughter that cuts through the haze of cigarette smoke. At least a few times, Marie, the black-haired barmaid, makes it over to our table to plop a fresh Pabst in front of me, sent compliments of one of the crew from various parts of the room. The jukebox belts out song after country-western song, many of which start out promising but lose my attention after the first refrain. I take part in the ongoing pool challenge, winning a couple before being put in my place first by Sully and later by Jim, both of whom I figure must spend a lot of their winters practicing. In addition to the *Mercury* crew, there are a few regulars here this Friday night. Some of the crew try their luck at wooing a couple of women sitting at the end of the bar who may or may not be attached to someone. The other men look like farmer types and they keep to themselves at a table in a back room. The cold beer continues to flow and everyone is having a great time.

Around midnight, the screen door opens to present an unusual sight. There enters a man dressed in a knee-length raccoon coat and a red baseball cap. This could be Charlie Brown on his way to college, I think to myself. As he walks through the haze, he is revealed to be none other than Ray, the steward. He is greeted by the crew as the Second Coming, and his furry coat is soon presenting its back to us from the bar. In short order his raucous cackle blends into the gales of laughter that engulf us all and I don't even notice when he disappears into the night. However, at some point I do notice that the bar clock is getting further from midnight and closer to my five-thirty wake-up call for breakfast and I decide to join a couple of guys who are returning to the ship. We safely negotiate the ladder and I am soon nestled in my lower bunk, trying to control the tempo of the polka band in my head. After a while, I notice Mike hovering above my bunk. He is talking about how great Rolling Rock is and is inviting me to come into the galley for a bottle. When I decline, he becomes angry and hurt. "What's the matter? I'm not good enough for you to have a drink with me?" I finally accommodate him by taking a swig from the bottle he is holding and telling him that Rolling Rock is the finest beer in the world, and he goes away placated. At this point I notice that the polka band in my head has been replaced by the caterwauling coming from the galley as Bughouse and Rodger D. Rodgers the Third have returned to set up shop and sing the night away. Caressed by the seasick country blues, I manage to drift off to sleep, only to awaken in the now quiet darkness to recall some of the stories Bughouse has told me about Ray and his binges.

Variations on these themes occupy my mind until one of the deckhands calls us up at 5:30. I roll slowly out of my bunk, expecting mortal damage, and am amazed to find myself able to function far better than I could ever have wished. Bughouse, on the other hand, struggles out appearing considerably worse for the wear. He gums a mushy complaint about his squirrely head while fishing in a scum-laden paper cup for his false teeth. I do a double-take as I notice he is still wearing his signature blue-striped suit with the VFW lapel pin that he left the ship in yesterday evening. I don't doubt that he left it on in the hopes of returning to Marie's with Rodgers after breakfast. We stumble through the passageway toward the galley, noting only that the muggy air of summer has made a return. Mike, the second cook, seems undaunted either by the humidity or by a night of Rolling Rock as he turns out final preparations for the crew's breakfast in the already-warm galley. Although not a great many of the crew attend, breakfast proceeds flawlessly and Ray makes an appearance at the end as he begins preparations for dinner. I manage to hit several of my cabins for maintenance immediately after breakfast and reward myself with a rest. My dreams are again interrupted by the long blast of the whistle signaling that the *Mercury* is departing the dock for Lake Erie, where, with fortune, a summer breeze might find us. I rest with my eyes partway open to view en passant the swing bridge, the dry dock, and the large, white lighthouse that marks the entrance to the channel.

Somewhat refreshed, Bughouse and I return to the galley around eleven o'clock to once again find the place in full swing for dinner. The stove is full, with corned beef asimmer in one pot, cabbage aboil in another, and vegetable soup asteam in a third. Ray has taken great pride in surpassing the efforts of tired Bill Giddings, and I have heard the crew voice their appreciation of the change on more than one occasion. As I set about my chores of coffee making and dishwashing, I notice that Ray's cheerful mood has colored his face and causes him to briefly bubble into snatches of a song that goes something like:

Oh my sweet darling hillbilly wife
Done left me six months ago

I figure, what the hell. If he's happy, so much the better for everyone. But then I watch as he picks up the boiling pot of cabbage and directs me to open the door to the deck so that he can pour some of the excess juice over the side. I obediently hold open the door and watch as he, attempting to clamber over the door's high bulkhead, catches his foot and lurches forward toward the railing. Ray hits the railing and goes down in a heap, releasing the boiling cabbage and its pot into Lake Erie. I stand shocked, still holding the door, looking down on Ray, who is lying motionless on the deck with some of the cabbage juice soaking into his shirt. After a short minute as Bughouse and Mike have joined me, he opens his eyes, pushes his wire-framed glasses up onto his nose, stirs a little, and breaks out into a plaintive singsong:

Broke my leg
I've broke both my legs

But after a few repetitions, we determine that Ray can support himself so we hoist him up and walk him gingerly back to his cabin, where he sits in a chair to gather himself. A little shaken up, we return to the galley and our normal duties. Mike sets about investigating the corned beef and the soup and thinking about what to do with the rest of the fast-approaching dinner meal. But we are all surprised a couple of minutes later to see Ray come walking back into the galley with a couple of cans of sauerkraut that he opens and puts in a pan to make up for the lost cabbage.

A few minutes later I step out the door to dump the kitchen wastes to feed the fish and seagulls and slip on the cabbage juice on the deck. Unlike Ray, I am back on my feet quickly enough to watch the metal garbage can join the cabbage pot on the bottom of Lake Erie.

During the serving of dinner, I notice Ray making brief forays into his cabin just off the galley. Before the last man has been served, he has disappeared behind the closed door permanently. During our afternoon siesta, Bughouse wonders aloud about Ray's condition, worrying about his wild temper. It is in the midst of this reverie, while I am praying for a cool breeze off Pelee Island, that we are awakened to a banging on the cabin screen door and a voice rasping, "Get up. Get up! We've all overslept and the crew's in the dining room, waiting for dinner." Bughouse checks his watch and yells back, "It's two-thirty, Ray. We already served dinner."

Although Ray walks away, he's back pounding at our door a couple of minutes later, hollering, "Let's go! I told you guys to get up. You want the captain to fire the bunch of us?"

Bughouse ignores him but, with tales about Ray's past behavior fresh in my mind, I think it best to meander out there to see if anything *is* happening. And a good thing I do, because, just as I'm leaving the cabin, Ray comes down the deck for the third time, muttering to me that I'm lucky I'm moving and then yelling to Bughouse, "Won't get up, eh? If you're not in the galley in five minutes, you're fired." Bughouse's protests go unheard and I enter the dining room to see a single crewman sitting in a chair, watching TV. Right behind me I hear Ray say to the confused fellow, "Don't you worry. We'll have your dinner in a jiffy. The boys 'n me, we overslept."

In the galley, Mike is attempting to maintain a sense of order to the day's events. In an attempt to let Ray know that dinner is truly past, he proudly unveils a cheesecake that he has made for supper.

"Supper?" Ray says incredulously. "Sheeit. We haven't even served dinner and you're baking for supper. On this ship we go one meal at a time. Better give 'em this right now," he declares, hacking into the uncooled cake with a butter knife, plopping great globs into soup bowls sitting nearby. Mike watches, mouth agape, as Ray drops the puddingy mess that was his masterpiece onto countertops and the galley floor itself.

Undaunted, Ray continues his rush to dinner. "Soup. Jesus Christ Almighty, almost forgot the soup. Can't have dinner without the soup. He disappears into the tiny pantry and emerges with two large cans of mushroom soup. He seizes a butcher knife, hacks off the tops of first one then the other, and commences to pour the contents directly onto the stove, neglecting the pan entirely. Then a gleam comes into his eye and, still wielding the knife, he turns to me and says, "Bughouse ain't here yet? Well I'ma gonna get him." Scared now, I follow Ray at a safe distance down the deck and watch as he bursts into our cabin, yelling, "So you're not gonna work, eh? Well, your job's finished here." I watch from the doorway, relieved that he no longer has the knife, as he begins pulling Bughouse from the top bunk. Bughouse is mouthing things like, "Take it easy, Ray. We're your bud-

The ill-fated *Mercury* after hitting the Grand Island Bridge, 1975
(Historical Collection of the Great Lakes/Bowling Green State
University)

dies. Go back to bed." But Ray is on a mission and, still tugging, he
screams:

"Pack your bags. You're going over the side."

At this announcement, I decide that the time has come for me
to inform the captain of the situation. I walk to his cabin in the forward end and, not finding him, up to the pilothouse. When I relate
the situation to Clark, he chuckles and says, "Yep, sounds like you're
having a lot of fun back there." Not comforted by his casual response,
I go back aft to discover that the captain has already been there, thrown
the causative bottle off the stern, and confined Ray to his quarters.

Thus rescued, Mike, Bughouse, and I pitch in to clean up the
mess and scrape together an impromptu supper for the crew. While
Bughouse is already laughing about this as just another day in his life,
Mike and I are still in shock at what we have witnessed.

SS *Mercury*

Built	1912
Builder	American Shipbuilding Company, Lorain, Ohio
Owners	Standard Oil Company; Cleveland Tankers (1957)
Names	*Renown, Beaumont Parks* (1930); *Mercury* (1957)
Length	390'3"
Beam	52'
Draft	25'
Engine	Triple expansion steam
Boilers	Two Scotch oil-fired
Capacity	43,790 barrels
Cargo	Gas, oil
Crew	30

After supper is over, Bughouse and I are again resting in our cabin. Out of nowhere, he says, "Say, you know, one time on the *Rocket* when he got like this he got out of his cabin and came after some of the crew. Tried to get 'em to come fix supper at nine o'clock at night."

The thought sends me scrambling to lock the screen door. Unfortunately, a half hour later, when I try to get out to go to the bathroom, I discover that the lock has frozen shut and we are trapped in our cabin. It takes us another fifteen minutes of pounding and yelling before the first engineer happens by and is able to extricate us. We decide to simply prop a chair against the door for the rest of the night.

It is a week after this day that I receive word from Smoky that I am being bumped off the *Mercury* and back onto the beach. I spend the rest of the afternoon in my bunk, at first stunned and then crying at the unfairness of being torn from something I feel I have become a part of over these two months. Bughouse tries to cheer me up in his own way by saying, "I know that guy. He's a bum and probably won't even get here for another week." Then I listen as he and Rodger reminisce about a deckhand named Harry they both knew. "Sonofabitch didn't know when to get off," muses Rodger. "Thought he could make it to the end of the season and get the bonus."

"Then, the last trip, only one more day to go," Bughouse says, picking up the thread as though he's memorized the tale, "he wuz gonna make it off ok. But he just couldn't stay away from that open hold."

"Open and empty, so he fell all the way down," adds Rodger.

"Poor Harry," laments Bughouse.

In the depths of my despair, I'm hoping to spend at least one more trip aboard the *Mercury*. At the same time I'm beginning my plan to follow up on a suggestion from Clark, the second mate, one of the more stable of the loony tunes crew of the *Mercury*.

"You know what you should do, kid?" he says when he hears of my being bumped. "You should get out of the NMU and ship with the steel carriers. Their strike's over. They have a lot more ships on the lakes and hire a lot of college kids."

"So is there a hall in Detroit?"

I don't think so," adds Jim. "Think it's in Toledo. You'd have to call."

Finally, Smoky gives me the word: my replacement will arrive tomorrow, so I am to get off the *Mercury* where I caught it, in Toledo. As I prepare to climb down the ladder for the last time, Smoky calls me up to his office, where he pays me my last check. He hands it over to me and then quickly takes it back to rewrite. "Almost gave you a hundred dollars too much," he says. "Doesn't matter. We would've put a stop payment on it and you couldn't have cashed it anyway."

And this leaves me with one more tale to tell my cousin Tom, who has bravely agreed to pick me up and save me from an otherwise interminable bus ride home. As he points his '64 light blue Plymouth Fury with the 318 toward the Motor City, I prepare for reentry into a world I have left far behind.

CHAPTER 5

Steamboat IV

Days of Rage on the SS *John Hulst*

The drive back to the city of Detroit passes swiftly as I share all too vivid recollections of what I have come to call Black Saturday. The barren and desolate road crawls along, punctuated by the flare-ups of the natural gas being burned off by fuel the *Mercury* and her siblings have recently delivered. For his part, Tom brings me up to date on the goings on of our friends and relatives. The city itself is quiet, still trying to dig out from last summer's insurrection. The Tigers, led by the pitching of Denny McLain, are rolling toward what could be their first pennant in over twenty years. By the time we have reached the city, it is another magical summer night and we rendezvous at Angel Park with the rest of the east side world youth movement. The latest from Cream blares from someone's car speakers and, mercifully, there has been a delivery of much more meaningful and life-sustaining fuels, as far as we are concerned—beer and wine.

While my friends are easily amused by my stories, there is a much more important item that pushes news from the *Mercury* off the top of the agenda. In another week, the Democratic National Convention—aka The Convention of Death—is due to begin in Chicago. We have talked about making the drive and joining the alternative youth convention that the Fifth Estate has promised will be a referendum on the war raging in Vietnam. Inasmuch as one of our schoolmates, Rick, is currently serving in Pleiku as a medic and sends us periodic updates on his and his colleagues' wasted efforts in fighting the war, we feel obliged to do something about it. Besides, some of the best bands in the Midwest are supposed to be there, including the MC5 and the Psychedelic Stooges from Detroit. The major topic that swirls through the park that night is who's going and how they are getting there.

I stand amidst the buzz, torn in more ways in one. As I watch the lights of a ship crawl past Windmill Point and set a northbound course, I realize that I have been one of the major promoters of this trip. I have followed the advice of Timothy Leary, who visited the Wayne State campus in the spring and first asked if the mike was "turned on" to general laughter. Then he challenged us to challenge the system before turning the stage over to the MC5 and the ubiquitous John Sinclair. I have accepted the challenge and have spent my park time during this summer to incite my peers to tune in, turn on, drop out, and, above all, be there at the Convention of Death. But I also realize that my soul is firmly in the thrall of steamboating and quite consumed with the quest to make it to the upper lakes aboard a ship this summer.

Thus, when the smoke and the weekend euphoria settles, I find myself in the kitchen of my parents' house, calling the hall of the Steelworkers Local 5000 in Toledo, inquiring into the possibility of shipping out on an iron ore carrier. This is the place I have been referred to by my *Mercury* shipmates for a couple of reasons. First, they represent by far the majority of U.S. flag carriers on the lakes. Second, they don't require the exorbitant fees and year-round membership that both the SIU and NMU do.

To my amazement, I find that there is a real person on the other end of the phone and that he is saying I can register without coming to Toledo. I am even more amazed when, later that day, a call comes from the hall, wondering if I can take a galley position on the steamer *John Hulst*, due past Detroit around ten tonight. My bag from the *Mercury* not yet unpacked, I have time to call my friends and tell them the news that I will try to be back in time to travel with them to the convention or meet them in Chicago if my ship should be heading for the steel mills there.

It is approaching full night as my father drops me off at the Westcott dock, just the other side of the Ambassador Bridge. Although I have never been here, I recognize the site as being near the former dock of the *Aquarama*, the passenger ship captained by Morgan Howell that gained notoriety for its speed and threat to small craft while on the Detroit-Cleveland run in the late fifties and early sixties. The other ship docked adjacent the Westcott is the fire-engine-red Detroit fire-boat *John Kendall*, the same ship that only last fall saluted the departure of the *South American* from the Bates Street dock.

The *John Westcott* is well known by both mariners and ship watchers around the Great Lakes as the floating post office that serves ships from around the world as they ply the seaway past Detroit. It is recognized by mail buffs as the only ship to have its own zip code. In addition to mail, the *Westcott* delivers local papers and miscellaneous supplies to ships. What is truly amazing is that the great freighters don't even slow down for their deliveries by the tiny mailboat. I can recall watching from the middle of the Ambassador Bridge as the *Westcott* made its approach to a giant ship and slipped under its wake to nestle up and make its deliveries before moving on to the next ship cruising in either direction.

Now I find myself entering the cramped, dimly lit office that houses the packages that are both coming from and destined for sailors aboard the ships that travel through the Straits of Detroit. I announce to the man behind the desk that I am here to catch the *John Hulst*. "*Hulst?* Haven't heard from her yet. Have a seat," he says, pointing to a dilapidated couch in a corner of the room. I comply and pass the time noting the names of ships as they are entered on a large blackboard:

Henry Ford	10:30	
Richelieu	10:35–laundry	
Pontiac	10:45	
Steinbrenner	11:00–5 papers	

The ship-to-shore radio crackles with ships calling one another or the *Westcott* office itself to let them know of their estimated time of arrival. In the meantime, I wander outside to watch the two-man crew of the *Westcott* shuffle packages, laundry bags, paper, and mail bags onboard for their next foray into the river. I watch from the dock as the *Westcott* rendezvouses with three ships in the space of twenty minutes before returning for another load for the next convoy. I realize for the first time that this is another marine industry that does not have the luxury of shutting down for the night. The *Westcott* is up and running around the clock from the start to the end of the shipping season on the Great Lakes.

The *J. W. Westcott* delivering mail to a vessel in the Detroit River (Dossin Great Lakes Museum)

After watching the ship go out and return from three runs, the dispatcher tells me he has heard from the *Hulst* and she will be coming by in a half hour. I watch as the mail boat completes one more run before the deckhand motions me to get on board and then things go very fast. The captain brings the motor to life and before I know it, the *Westcott* is nestling up to a seven-hundred-foot-long ship to complete a routine delivery of mail. I am instructed to stay inside the tiny cabin while the deckhand completes the delivery via rope and bucket to the wall of steel moving at ten miles an hour only five feet from where I am sitting. That complete, the *Westcott* gives a short honk of her horn, answered by an equally short blast of the ship's whistle, to let her know we are pulling away. Then the *Westcott* sweeps a few hundred feet across the river to intercept the *John Hulst*, my ship. The

The *John Hulst* in the Detroit River (Dossin Great Lakes Museum)

deckhand cautions me to stay inside until the ladder connecting the *Westcott* to the *Hulst* is secure. Then he quickly signals me out of the cabin and up the ladder to the deck of the ship while my bag is being hauled up beside me. Because the *Hulst* is light of cargo heading up, she is high out of the water and there is a lot of ladder to climb. With every step, my eyes are focused on the rust-red hull of the ship that I can reach out and touch. I am careful not to look up or down and keep going one step at a time. Finally I reach the deck and am assisted over the wire railing by a couple of hands. Then, as the *Westcott* and *Hulst* exchange short toots, I look down to see the little mail boat veer off toward yet another ship and I realize that I am aboard my first ore carrier and am northward bound to boot.

As the hour is approaching midnight, someone quickly shows me to my quarters in the after end. The access to the room, on the main deck, is from an inside corridor. The room itself is long and narrow, illuminated by a light from the bathroom—the first time in four ships that I actually have an attached bath. As I hastily throw sheets on my upper bunk, I take note of the disheveled state of the room. Although I am relieved to find no evidence of the tobacco slurry that seemed to permeate the cabin on the *Mercury*, I find stray articles of clothing hanging from every available knob, pipe, and porthole clamp, to the point that the view of the river is obscured. But the bunk is comfortable, the sheets fresh, and the river generally conducive to sleep, although I find myself awakened throughout the night by a strange whistle that serves to remind me that I'm not on the *Mercury* any more.

Further evidence of this fact is found when I meet my roommate in the early morning as we both respond to a call to "Drop your cocks and grab your socks" from the other side of the door. Denny is a kid about my own age and size with straw-colored hair who attends Michigan State. He shows me around the galley and introduces me to the chief steward, Pat, who is himself youngish looking. Pat clarifies our responsibilities—I am dishwasher and Denny is the waiter and we share the task of making up the beds of the officers fore and aft. In the midst of our breakfast preparations, Denny fills me in about shipboard life aboard the *Hulst*. I learn that, unlike on the *Mercury*, there are several crew close to our own age and, as breakfast is served, I observe that there doesn't seem to be one saltwater veteran among the lot. Moreover, a lot of the crew are wearing dark green coveralls emblazoned with the USS logo of United States Steel on the breast pocket. These guys seem a pretty sober lot compared to my previous shipmates. The fact that there are almost fifty ships sailing in the U.S. Steel fleet on the lakes this summer means that there are close to 1,500 sailors out here dressed pretty much the same.

By the time breakfast is over and I reach the deck, I am immediately taken with the fresh breeze that lets me know that we are Superior-bound on the blue waters of Lake Huron. As we gaze at the waves tranquilly lapping against the ship's side, Gene, the genial forty-something second cook, tells me that I'll have a lot of time aboard the *Hulst* to enjoy the water. She is known as one of the slowest ships on the lakes, with a top speed of only eight miles an hour.

Pat's meals are also different from those I've experienced aboard my other ships. He tries to serve them in a family style by putting bowls of potatoes and vegetables on the table so that the crew can serve themselves seconds. The talk around the mess is peppered with calls to "pass the gravy boat" and "some more peas and carrots over here."

As the evening finds the *Hulst* still laboring through Lake Huron with no shore in sight, Denny guides me to the forward housing, where we descend a level below the main deck to the deckhands' quarters. He introduces me to Dave and Jerry, a couple of eighteen-year-olds on their first ship, and to Jackie Bates, who, at the age of twenty-three and bearded as well, takes delight in serving as our shipboard mentor. In addition to being the oldest, Jackie is also the "Bull deckhand"—the one with most seniority. This is an honorific that is recognized by the union and carries with it certain privileges. He is also the only one among us who is planning to sail the entire season and work his way up the system. Over cans of Hamms, he explains that the ritual of the deckhands is to play the game of hearts for money, with the losses feeding the beer kitty. Although alcohol is technically prohibited aboard ships of the USS fleet, the captain of the *Hulst* is known for not enforcing the rule as long as there are no problems. I choose not to share my experiences aboard the *Mercury* with them at this time. After a few rounds of hearts, I discover that Jackie can also play the guitar and knows a lot of Beatles songs to accompany his stock of country and western. As he knocks off a couple for our entertainment, I find myself transfixed by the difference between the crews of the *Mercury* and the *Hulst*. This will be a very different experience, I think, as we bid our adieus and head back to our bunks for the night.

While we sleep, the *Hulst* chugs through the St. Marys River and arrives at the Soo Locks around 4 AM. My first passage into Lake Superior is made in my sleep. When I stick my head out the now open porthole window I notice the cool air and a lot of grey-white water. We are in Whitefish Bay and land is slowly disappearing. The sheer awesomeness of being part of this inland ocean buoys my spirits throughout the day. And the night. And the next day. For the *Hulst* will take over two full days before arriving at Two Harbors, Minnesota, a mining terminal about sixty miles east of Duluth. While the ship glides back and forth beneath the giant red chutes that drop raw iron ore into her holds, Denny and I find time to stroll uptown to a bar that serves Hamms even to fuzzy-cheeked youth of our countenance and bearing. We drink in memory of our deckhand friends who can't be with us because they are responsible for helping winch the *Hulst* up and down the dock to different chutes, a process that will keep them busy all day, until the ship is loaded and ready to depart. However, Jackie surprises us after a while by joining us for a couple quick ones. He explains that, since only two deckhands are needed for the moving operation, he is exercising his right as Bull deckhand to join us. Over a round of the watery brew, he tells us the story of the *John Hulst*. She was built in 1938 at the Great Lakes Engineering Works on the Rouge River and named after one of U.S. Steel's foremost engineers. Her claim to fame is having the first steam turbine engine on the Great Lakes, and perhaps on any ship anywhere, that provides power directly to the propellor shaft. The steam for that power comes from burning coal, which contributes to the occasional dusting of the crew bench on the after end. The *Hulst* was the first of four such ships built for U.S. Steel that year, and her sisters—the *Governor Miller, William A. Irving,* and *Ralph A. Watson*—are passing us every now and again, also going very slow. When these vessels were built, they were among the longest ships on the lakes, at over six hundred feet. The newer ships now are easily one hundred feet longer. Jackie tells us that the *Hulst* is also the first ship to be equipped with tunnels linking the forward and after ends, allowing passage for crew in rough weather.

We arrive back at the *Hulst* more diluted than drunk, smuggling several six-packs of Hamms on board for the downbound trip. The watchman at the ladder looks the other way, knowing full well the need for diversion on the lake that the *Hulst* spends so much of her time in the middle of. As the ship labors her way through the midsummer tranquil sea of Superior, the beer helps fuel the multiple hands of hearts and singing in the deckhands' quarters. I am bonding with my peer group at an astonishing rate. The pace of the ship also gives me plenty of time to contemplate the calendar and realize that my impending date with the Convention of Death is quickly approaching. But, after witnessing the downbound locking through at the Sault—in daylight this time-and the wilderness of the St. Marys River, I am hard pressed to reject the entreaties of my new shipmates to make another run on the *Hulst*.

A couple nights later, as the *Hulst* approaches the steel mills of Lorain on Lake Erie, I am facing a monumental decision to quit the ship and make it back to Detroit in time to join the caravan to Chicago. But it's a beautiful summer night, full of a warmth that bathes our fledgling souls as the *Hulst* winds her way up the Black River.

By the time the ship has tied up under the Hullett cranes, it is full dark and I am facing the added impediment of transportation back to the Motor City. Thus, when Jackie and the deck gang finish their task of unbuckling and placing the hatches on the deck, I am relieved to hear him propose that we all go to a great bar he knows of just up the street. What I probably need more than anything is a couple of cold ones to help me make up my mind. Besides, I can always leave in the morning before the *Hulst* gets under way. So we pile into a taxi, Denny and I, Jackie and the other two deckhands, who have traded their responsibilities with a couple of the deckwatches for the short ride to funky downtown Lorain. The bar is located at the top of a flight of stairs. As we open the doors, we are greeted by your usual bar smells and a blast of honky tonk guitar. The night is warm and made for slurping cold ones. After a few, we watch, impressed. as Jackie mounts the stage and begins to play a few songs on a twelve-string guitar that has appeared from nowhere. He stands the place on its head and is glad to accommodate a few calls for encores. This results in a few gratuitous pitchers being sent over to our table, which we help him consume. Closing time comes all too soon and, as we make our way out into the warm night, Jackie suggests that it's too early to quit and I notice that Dave and Jerry are each carrying a case of Strohs. As we jump into a waiting cab, Jackie asks the driver, "Okay, so where do people go around here when they don't want to go home?"

The cabbie thinks for a second and answers, "The beach at Hole in the Wall."

"Is it close?"

"Get you there in ten minutes."

"All right. Let's do it," Jackie says, punctuated by a rebel yell. And then four more.

The cab drops us off at a park near Lake Erie. We can hear the soft whoosh of waves from the gravel parking lot. Jackie leads the way in darkness toward the beach, and the trip is without event until Dave trips going over the railroad tracks and crashes into Jerry, who falls with him amidst the great clashing of beer bottles breaking in their cases. We sadly survey the damage and count our lost soldiers before checking out our shipmates, who manage to continue the trek to the beach, sobered by the experience and shepherded by the rest of us.

The Hole in the Wall is almost deserted at this hour and we appropriate and rekindle the remains of a bonfire. Soon our spirits are

restored and we find ourselves up to our necks in Lake Erie. To pro-
pitiate the sailing and brew gods, a call and response chant emerges
that goes:

> This is our lake
> This is our lake
> We sail it
> We sail it
> We swim it
> We swim it
> We piss in it
> We piss in it
> We drink beer in it
> We drink beer in it
> YEEEHAAA!

One by one, we drag ourselves slowly onto the shore to suck from the
rapidly diminishing cases of Strohs. The false dawn gives us a rough
idea of the time and soon we are weaving down the streets of Lorain,
looking for a taxi without success. As the true dawn illuminates things,
we discover the loading docks and reconnoiter until we have found our
ship. By the time we have climbed the ladder, Denny and I realize that
it's time for us to get up for work. But Pat the steward takes one look
and waves us back to our bunks with the warning that we had better be
ready for dinner at ten-thirty. We gratefully careen toward our cabin.

A few hours later, we are back at work, I myself much the worse
for the wear. But as I make my way up the deck to catch the mate's
bunk, I notice Dave and Jerry working with the boatswain replacing
hatches and Jackie Bates, dressed in a casual suit, just getting back from
town after a quick visit to someone he describes as "a lady friend." I
am overwhelmed that he has that stamina and ability when it is all I
can do to put one foot in front of the other without tripping.

Back in the galley, I try to slake an overwhelming thirst by gulp-
ing a quart of chocolate milk. A mistake, I realize, as within minutes
I am back in my cabin, heaving my guts into the toilet. Denny, who is
a little better off, covers the dinner hour for me as I try to catch some
more sleep. But sleep won't come and I'm left with the realization that

I'm in no shape to carry through with my decision to leave the *John Hulst* and take a four-hour bus ride back to Detroit. Like it or not, I'm on for another trip to Lake Superior. I wonder if I should try and get off up there to meet my friends in the Windy City, but my head hurts too much to pursue this idea.

Later that afternoon, feeling better, I regain the deck to watch the *Hulst* approach the Southeast Shoal and Point Pelee Lights in Lake Erie. By the time supper has been served and the galley cleaned up it is evening and we are on deck watching the brightly lit rides soar and twirl amidst shrieks of pleasure that echo through the night sky above Bob-Lo. It is another warm night and several of the crew join us in watching the passage of the skyline of Detroit highlighted by the flashing red globe above the Penobscot Building, the blue-fringed top of the Gas Building, and the twinkling lights of Woodward Avenue that give way to subdued drumming and shrieks of humanity unleashed that emanate from the shores of Belle Isle.

Dave, drinking it all in and watching a Good Humor truck cruise the island, says, "Sure would be nice if we had some ice cream."

Denny says, "You really want some?"

"Hell yes."

And so, led by Denny, we snake back through the corridors of the galley to a door that only Denny knows how to open and just like that we are back on deck enjoying bowls of chocolate ice cream as we pass Windmill Point.

But the next afternoon, as the *Hulst* crawls through Lake Huron, Pat, the steward, confronts us with a union grievance that certain crew members got ice cream last night. He chides us for our unprofessional behavior and lets us know that, because of charges of preferential treatment brought by other crew members, he will have to provide ice cream to everyone tonight. And so, rebuked, we try not to enjoy our ice cream treat too much the second time around. Although, in honesty, we know that the first time was truly the most enjoyable.

It is daylight as we cruise the upper St. Marys River, drinking in the wild beauty while working our way with peeling knives through a bag of potatoes for tonight's supper. While not blessed, as was the crew of the *Columbia*, with daily access to fresh food, Pat the steward adheres to some sort of steward's commitment to freshness by providing potatoes on a daily basis. There is no place for instant potatoes on a Great Lakes ship. But the food we are served on the *Hulst* cannot compete with the daily feasts put on for the crew of the *Columbia*. On the *Hulst*, the entrees are simpler and tend to be geared more toward the meat-and-potatoes diet that these guys were brought up on. So we see a lot more meatloaf and boiled and mashed potatoes accompanied by canned peas and carrots. Gene, the second cook, is kept busy making fresh bread to supplement the store-bought stuff that is picked up as part of our weekly provision of food. Pat explains that his budget allows him to buy only so much every week and he has to deal with the going rate for provisions in any of the ports the *Hulst* happens to be in. A decision not to purchase a staple because of higher prices could put Pat and the crew of the slow-moving *Hulst* in the position of heading into Lake Superior with a dwindling food locker.

As the peels fly into newspaper at our feet and a couple of deer poke their heads out of some popple scrub on the banks of an island, I reflect that the crew of the *Hulst* reminds me more of factory workers than sailors. Deck crew and engine crew both wear green coveralls favored by grease monkeys. And everyone basically goes about doing their job on a day-in, day-out basis. If it weren't for Denny and the deckhands, I would get bored with these guys in a hurry. Not to say that these guys aren't nice, but compared to the crew of the *Mercury*, I feel like I am at some Baptist convention. One of the oilers, Charlie, is a young, pimply faced guy with a crew cut and black glasses. Although he's only twenty-three, he's already got one son, with another on the way. Later in the day as the *Hulst* chugs against the current into Whitefish Bay, he warns me about sitting for prolonged periods on the steel hatch covers as the chill of a Superior evening ascends. "Might get some piles in a hurry." Then he borrows Jackie's guitar and strums out a rendition of a song celebrating the passage of the *Hulst* through the Great Lakes to the tune of "Wabash Cannonball." One of the oilers up on deck, listening to the song, says, "Bet you don't know that this ship once exploded." He goes on to recount how the coal in the *Hulst*'s bunkers created a methane explosion in the Straits of Mackinac in 1944. "Tore up the after end here," he says.

That evening as we make our way through the big lake, we pass the time drinking the rest of our beer and playing hearts to help replenish our kitty. After a while, Jackie and I get to working on a song that has been building in my mind since I returned from California this past spring. Its working title is "California Wet Dream," and we begin working on some basic chords to bring a surf beat to accompany the words:

> Floppin' in a flophouse
> Sloppin' in a mission
> Here in California
> Everybody's bitchin
>   Refrain: Bonk a bong, Bonk a bong
>   Yeah Bonk a bong, bonk a bong,
> Do like the Californians
> C'mon baby let's go screwin'
> Wondring where we're going
> Wondring what we're doin'
> Here in California
> Everybody's screwing
>   Refrain
> Etc.

As the *Hulst* arrives in Duluth, I am confronted again with the decision that I have been successfully avoiding since we left Lorain. The siege of Chicago is officially under way and I had promised to be there with my buddies. I ponder my alternatives while on the bumboat on a drizzly, cool Saturday afternoon. The bumboat is the name given to an unheralded fleet of vessels that service the Great Lakes fleet at the ports of Duluth, Superior, and Toledo. So far as I know, they exist nowhere else on the lakes. Although I don't know how many they are in number, the bumboats flitter from one vessel to the next as they are tied up under the loading chutes, taking on their iron ore. The bumboat ties up to the ship's outboard side and a ladder is made fast. Then, any crew member with the inclination and time climbs down onto the deck of the tiny craft tucked into the side of the mother ship like an illicit calf whale. But inside there exists an emporium of delights designed to tempt even the most jaded sailor. Of course there are the utilitarian things like work gloves, waterproof boots, and mackinaw jackets. But beyond that are a variety of portable radios and even small, cabin-sized personal TV's. If that isn't enough, there is a row of magazines with titles ranging from *Hunter's Digest* to *Playboy* to *Crawdaddy*, along with some newspapers for the more literate minded. But we don't bother with such trivia and head for a few ragged chairs and crates in the back of the boat set up around a TV showing the baseball game of the week and within arms' length of chips, candy bars, and a cooler filled with Hamms. Because the bumboat has other ships to visit and will be here for two hours at most, we are obliged to compress our enjoyment and thus guzzle and chew at an accelerated pace. The bumboat serves those who have too little time or inclination to walk to the end of the dock and catch a taxi to the distant city, where we would have nothing to do once we got there. And with the weather the way it is, the bumboat is probably the best deal around. And so, around a tiny TV with a couple beers in my belly, I make the fateful decision that it would be foolhardy for me to leave the *Hulst* on this day for the shaky trek to Chicago, where I would be hard pressed to find my friends in the midst of thousands of freaks. I make my way carefully back up the ladder to the *Hulst* for one more trip down Lake Superior.

The next day is a Sunday, a regular work day for galley slaves Denny and myself but an off day for our fortunate deckhand brethren, who would be pressed into service only if we were in port. As a special treat, the captain invites the five of us up to his quarters to watch a soccer game on his television. To our amazement, he even serves us beer. Having flaunted one standing rule of the Pittsburgh Fleet of United States Steel, he invites us up to see the pilothouse—another place declared verboten by the authorities. Perhaps this Chicago thing is stirring some seeds of rebellion into the air we drink, I reflect as we troop up the narrow interior stairway that leads from his quarters to the wheelhouse.

My first impressions of this pilothouse are that it is much more spacious than the homey confines of the *Mercury*'s. There is also a lot more equipment as well as a chart table for the mate to work on. Framed on the wall above the chart table is a yellowed *Detroit Times* article that reads:

HULST BUCKS INTO WIND STARTING HER FIRST RUN

Bucking an easterly wind that pushed the big new freighter against the dock, the *John Hulst* finally swung out into the Detroit River at 8:30 o'clock this morning from the Great Lakes Engineering Works at Ecorse. The new Pittsburgh Steamship Company boat had been scheduled to start her trial at 7:30.

With some 40 aboard, including representatives of the Bureau of Marine Inspection and Navigation, the shipbuilding and steamship firms, the *Hulst* nosed out into Lake Erie for a run that will not bring the freighter back until tonight.

I am next captured by the tiny black ship's wheel that sits unmanned in the middle of the room. This is my first meeting with "Iron Mike," as the automated steering system is called. I watch, mesmerized, as the wheel adjusts to keep the ship on a preset course over the vast blue expanse before us. Although built thirty years ago, the *John Hulst*, with its silent, invisible turbines and its Iron Mike, resembles a ship of the future for me. Given the fact that it's almost thirty years younger than the other ships I've sailed, it is. But I also sense in the *Hulst* a ship without a soul. Whenever I walk the entire length of the ship through the long, narrow tunnels that flank the holds, the silence is eerie.

I admire the view of the slowly passing Apostle Islands and think about the fact that the innovations introduced on the *Hulst* have themselves been overshadowed by the next wave of technology brought on by the Second World War. Ships like those in the Republic Steel fleet, like the *White, Girdler,* and *Patton,* all built in 1945 using war monies, show much more character afloat than the plebeian *Hulst.* What's more, they are almost three times as fast. It is a running joke among our crew as we seem to sit still in the open lake like an island as the rest of the Great Lakes fleet passes us by. This, of course, serves as a great advantage to a ship watcher like myself. Over the course of these two voyages, I have been able to see dozens and dozens of ships from both near and afar—even more than in the *Cuyahoga* during the Steelworkers' strike earlier this summer. I have been able to observe the next generation of the fleet, ships built in the late fifties and early sixties, like the dashing *Wilfred Sykes,* the sleek *Patton,* and the downright handsome *Fitzgerald.* I wonder if they will lead us back to a place where ships can have their own character and not become merely another part of the machine that made them.

That evening, still miles from nowhere, the deckhands assemble on the hatches midships to celebrate a warm night in the middle of Superior. Jackie's guitar leads us through our world premier of "California Wet Dream" but the highlight is an elongated marching version of "Yellow Submarine" as we lead the crew around the deck and the guys in the pilothouse put us in their spotlight for an encore.

If the captain is drawn to his window to watch our antics, we never know. Although I have given up being with my friends in Chicago for this chance for one more trip on the *Hulst*, I don't regret it. At least, not on this magic Superior evening.

Early the next morning we pass through the locks and snake our way through the St. Marys. By midafternoon we are into Lake Huron when Gene, the second cook, comes to our cabin holding his hand in a towel. His face is red and he is flustered: "Fellas, I need your help," he says apologetically. "I just sliced the tip of my thumb in the salad I was making for supper. Can you guys finish it for me?"

"What happened, Gene?" I ask.

He is further embarrassed but finally blurts out, "I bought some beer back in Superior off the bumboat. Shouldn't a been drinking but I had a couple after dinner. Then this happens."

"Sure, Gene, go get that taken care of. We'll cover for you," we assure him.

And so, as Gene retires to his cabin, so are retired my fears of another Black Saturday, which only goes to reinforce my impression of the bland character of this crew, compared to the crazies of the *Mercury*. Later that evening, after supper has been cleared away and Gene is sleeping it off in his cabin, Denny and I make a preemptive strike. We use the same back corridor technique we previously used to get the ice cream and discover the remainder of Gene's beer. We confiscate the brew to add to our rapidly diminishing supply in the guise of protecting the crew from any further bad behavior from Gene. We are confident that, when Gene recovers, he will be too ashamed to ask us if we know anything about it.

> Drop your cocks and grab your socks.
> Rise and shine for the Pittsburgh line.

This is the call that begins what will be my last day aboard the *John Hulst*. The ship is in the lower St. Clair River, approaching Lake St. Clair en route to Lake Erie and Lorain. I pass the morning and afternoon going through my chores and, by the time late afternoon has arrived, we are approaching Lorain Harbor and my bag is packed. The only glitch is that the ship will have to navigate the Black River for almost two hours before we are docked, a journey that could well jeopardize my plans to find transportation home tonight. But Pat the steward comes to my cabin with the news that the captain has okayed my request to disembark on a supply boat at the mouth of the river. And in a jiffy I'm out on the deck, watching as the *Hulst* crawls into the narrow river mouth. Jackie, Dave, and Jerry are already on the deck, unclamping the hatch covers with the boatswain. I have a chance to shake hands with them and Denny before I hustle off the *Hulst* the same way I got on—by ladder.

It takes a few seconds before I am on land and walking in downtown Lorain. I find the bus station and make a decision to catch the next one to Cleveland, from where I hope to be able to catch a plane back to Detroit. I am anxious to regroup with my buddies and find out what has happened in Chicago over the past several days. With an hour to kill, I take refuge in a local bar, where I am served a Strohs with the label partway torn off—the signature and badge of shame that I have been identified as under twenty-one and thus served a 3.2 beer.

The bus ride to Cleveland is swift and uneventful and I quickly make connections to an airport near downtown that has a connecting flight to Detroit City Airport, close to my home. Before I know it, I am gazing down at Lake Erie and the tiny red-and-black toy boats that make up the Great Lakes shipping fleet. A call from City Airport produces a car full of bandana-wearing, long-haired hippies obviously out of control. These are not the same tame friends I last saw a few weeks ago in Angel Park. They have been to Chicago, have slept in the park, watched rock and roll bands, marched on the convention, and been tear-gassed and rousted by the police, who will now and forever be referred to as "Daley's motherfucking pigs." Thus radicalized, we drive across the bridge to a party in Windsor where the major entertainment is watching the live coverage of the last night of the Convention of Death. We drink beer and watch protesters try to storm the convention only to be repelled by waves of police charges. Throughout, the chant of "The whole world's watching" mingles with the gas-hazed images on the screen. Everyone, including my friends who have just been a part of it, is shocked at the rising levels of violence captured before our eyes. I watch, astonished and sobered, as my brothers and sisters succeed in bringing the war back home to the streets of the country referred to as "Amerika" in the underground press.

Monteith Professor Otto Feinstein speaking at a rally in Detroit after returning from the 1968 Chicago Democratic Convention where he served as an alternate delegate (Walter P. Reuther Library, Wayne State University)

The spirit of Chicago permeates the waning days of summer as the underground media goes to work to help balance the establishment news stories coming out of the Windy City. I attend a concert at Meadowbrook that features some of the hottest bands coming out of the Trans-Love network managed by John Sinclair and the Artists Workshop. At one point, someone announces that the park management are refusing to let the MC5 in to play and a near riot erupts until someone announces that they are in. The music is really secondary to the chance just to be with thousands of other people who share our culture of youth. To be sure, the availability of weed and beautiful young girls only adds to our appreciation of the atmosphere. As Iggy and the Psychedelic Stooges take the stage for their mind-numbing set, I can think of no place I'd rather be. Except maybe on a ship in the middle of Lake Superior with a bunch of crazy friends.

SS *John Hulst*

Built	1938
Builder	Great Lakes Engineering Works, River Rouge, Michigan
Owner	Pittsburgh Steamship Company (Division of U.S. Steel)
Length	611'6"
Beam	60'
Draft	32'6"
Engine	Steam Turbine
Boilers	Two Babcock & Wilcox coal-fired
Capacity	14,150 dwt
Cargo	Iron ore
Crew	32

The advent of fall brings a long-awaited treasure to Detroit—a World Series victory for the Tigers. A few hours after Bill Freehan catches the last St. Louis pop-up, Sam and I drive downtown to attend a Detroit Symphony concert at Ford Auditorium. We struggle through a traffic jam and park my old Plymouth in an alley. We make our way through the throng of partyers who have shut down all traffic on both Woodward and Jefferson. When we get out of the concert a few hours later, we are surprised to find the streets empty and downtown virtually shut down. The next day's papers tell the story of the party that got out of hand and the shops that were looted before the police unleashed the tear gas. While the *Detroit Free Press* headlines "We Win" with pictures of Mickey Lolich and Jim Northrup, the *Detroit News* tells of the thousands who jammed downtown to celebrate and of the happy hours of looting and rioting that ensued before law and order was restored.

CHAPTER 6

1969

The War Comes Home

Well it's 1969 okay
All across the USA
Another year for me and you
Another year with nothing to do
   "1969"—Psychedelic Stooges

Within a few weeks I am back in the cozy confines of Monteith College and am engrossed in a variety of studies. I have no idea of what I want to do with my life, which makes college a pretty good place to be. Wayne State University Prez William Rae Keast has reiterated his position to continue exempting every student from the immoral military draft, which elevates him to near-hero status. The campus newspaper, taken over by a gang of hippies last year and renamed the *South End*, has been taken over by a gang of Black Panthers this year. Although the name has not changed, a logo of a black panther helps to redefine the front page. Almost weekly there are teach-ins and protests related to the war in Southeast Asia. A professor at one of our seminars arranges for a U.S. Army deserter from Vietnam to sit in and relate his experiences. This is the first time I have heard tales from the front firsthand. Letters from my friend Rick, who served as a medic, were much more banal and did not really ask the question now made famous by Norman Mailer's *Why Are We in Vietnam?* This theme, of course, provides a treasure trove for our professors to plunder, and we spend an entire semester studying the Faust legend and how it has shaped our twentieth-century psyches.

On another front, I have my first serious crush on a girl since high school and am devastated when she attacks me in the midst of a pseudotherapy group conducted by a shaman professor. Some days, college life is all too real and I long for the camaraderie of the *Mercury* crew, who, I'm sure, have all suffered similar fates at the hands of the opposite sex. Which is probably the reason that crews for ships like the *Mercury* exist in the first place.

Horst, Tom, and I are confreres at Monteith. We find ourselves in the same seminars and form ourselves into a team to do some research and write a couple of papers. Tom lives with some people in an apartment on Woodward who are practicing war- and draft-resistance in a very serious way. Others from our class are beginning to show signs of being a part of the age of Aquarius. When I inquire of Horst what became of one of our seminar mates, Glenn, he replies with a laugh, "Oh, that cat. He dropped some acid and got on his bicycle and took off down Woodward. Said he was going to Florida." One evening a friend and I decide to check out an event hosted by Trans-Love Energies. The gig is a celebration of no school tomorrow because of an antiwar rally that is supposed to shut down the campus. We walk into the Pontiac Building—more of an open hall on the edge of campus—and discover some pretty strange folk hopping around to the postmodern Polish wedding marches put down by a group introduced simply as the Pigfuckers. Then the Psychedelic Stooges take the tiny impromptu stage and their leader Iggy turns the place upside down. Fortunately a security guard is on hand to stop him from toppling a metal coat rack into the audience and wrestles him off the premises. Then the legendary MC5 bring it home with a free-for-all that culminates with everyone on stage playing some instrument or another handed out by the psychedelic guru himself, John Sinclair. After, my friend and I stagger down Cass Avenue, drunk on sound, trying in vain to recover our hearing. The next day at noon, on my way to a teach-in, I again see the Pigfuckers performing on the mall. I decide to give them a pass this time. And so life at the big city school seems to go.

Because I still live at home, my week nights are divided between parties with my old high school friends and new college friends. My friend Rick is newly back from Vietnam. A part of me is jealous for his experiences. Even though he is suffering, I see him as a part of the real world swirling around me, full of people who are saying and doing important things. It is the young people with these types of experiences who are writing the stories that fuel the revolutionary rhetoric of papers like the *Village Voice*, *Fifth Estate*, and *South End*. Rick is using his GI money to enroll at Macomb Community College and often comes down to Wayne to sit in on the protests. He doesn't seem to have a lot to share about his experiences in 'Nam. Through the winter, he is prone to sit in the basement of his parents' house and listen to Miles Davis's *In a Silent Way* while sipping Jim Beam and Coke. He is not a leader but more of a silent witness to a war almost impossible to describe and the times that have become almost impossible to escape.

As winter yields to the bitter early spring of Detroit, we often spend evenings driving around quiet Belle Isle in his newly purchased '65 Mustang, sipping Boone's Farm apple wine. The island is almost empty of humans at this time of year and becomes a refuge for us from the mad world. We drive down Tanglewood with the lights out, watching for deer as our eyes adjust to the natural light. Occasionally we coerce some other friends to join us, but most of the time we manage on our own.

On the Monteith front, Professor Joe Armstrong is organizing an end-of-year field trip to the dunes of Lake Michigan. So I join a bunch of students and hangers-on in a caravan of beetles, motorcycles, and microbuses to a sandy campground on the shores of the lake near the Indiana border. It is early June and the weather has moderated enough to be pretty nice. We set up our tents and Joe leads an eco-expedition across the dunes. I enjoy this experience all the more because I have learned how not to enroll in his classes. He is too exacting a teacher and hard a grader for my student lifestyle. So I take the same classes from other profs who establish their anti-establishment credentials by announcing at the beginning of the quarter, "All right, I just want to let you know that everyone in here will get an 'A' or a 'B,' whether you show up or not." And then I sit in on the truly informative and fascinating classes of Joe Armstrong, which include expeditions into the alleys of the Cass Corridor to explore flora and fauna. This is the Monteith spirit at work.

As darkness falls over the dunes, bottles of various types of cheap wine begin to appear and a bonfire is set. A group of sophomores heads over the last mound of sand and finds the lake, whitecaps visible by their whiteness in contrast to the black water. We worship at the altar of the lake and return to our campsite no worse for the wear to a brief astronomy lesson by the prof before he retires, grinning, into his tent with the prettiest student. And thus passes another school year.

CHAPTER 7

Steamboat V

"The Ford Got Hot . . .":
The MV *Henry Ford II*

The summer of 1969 shimmers forth in a blaze of glory. I help my cousin Tom, now known to us as Martinez, celebrate his graduation, and even find a girlfriend to join the ruckus. My high school friends and I have discovered a pocket park just down the street from the mayor's Manoogian Mansion on the river and we christen it our own people's park. There is enough room there for a game of Frisbee or even soccer as well as a grill. The amazing thing is that the park is basically uninhabited most evenings when wc go there. The down side is that the neighbors are not slow to call the cops if we get carried away and start a small bonfire. I get to know our people's park pretty well because the Local 5000 Steelworkers in Toledo has not returned my calls for a ship to work on. I have little alternative except to hang out at the park. The days are scorchers—hot and dry—and the nights bring only the descent of the Midwest mug upon us. Great beer-drinking weather, even if we can afford only the cheapest stuff. Gambrinus, at a dollar for an eight-pack, is a favorite even though there is often a different sort of price to pay the next morning. So long as it's cold, we put up with it.

I finally determine to face the matter directly and drive around in my car until I wind up in front of the NMU hall, now relocated west of the bridge on Fort Street. Although the union has new quarters, the furniture and the smells have been moved intact from the old hall. Even Louis Streho is still there and he remembers me. Too well. He puffs at the end of a stogie and regards me skeptically as I make my request for a ship. Then he rumbles through a nearby cabinet and pretends to read my file. He looks up from it, rolls his eyes into his forehead, and then sneers at me, "You owe the union $240 in back dues. No dues, no jobs." I am truly shocked to learn that the union has continued to charge me dues since I got off the *Mercury* almost a year ago. Louis tells me, "Should've retired your book when you got off the *Mercury*. I can't ship you out until you pay up."

But as I return, dejected, to my car and begin to pull away, he walks up to my window and says, "I'll give you one more chance. Passenger porter on the *Henry Ford*. Temporary for just one trip." He hands me a slip of paper with directions. "But you'll have to make up back dues through your salary, starting with your first check." I accept the berth with some mixed feelings. I'm happy to have the job but troubled at the prospect of having to make up all these back dues he keeps jabbering about.

My letter from the hall takes me through security at the nearby Ford Rouge plant to a company doctor for a physical. I am surprised to find that I need to apply for employment with Ford as a part of working on one of their ships. I have never had to do anything like this since my initial physical for my "Z" card with the Coast Guard. After a couple hours of processing, I head home to pack my bag, happy to be shipping out again at last. By 7:30 that evening, I'm back at the Rouge, complete with bag and girlfriend hanging all over me. I disengage her, much to the amusement of a security guard, and begin a long, hot walk through the plant and mountains of dust-laden coal and iron ore to the dock.

Once up the gangway, I am amazed at how different the *Henry Ford II* is from any ship I've yet been on. The gangway is broad and well constructed and there is an elevator dockside to lift stores directly onto the deck. My experience on the *Hulst* last summer introduced me to the workings of an ore ship, and the *Ford II*, although built almost fifteen years earlier in 1924, is similarly designed. Robert E. Lee, later curator of the Dossin Great Lakes Museum, discussed Henry Ford's vision in an article he wrote for *Telescope* magazine in 1975:

> The American people had become used to looking for the unusual in any project undertaken by the senior Mr. Ford. When he announced that the Ford Motor Company would have two ships built for its steel production operations at the Rouge, it was more than a routine announcement to the shipping industry. The contracts were given to

the Great Lakes Engineering Works for the construction of the *Benson Ford* and American Shipbuilding Company for the *H-II*, as she's come to be known. They were practically sister ships—up to a point. Both were 62 feet wide; the *Henry* measured in three-tenths of a foot shorter than the *Benson* at 596.7 feet, but the *Henry* was one-tenth of a foot deeper than *Benson*, which was 27.8 feet. Both had the same power plant.

The power plant referred to is a Sun-Doxford opposed-piston diesel engine built in Chester, Pennsylvania. In addition to being the first diesel-propelled ships on the Great Lakes, the *Henry* and the *Benson* are the first to be equipped with all-electrical systems, including winches, steering, heaters, and stove.

The *Henry Ford II* is one of six ships in the Ford fleet. Also built in 1924, the *Benson Ford* is almost an exact replica of the *Henry* in dimensions, although lacking her appointments. The oldest ship in the fleet, the *Robert McNamara*, built in 1909, is used exclusively on the Toledo-Rouge coal run, and tries to run year-round. The remaining three vessels, the *Ernest Breech*, *John Dykstra*, and *William Clay Ford*, were all built in the early fifties and kept busy on the iron ore runs to the Rouge.

The chief steward who welcomes me aboard introduces himself as Jim. He is attired in a formal black uniform, similar to one I remember Beauregard wearing on the *South American*. He invites me into his sumptuous quarters in the after cabin to talk about the role I will be performing starting in the morning. He tells me his job is entirely administrative—making sure that the galley crew work to satisfy the needs of passengers and crew alike. He spends no time in the galley cooking and consults with the first cook on the menus for the week. Save for the *South*, no other ship I've been on has had this type of position. On all my other ships, the steward has also served as first cook and, while generally regarded as the person responsible for the comfort of the crew, has confined his efforts to the galley. But here on the *Henry Ford II*, there is a steward assigned to look after our comfort. He directs the first and second cooks, two crew porters, a dishwasher, and me, the passenger porter. The first cook tends strictly to making the food from menus provided to him by the steward. Pretty wild.

"And your job is to make sure that the guests of the company are comfortable and have everything they need," Jim continues. "The

The *Henry Ford II* under construction in the American Shipbuilding Company yard in Lorain, Ohio, circa 1924 (Historical Collection of the Great Lakes/Bowling Green State University)

Ford Motor Company is one of a few that provides this type of excursion to friends of the company. Your job has nothing to do with serving the crew. Your whole purpose here is to make sure those six people coming on board tonight have everything they need when they need it. I know that you're assigned to us for only this trip, but I know that if you do your job well, there will be more to come this summer."

He then takes me around the fantail of the ship and shows me the cabin I will be sharing with three other crew. The cabin has some of the same dark wood I've noticed in the steward's rooms, but none of the amenities, let alone space. He notices my interest and says, by way of acknowledgment, "English oak." I nod, feigning appreciation, and stow my gear in a closet made of the same wood and make my bunk, which I notice is also made of wood.

A while later, I escape the oppressive heat of the cabin for the infernal heat of the deck. The evening is beyond warm, and as I watch the Hullett cranes rip into the body of the *Ford II* to extract its mineral riches, I can barely imagine the cooling breezes of Lake Huron, where we will be heading.

Up forward I notice that the elevator has sprung to life and lifted six people onto the deck, where they are being met by Jim. He escorts them up one flight into the forward cabins that he has identified to me as the passenger quarters. I am told by one of the deckhands that the *Ford II* will be unloading all night and will not sail before daybreak. I retire to my cabin, get directions to the washroom, and take a quick shower before bedding down. The quarters are as cramped as those of the *South* or the *Columbia* and don't have the cooling benefit of being under the waterline. I sweat through the night, warmed by the boilers that feed the steady throb of the idling diesel engine that is housed on the other side of the oaken cabin wall.

The early morning call from Jim finds me rumpled, crusty, and ready for duty. He leads me forward up a flight of exterior stairs and through a door into a suite of three separate staterooms that occupy what I imagine to be the entire deck. He indicates with a finger to his lips that behind these doors are the three couples, still sound asleep, and then points to a doorway that opens to a formal dining room with eight seats around the table. I take it that this is where most of the meals will be served. Jim then he leads me up a wide flight of steps into the guest lounge. The wood is more of the baronial variety I have been exposed to in my quarters on the after end. But this has been filigreed and burnished, and when Jim once again notices my roving eye, he speaks the words "Santo Domingo mahogany" to enlighten me. The furnishings and hanging tapestries match the wood and are consistent with what I have been exposed to in my high school days working at the country club and have seen at the Detroit Institute of Arts. He shows me an alcove that serves as a bar that is touched with nuances of art deco, but only nuances. In short, I've seen no captain's quarters to match these in luxury. As we look out through the large plate glass windows onto the bow, Jim reviews my role once again. It is my job to anticipate and meet every craving that these guests of the Ford Motor Company might have. In addition, I am to make the beds, clean the rooms, run snacks from the galley, and, above all, make sure that the ice chest behind the bar never ever runs close to low.

My very first duty, Jim now tells me, is to provide the guests a requested 7:30 wake-up call so that they can watch our departure

The passenger lounge of the *Henry Ford II* (Historical Collection of the Great Lakes/Bowling Green State University)

from the dock and down the Rouge to the Detroit River. I bide my time tidying up the salon and gazing out the large windows that look out on the deck. The Hulletts have stopped their feeding of iron ore from the Ford's holds. I watch, intrigued, as the deckhands close the hatches with a cable device that pulls them shut from each end of the hatch. My first exposure to telescoping hatches. At first glance, it doesn't look as easy as the deck crane operation I'd witnessed on the *Hulst* last year.

At the appointed time, I rap softly on the three bedroom doors, make sure the occupants are awake, and invite them to come to the dining room for breakfast. I stand by in the foyer as the guests make their toilets and introduce myself as their porter when they emerge to lead them into the dining room. In the meantime the first cook has arrived with covered platters of food and has set up the room. As I make sure that they are comfortably seated, the *Ford*, with a mighty blast of its electric whistle that sounds more like an air horn, casts off its lines and backs to the turning basin from where she will begin her descent of the Rouge. While my charges are noshing around the white tablecloths, I grab a quick something from the crew's mess and park myself at the rail outside the stateroom door, awaiting my next orders.

It is already hot and I seek shelter in the shade of the overhang as the *Ford II* cuts her way past junkyards and chemical graveyards through the simmering brown lifeless soup that is the Rouge. I am sweating as we pass under the final lift bridge and enter the relatively benign, blue-green waters of the Detroit River. I find myself looking forward to the trip north, especially the cooling waters of Lake Huron a few hours ahead.

The *Ford II* makes good time through Lake St. Clair and the St. Clair River and, shortly after noon, we are cruising along the coast of the Blue Water Lake. In the intervening hours, I have made up the rooms and made the acquaintance of our guests. They are three middle-aged couples, all on their first company cruise. Three sets of men and women all wearing casual clothes and not standing out in any way that I can discern from one another. I don't recognize their names as among the Detroit elite, but I'm sure they must be important to somebody somewhere to be guests of the company on a trip of this nature. Since the demise of the *South American*, there are no public cruises on any of the Great Lakes, a fact that makes this trip all the more valuable. The men and women are all obviously enjoying their good fortune at being on the *Ford* and appear quite easygoing and good-natured. Once again my experience as a caddy and pro-shop staffer at the country club has made it easy for me to converse with them. For the most part, once I've made up their rooms, my duties consist largely of replenishing the ice buckets that are fighting a losing battle with the warmth of the guest quarters. I hope that the cooling temperatures of the upper lakes will help take care of that.

But, aside from that, I'm basically on call and bide my time as the long summer day becomes longer with every passing mile into the northern latitudes. As the ship settles down for a night on Lake Huron, I see that the ice buckets are full and head back to my still hot cabin for another round of fitful sleep to the pounding rhythm of the diesel.

That same diesel can do twelve miles an hour, one of the oilers proudly tells me the next morning as we steam toward the Straits of

Mackinac. This is 50 percent faster than the sluggish *John Hulst* and about the same as the *Mercury*, the *South American*, and the *Columbia*. He invites me down for a quick look at the history-making engine. Only the fact that I had seen the engine room of the *Hulst* last summer prepares me for the absence of motion in that of the *Ford II*. But, unlike the cool green electrical generators that powered the *Hulst*, I am confronted here with what looks more like the *Mercury* or *South American*. There are four large units that reach up toward the ceiling and house the pistons. But, because they are enclosed, I cannot see them go through their circular, mesmerizing dance. My guide points out that this design allows the *Ford II* to run continuously at a very low rpm rate—fifteen to seventeen per minute—and to reverse direction in four seconds. I can only stare at the source of the throbbing that has kept me half awake these past two nights. But I am able to console myself with glimpses of the smaller engines that filter the water and perform other odd jobs aboard the ship. My biggest reward is being able to see the shaft turning toward the ship's propellor at the stern.

I contrive to ensure that I am with my guests on deck as we slip past the Grand Hotel of Mackinac Island to starboard, past Fort Michilimackinac of Mackinaw City to port, and directly under the almighty awesome alabastered Mackinac Bridge. A short time later I quietly congratulate myself on entering my fifth Great Lake as a sailor as the straits yield to the azure skies above northern Lake Michigan.

A few hours later I watch, fascinated, as the deckhands work with a cable and quiet electric winch—no hissing steam here—to telescope the hatch covers back to open the holds of the ship for her next cargo. We are about to tie up in the port of Escanaba in Michigan's Upper Peninsula, where the *Ford II* will load taconite pellets—little black marbles of processed iron ore—all night long.

By 7 PM we are tied up, and I receive a brief reprieve as my charges decide to march up the street to investigate the wonders of downtown Escanaba. I take advantage of the break to kick back and enjoy the warm summer evening on the deck. Walking up the street does not appeal to me at the moment, my being broke and still underage influencing that disinclination. The *Ford II* is not scheduled to begin loading for a few hours and I choose to enjoy the quiet time on the after end as the sun sets on Little Bay de Noc. I pass some time in desultory conversation with a few of the crew who have not elected to go up the street on such a beautiful night. But my job has almost

The *Henry Ford II* under way (Thomas Manse Collection)

set me apart from them and the fact that I am on as a "temp" gets in the way of any effort to strike up friendships. Finally, Jim calls me into his cabin and offers me a glass of whiskey. It is strange for me to be sitting in these posh surroundings drinking the hard stuff when I have become accustomed to hoisting beers with crew closer to my age. But we sit and talk for a while about college life until he reminds me that the guests could be coming back soon.

As evening descends into night, I make sure the ice is topped up and once again head back to my quarters for what I hope will be a cooler sleeping environment. I immediately notice, to my dismay, that the diesel at rest still throbs like the diesel under way. And the Upper Peninsula is not really that much cooler than Detroit at this point in the summer.

On the third day I arise to discover the deck crew of the *Ford II* already at work closing the hatch covers. The day is fresh and the

MV *Henry Ford II*

Built	1924
Builder	American Shipbuilding Company, Lorain, Ohio
Owner	Ford Motor Company
Length	611'
Beam	62'
Draft	32'
Engines	Sun-Doxford Diesel
Capacity	14,000 tons dwt
Cargoes	Iron ore, taconite, coal
Crew	31

breeze from the north invigorating. I go through my routine insuring that the guests enjoyed their night in Escanaba and are in good shape to enjoy another passage through the straits. One of the wives confides to me that they stayed out until well past closing time and might need a little recuperation time. I take the hint and retire back aft for a little R and R of my own.

It is after the dinner hour, around midafternoon, when I am summoned to the steward's quarters for a message. But when I get there, Jim is content to have me sit in a leather chair and talk for a while more about some of the ideas that we surfaced the evening before. Although he doesn't offer me any hard liquor this time, I am uncomfortable in this setting. While it could well be that he is simply a person in need of intellectual discourse, something in the back of my mind questions whether he isn't seeking another sort of stimulation as well. After a half hour or so of discussion of college-level ideas ranging from the Greeks (careful!) to Vietnam to the Detroit riots, Jim says casually, "Oh yeah, the captain has called for a fire and boat drill at 3 o'clock. You've got to go back and let the guests know so they won't think it's the real thing." I look up at the clock on the wall that tells me I've got about ten minutes to perform this duty. As I excuse myself, Jim adds, "By the way, make sure that you've got yourself ready for the drill, too. The old man has got a thing about everybody being at their station."

196

Before I head forward to the guest quarters, I stop by my cabin to grab the life preserver and double-check to find my station—number 4—on the port boat deck. I throw on the preserver and then walk quickly forward and up the stairs to the guest cabins. I check the lounge first and find no signs of life. Then I turn to the teak doors of the staterooms and begin to knock. Simultaneous with my knock I hear the ship's electric horn begin to blast out a series of long and short blasts accompanied by an interior bell that commences to clang in my ear. Of course, just at this time, the doors of all three staterooms open to see me standing before them in my life vest, looking very perplexed as I try to shout over the noise, "Fire and boat drill! Fire and boat drill!" There is a lot of screeching and yelling and, as the first mate finally appears to take charge of this station, I decide that it's probably a good time for me to head to my station on the after end. I stand by and admire Mackinac Island as the lifeboat is let down a few turns and then cranked back up. This time through, my feeling of exhilaration is decidedly tempered by the events in the staterooms.

Looking back on it later as I sit with Jim in his quarters, I'm sure that the guests couldn't have heard all of what I was yelling and chose to let the image convey the story they most feared. Although Jim is conciliatory, he is also brutally pragmatic. "It looks as though the guy with the weak heart didn't really have a heart attack. The Cap thinks he'll be fine with some rest." Then he looks at me crookedly and says, "But we blew it. There's hell to pay and I can't lose my job over this. I'm sorry to do this, kid, but the old man told me that someone's got to take the blame."

I walk out on the deck and gaze over the railing at the expanse of blue water as we enter Lake Huron for what assuredly is my final time on the *Ford II*. My feelings vacillate between rage and self-pity and my thoughts swing from those of rampage and shipboard mayhem to simply ending it all over this very railing. Later in the evening, after supper, I offer my not-quite-heartfelt apologies to the guests, who have decided not to question the official version of events they have been fed by the captain. I am sure that they have been assured that a head—specifically mine—will roll in atonement for this stain on the Ford Motor Company. As night falls, I look toward the forward end to see the guests obviously fully recovered and capering about on the balcony of the second deck as though they are in the play *South Pacific.* While it may be for them, for me it is anything but some enchanted evening. I retire to my boiler-warmed bunk, not really caring whether their bloody ice chest is filled or their glasses are clean.

I manage to get through the next day without further damage and, by the time the *Ford II* is entering the Rouge, I am on friendly speaking terms with all the guests, with the possible exception of the wife of the man whose life I may have shortened. Along with the steward and the captain, I stand by the elevator to see them off and to wave my farewells. Then I turn to my own quarters to gather up my GI duffel, a gift from my friend Rick by way of 'Nam, and prepare to reenter the city. Jim sees me off at the gangplank with an apology. "I wish things hadn't happened that way. I was hoping we could keep you on. But that's the way the cookie crumbles." I walk my way down the gangplank construction and through the dusty hot yards of the Rouge, thinking that maybe it isn't such a bad thing that I won't have to sail with a guy like him anymore this summer.

In my distressed state of mind, I have failed to notice that it's ten o'clock on a Saturday night in Detroit and I am on the far west side. Phone calls to home and to friends' houses only confirm that everyone is out trying to escape the heat. I wait in the muggy night for a bus to come that will bring me back to the east side, where I will be free of these monsters and be safe. But the buses are slow in coming and it is well after midnight when I regain the sanctuary of my parents' house. It is now too late to catch up with my friends. I take a cool shower to temper the muggy warmth of the night and head to bed, grateful to be free of the throb of that goddamned diesel.

The summer of 1969 drags on. The friends I had left less than a week before are not doing anything new. *Rolling Stone* magazine and the local underground radio station, WABX, talk about this monster concert coming up somewhere in New York called Woodstock. I figure my paycheck from the Ford job would just about get me there and halfway back. With none of my friends in any better shape, there is no impetus to go. The days continue to stay hot and we gravitate to the river almost every night to sip ice-cold Boone's Farm apple wine and hobnob with hundreds of our set also not going to Woodstock. To make matters more difficult, the Local 5000 Steelworkers are not returning my calls with offers to catch ships anywhere. The word "recession" keeps popping up and the auto industry is simply not keeping up its demand for iron ore. With my newly cultivated environmental consciousness, I have mixed feelings about this lack of development. I have become aware of the enormous costs that every automobile places upon our culture and how it affects our quality of life. I have seen Minnesota's mountains flattened by mining equipment and witnessed iron-ore tailings floating into Lake Superior. Most significantly, I have contributed to the fouling of the Rouge and Cuyahoga Rivers and the lifeless, limpid waters of Lake Erie. On the other hand, I have become somewhat reliant upon the industry that plays a vital link in connecting the ore to the mills and don't quite know how I will be able to return to Monteith in the fall without some other work.

Having watched my father come home exhausted from Dodge Truck for all of my childhood, I am reminded of a vow I made to myself to stay away from factory work. Now for the first time I am faced with a test of that resolve. When I get to the point that I can't even afford to buy my own bottle of wine at night, there is no contest. So I scramble along Grosbeck Highway and come up with a job in a small factory that makes some kind of metal clips. The hours are 11 PM to 7 AM. I am expected to sweep the place up and occasionally remove spools of these clips from the machines that bang them out at the rate of what seems like several billion per hour. I manage to make it through a couple weeks before the insane hours and the noise and the low wages force me to call an end to it.

But at least I have enough spending cash to go along on a trip to Beaver Island in Lake Michigan. It turns out that Gail, a St. Bernard's classmate, has family on the island and regularly summers up there. So a bunch of us pile into Bob's Plymouth with the 318 and make a late-night drive that gets us into Charlevoix before 7 AM. We grab some breakfast and get our tickets at the boat dock and at 8:30 I am once again on Lake Michigan, this time for a three-hour cruise. Beaver Island proves to be a wild and crazy place for people, young and old alike. I quickly assimilate into the Irish tradition and learn to stay out of the Shamrock, where the beer can be expensive, and stick with the groups who have a steady supply of brew at all hours. Someone knows someone who offers us an A-frame to stay in for the two nights we will be here. Just an A-frame—no furnishings, running water, or bathroom. So we use the woods as toilet and the lake for cleaning up. This actually seems to aid and abet our scruffy lifestyle.

The real draw of Beaver Island, though, is the evening parties that often stretch into the dawn. One we attend is held on a remote beach, where a huge bonfire is the focal point. Everyone just sort of hangs out there and drinks. Occasionally, someone that nobody knows attempts to walk through the fire. It is interesting to watch but not something any of us are tempted to follow.

But all too soon we are back on the streets of Detroit and I am once again faced with the money situation. For the first time this summer, good fortune smiles her face upon me and I follow up on a lead my mother gives me and land a job with a trucking company that delivers voting machines to every precinct in Detroit.

The job is union and means I will be making good money—better than aboard the ships. As I quickly discover, however, there is hard work for the money. The voting machines to be delivered are roughly four feet high by four feet long and eighteen inches wide. They each weigh over a ton and must be delivered to schools and churches that were not built with the idea of housing voting machines. To make the job more difficult, the machines are to be delivered to the precise location of the precinct. This means that it is our job to move the machines up and down flights of stairs and around sharp corners in church basements. The machines are on casters so that we can use a system of ropes and tracks, called skids, to move them around.

The company has hired two crews of five men each to man two trucks carrying twenty machines at a time. Some of the smaller precincts receive only three or four machines, while others will get as many as ten or twelve. We start at seven in the morning at a warehouse on the east side, where we take on the first load. In this game, the truck drivers are top dog and are responsible for seeing that the loads are delivered to their final destination. The company owner is on hand to personally oversee the operation and help plot logistics. I am one of the grunge laborers on this job, responsible for doing whatever it is that the driver decides to get the machines where they have to go. The drivers are generally good guys who take a hands-on role in getting the machines on and off the trucks, up and down the stairs, and to their final destination.

And so we spend the hottest days of the hot summer cruising through the city, going to every neighborhood and getting the machines into place. There is not a whole lot of room for slack in this operation. We are driven by the date of the approaching primary for something or other and there are nights when I don't get home until well after eight, too worn out to do anything but eat and hit the sack. But on the job we manage to make time for the union-designated coffee and lunch breaks and stop at some of the best small restaurants in the city. We eat well and also find time to enjoy ourselves in spite of the hard work. I especially enjoy the travel time between stops, when I feel I'm being paid to sit and shoot the breeze with the driver.

The voting-machine job saves my butt for another summer and I manage to put away enough money to secure myself for the next quarter or two at Monteith but nowhere near enough to transfer to U of M or MSU, where I would have liked to have been at this point in time. Likewise, the hovering specter of the military forces me to abandon plans for a year off for travel, and I am forced to continue on with my conscription-free studies.

It is after a still hot, late summer day of boring routine frolic at Metro Beach that a bunch of us arrive at Gail's to see if she wants to come out and party. But she emerges through the front door looking distraught and snaps, "Why are you guys all laughing?"

"Why the hell shouldn't we be laughing?"

"Didn't you hear? Raymond Parks was killed in Vietnam."

My world stops as the shock sets in. And it gets worse. At some point in the night I am riding on the front hood of Rick's Mustang, feeling no pain—feeling nothing whatsoever except a fervent wish to awaken from the nightmare. Then I recall passing out at one of the riverfront parks and awakening to go home and be confronted by my mother, who yells at me for coming home drunk. My only response is, "They killed him," as I run crying up the stairs to my room.

Raymond Parks was the third of our old St. Bernard's clique to go to Vietnam. His was the house that became the unofficial party hangout while Rick was in 'Nam. He was a quiet, reserved kid, a magnet for the girls. He entered the army just over a year ago. I am shocked almost beyond belief as Rick and I visit his mother to try and offer comfort and to seek some kind of comfort ourselves.

The next week is more of the same as our gang gathers to mourn. Finally the body is sent home and there is a funeral at St. Philip's on Lenox. I cannot sit through the sermon as the priest fails to confront the truth of the matter and declares Raymond a defender of the American spirit who gave his life for his country. Bullshit is all I can think as I leave the church. I am ashamed at not having the courage to stand up and call the priest a hypocrite and a sellout to his face in front of the congregation. But out of feeling for Raymond's family, I don't. At the cemetery I watch the twenty-one-gun salute with the same emotions—too angry to do more than drink E&B beer and mourn and silently curse the people responsible for putting my friend in that place where he had no business being. My antiwar and anti-American sentiments are solidified through this experience of the death of my friend due to friendly fire in Vietnam.

CHAPTER 8

Steamboat VI

Deckhand at Last
on the SS *Paul H. Carnahan*

In the middle of fall before Thanksgiving my east side friends and I rent an apartment on Lincoln Street a few blocks from the Wayne campus. The purpose of the place is primarily for get-togethers and parties but, as the only member of the group attending Wayne, I begin to use the house as an alternative to the home environment. Although the cost of the shared rent is low, I find that I have underestimated my budget and am once again beginning to run out of money. The perpetually looming conscription of the U.S. Army really doesn't give me the option of taking a quarter off and being exposed to the killer draft. Between the nevermore face of Raymond Parks and the deranged behavior of the recently returned Rick, I really want no part of Vietnam. I explore the possibilities of becoming a conscientious objector or moving to Canada, whatever it takes to avoid participation in the Great American Death Machine.

And so it is as my last final is taken on December 9 I am on the phone to the Steelworkers 5000 in Toledo. Instead of the steady diet of "no" responses I found during the summer, the man on the other end of the line asks me what sort of job I want, galley, engine, or deck. I have my choice. Having burned for three long summers to shed the galley whites and join the deck gang lets me answer without even thinking. It is settled in a matter of moments: I will catch the *Paul H. Carnahan* at the Zug Island dock of National Steel, right here in Detroit, this very evening. It is truly amazing how one's fortunes can change with the seasons, I reflect as I pack Rick's army duffel for another round of adventure.

It is dark as my father drops me off at the entrance to Detroit's riverfront monument to the industrial revolution. While the Ford Rouge plant is renowned for its sheer size and raw-ore-to-finished-auto capabilities, Zug Island stands belching defiant on the riverfront, J. R. R. Tolkien's land of Mordor come to life. As I report to the guard shack at the gate, I gaze up at the conglomeration of tanks, smelters, pipes, and cooling towers silhouetted against the shrunken night sky. The guard confirms that I haven't been here before and summons a Jeep to ferry me through the rumbling labyrinth to the docks.

My first impression is that the *Carnahan*, even dwarfed by the towering Hullett cranes, is a huge ship. She sits there tied to the dock and is illuminated by a few dockside lamps so that I can see that her hull color is iron-ore red. My excitement mounts as I climb the ladder attached to the stern and meet the watch, who directs me to a passageway that leads to my quarters. The deckhand quarters on the *Carnahan* are located in the stern section. I find the room is spacious, with one set of bunks, a writing desk, a sink, a couple of lockers, two portholes, and nothing else. The walls are painted a mint green.

The watchman who directed me here has told me to report to the mate as soon as I am settled. With my bunk made and my clothes stowed, I head forward past the monstrous cranes as they swoop open-mouthed into the belly of the ship and emerge dribbling pellets of what I take to be taconite marbles to be deposited on the shore. Like everything else on Zug, the cranes appear decrepit and fearsome, like something out of a Dickens novel.

I discover the mate in his cabin on the second deck forward and find him to be a likeable man. He welcomes me to the crew, accepts my "Z" card for his paperwork, and tells me that I'll probably be called out to work sometime after midnight. As I retrace my steps to my cabin in the chilled December air, I find myself wondering if I chose the right time of year to leave the warm confines and regular hours of the galley.

Returning to my room, I meet my roommate, a tall skinny fellow who reminds me of Ichabod Crane. A smattering of conversation causes me concern that I've drawn another Bughouse Schultz. But I'm at least able to determine that this fellow is closer to my age and doesn't smoke or chew. Although he introduces himself as Ed, he confides with a gape-mouthed grin that he is known to the crew as Smiley. What else would you call someone who gleefully pops out his teeth with a cackle? With his plates back in, Smiley relates that he is still on duty and has to return to the deck. He expects to be up and working around the clock as one work day feeds into the next. For my part, I decide to try to catch a few hours of sleep before my call comes.

The call doesn't come until 4 AM. I pull on my work clothes in the dead of night and make it out onto the deck full of early winter chill and soul-shrinking damp. Smiley directs a rotund fellow with glasses my way. He introduces himself as Mike the boatswain—pronounced "bosun"—and directs me down a ladder into the ship's mammoth hold, from which the cargo has almost been emptied. The task is to shovel and sweep as much of the remaining cargo as possible into a pile that the Hullett can pick up. The work gang down here consists of maybe a half-dozen guys, at least three of them dockside workers employed to work at the mill, not on the ship. After an hour or so of this, we have progressed through two of the ship's three holds and I am called up to help the boatswain and the deckhands replace the hatch covers. My job is to use a long-handled wrench to secure clamps that connect the covers to the deck itself. There seem to be hundreds of clamps per hatch and at least twenty hatches running the length of the deck. My arm quickly tires as the false dawn yields to more darkness before actual daylight creeps ashen grey behind the town of Sandwich west across the river. Near eight o'clock, Smiley and John, the other deckhand, are dispatched to the dock, where they detach the cables that hold the *Carnahan* to land and quickly scramble up a ladder held over the side. With a short blast of the whistle, the *Carnahan* is off for northern waters.

After a break for breakfast, all three deckhands are set to the task of finishing the clamping and securing the remaining hatch covers. While we are doing this, Mike the boatswain is dragging out a three-inch black hose that he uses to begin hosing down the deck. Smiley directs me to a locker in the forward end, where we don yellow rain gear. He also finds an old pair of long rubber boots for me to throw on. They are much used and torn in a couple of spots and too tight as well. Smiley watches me struggle, cackles, and says, "Gonna have to get some new ones up above." The hose is so long and heavy that it takes at least two people to maneuver it along the deck. While Mike and John perform that task, Smiley and I shovel small piles of taconite pellets over the side into the frigid grey chop of Lake St. Clair. By noon, when we break for dinner, my arms ache and I'm wondering how much more there is to this job. For the first time in all my sailing experience, I find myself digging into the potatoes and meatloaf before me. I have never worked so physically aboard my previous five ships nor under such cold conditions out of doors. I have found an appetite on the deck of the *Carnahan*.

Fortunately, as we go back to work, the day is not too cold and we are able to enjoy the passing sights of the St. Clair River. Finally, at about 1:30, the deck hosing is completed and Mike tells me I am knocked off for the day, having put in my eight hours. I retire to my warm cabin, exhausted but secure in having attained the answer to that question asked on a warm summer's night on Belle Isle so many years ago: "Just what do people who work on freighters do?" I realize now that ever since that question formed I have wanted to work on deck, the most visible part of the ship.

I immediately take to the life of a deckhand aboard the *Paul H. Carnahan*. This is by far the newest and cleanest of the ships I have sailed on, with all kinds of space for the crew. On the after end, where I am housed, there is, in addition to the galley, a rec room with a TV and couches. There is another one up forward for the crew that are housed up there. There is fresh paint everywhere and I feel like I'm on a brand new ship.

I make the acquaintance of Ray, an oiler, in the galley one afternoon. He has been on the *Carnahan* for four years and brags about this being one of the best on the lakes. He says that the *Carnahan* routinely runs at sixteen miles an hour, making her easily the fastest among those I've sailed and actually twice as fast as the *John Hulst*. Like the *Hulst*, the *Carnahan* is powered by a steam turbine, but, unlike the 1938 vintage model on the *Hulst*, the Westinghouse turbines of the *Carnahan* were put in place when she was converted to lakes use in 1961. Also, unlike the coal-burning *Hulst*, Ray points out that the *Carnahan* burns oil.

Ray walks me down the hall to the rec room, where he points to a framed photo on the wall. The picture is cut from the *Detroit News*, dated November 2, 1961. It shows a smiling woman wearing a fur, a bowl-shaped hat, and long black gloves. Nestled in her arms is a large bouquet. She is waving from the Aquarama dock at the foot of West Grand Boulevard while in the background the beflagged

The christening of the *Paul H. Carnahan* at the foot of West Grand Boulevard, Detroit (Dossin Great Lakes Museum)

Carnahan serenely floats. The caption below identifies the woman as Mrs. Carnahan, wife of the president of National Steel, who has just "belted the nose of the ship with a bottle of champagne and waved her away."

Ray lets me admire the picture as he tells me more. I learn that, before she came into the lakes, the ship we are on was known as the *Atlantic Dealer*, a T2 tanker built in 1945 for the ocean trade by the U.S. Maritime Commission. In 1960, the ship was towed up the Seaway to Lorain, where she was rebuilt with a new midbody cargo section that lengthened her to 730 feet. The *Carnahan* is as large as ships that transit the Soo Locks can be. Not only is she twice as fast as the *Hulst*, she can also carry twenty-four thousand tons of cargo—ten thousand tons more than the silver stacker. This means that, in any given ten-day period, the *Carnahan* can deliver three times the cargo of the *Hulst*.

Because she was built for the ocean and not the lakes, the *Carnahan* also appears different from traditional lake freighters. She has a high, pointed bow over which her white superstructure towers. The after cabins are supersized as well and make the ship look smaller than it actually is. The black smokestack is embellished with a white star with a red "H" in the center. The "H" stands for Hanna Mining Company, a subsidiary of National Steel Corporation. These last three words appear in eight-foot-high letters along the length of the vessel.

The passage of the Soo Locks is made in the dead of night. Because only two deckhands are required to assist in this operation and I am the most recent acquisition, I get to sleep through the whole thing while Smiley and John get the call. Their reward is an hour's worth of overtime.

I am not so fortunate when, twenty-four hours later, still in the dead of night, all three deckhands are called out to begin unclamping hatches and preparing for loading at the Allouez dock in Superior, Wisconsin. As we enter from our warm cabin onto the deck, the approach of winter is evident in the damp chill that reflects off the steel deck and seeps through our bones. The sky is black and the wind seems to be coming off where I imagine the lake to be. After a spell with the wrenches, unclamping the hatch covers, we are called to the bow to stand by the starboard side of the first hatch. While the *Carnahan* creeps toward the dock underneath the massive loading chutes, Mike shows me how to mount and sit astride the boatswain's chair. This contraption consists of a slender swing seat attached to a thick rope suspended from a simple pulley and a swing-out boom/pole. Its purpose is to get crew to the dock before the ship touches so that we can catch the lines to tie the ship to the dock. I watch as first Smiley and then John perform the ritual of being suspended over cold open water as the ship closes in with the dock. And then, before I can catch my breath, Mike is gesturing to me to climb aboard. I jump up to the top of the hatch, park my buns on the seat, grip the line with two hands, and, with a gentle push from behind, am airborne, floating toward the side of the loading chute at what seems like fifty miles an hour. I am totally in the hands of Mike and the deckwatch, one of whom has the responsibility to make sure the boom/pole doesn't extend me too far toward the chutes and the other of whom has the responsibility to lower the chair when it's safely over the dock and not a moment before. We are further aided by a searchlight fixed on the proposed landing area, manned by one of the mates

Riding the boatswain's chair over the side to the dock (Author's collection)

working overtime. The entire operation takes all of twenty seconds before my feet touch the scrabbly surface of the dock and I feel safe enough to let go of the rope so that the chair can be pulled back aboard. At the same time, Mike is waving me to get to the stern. I walk slowly along the dock in the darkness, knowing that there is no safety railing and that the dock itself is treacherous, filled with broken asphalt and random piles of iron ore. By the time I get to the stern, a watchman on board is holding up the end of a line for me to see. He intends to throw it down for me to catch. He does, and although I don't manage to catch it, I do retrieve it before it slides back into the water. I then begin pulling on the line and, when it is taut, the watchman begins to pay out a very heavy two-inch-thick steel cable that I am expected to wrestle to the dock and slip around a designated bollard to secure the ship to the dock. As the full weight of the cable is released, I feel a surge of panic as its weight drags me toward the edge of the dock, where the mighty propellor of the *Carnahan* is churning slowly away. I think for a split second about just dropping the cable but then, with a superhuman effort, regain my footing and manage to bring the thing up and into my hands. The end of the cable has a large loop, which makes it easy for me to drag to the bollard. I drop it on and signal to the watchman, who immediately picks up the slack and begins to winch the ship into the dock. I stand by and watch, dazed and shaking from the experience. But, before I can collapse, the watchman is waving me to pick the damn thing up and get it to the next bollard, thirty feet further down the dock. This time I know enough to secure my footing before I pick up the cable, and secure one arm to a railing I have discovered placed near the bollard to support deckhands engaged in this very activity. I once again manage to successfully lug the thing and get it over the bollard. This time, the Carnahan seems to be at the right place and we three deckhands clamber back up a ladder onto the deck of the ship, which is about twenty feet higher than the dock before loading.

But, instead of getting a chance to take a break, we are immediately put back to work unclamping and removing hatches. While any one crewman can unclamp the hatches using the heavy, unwieldy wrenches, it takes two crew to assist the boatswain in getting the hatches off and onto the deck space provided for them. The boatswain operates a crane called the iron deckhand that runs on two rails the length of the deck. The iron deckhand straddles the hatch while two hooks descend to attach themselves to the top of the hatch. The crew members are responsible to stand, one on either side of the deck, and insert spikes into holes that connect the covers to the hatches themselves. The purpose of the spikes is to assure a level lift and minimize swaying of the heavy hatch cover. With the spikes in place, the iron deckhand lifts the hatch cover and slowly swings it over to adjacent deck space, where it is set. Three to four covers are set atop one another. They are all numbered so that they can be reattached to the corresponding hatch when the hold is full.

Again, because I am the junior deckhand, I get stuck with the unclamping while the other two deckhands assist Mike in the easy task of setting spikes in the hatch covers. Eventually, they overtake me and have to come over and help unclamp all the hatches. By the time the sky has turned to grey, the hatches are off and the first chuteful of iron ore is skidding into the hold of the ship. The boatswain knocks John and me off and assigns Smiley to the dock to assist in any dockside moving the ship will have to do for repositioning under the chutes. His task will consist of standing on the dock and every so often moving the cables from bollard to bollard so that the ship can move without need of the engine. John and I grab some breakfast and head back to our respective cabins to catch some sleep before we are called back out later in the day. I hit the bunk exhausted but alive. I am finding that the job of deckhand is challenging but I truly love being where the action is.

The *Carnahan* loads the red iron ore until late in the day. First John and then I am called out to take a shift on the dock, to stand around and try to stay warm. Occasionally the mate on watch directs me to shift the heavy cables from bollard to bollard. At one point, he leans over the rail and asks me to read the number painted on the ship's side. These numbers represent the draft of the ship at the stern. There are similar markings on the bow and there is the Plimsoll line in the middle of the ship, which indicates the maximum draft the ship is certified to carry cargoes. Eventually I am called up on deck, where the boatswain has already begun the process of replacing some of the hatches over the slowly filling holds. I hear the mate remark to the boatswain that our stay here has been prolonged by frozen iron ore that is sticking to the chutes above the ship. We busy ourselves clamping the hatches down, and after a quick supper break we are directed to spots on the bow and stern to monitor the thick lines that are connected to two tugs assigned to pull the *Carnahan* free of the dock and back into the harbor. The tugs make quick work of turning the *Carnahan* around, and when the forward tug sounds its all-clear whistle, we rapidly release the lines and set our ship free. With the *Carnahan* on its way back to Lake Superior, we set back to securing the final hatches and stowing the deck gear. Because it is already full darkness and the night is cold and we have already put in more than our eight hours, the boatswain knocks us off for the night, promising that we will hose down the deck first thing in the morning. We return uncomplaining to our cozy cabins, ready to sleep the night away while the *Carnahan* works her way through Superior. The next morning finds us riding out a storm in the middle of the lake. It is too rough for us to be out working on the deck, so the boatswain basically ignores us, saying that we'll hose down the deck when it calms down. I look out from the stern cabin doorway at the waves battering the *Carnahan*. Spray from the waves clears the pilothouse and I can feel their pounding ripple through the frame of the ship to my feet. This is the first time I have been witness to a ship "working" in a storm and I can see the *Carnahan*'s deck twist and turn before my eyes. I finally understand why the tunnels connecting fore and aft are necessary.

Before I know it, night has fallen and the *Carnahan* has made it through the storm into Whitefish Bay. I find myself riding the boatswain's chair over the side as the *Carnahan* enters the Soo Locks. I take the line attached to the stern cable and begin the long walk into the lock beside the ship. It is another cold, dark night with a taste of snow in the air, but I feel great taking my ship out for a walk. After a while of slow-paced walking, the *Carnahan* gets the green light to enter the MacArthur Lock, right next to the viewing stand. As I turn over my line to the Corps of Engineers lockworker, I try to imagine what the now-empty stand would look like on a hot summer's day, filled with people. I fail and am happy when I am directed to climb over the ship's rail as the *Carnahan* begins to sink between the concrete walls. It takes less than fifteen minutes before the ship has been lowered thirty feet and the gate silently swings open and we give a short toot to tell the lockhands to release the ship to the St. Marys River and we head toward Lake Huron.

By the following evening, the *Carnahan* is at the dock at Zug Island and racing through an unloading. My work on deck makes me more aware of the overwhelming awesomeness of this place of fire and brimstone. And my budding awareness of ecology makes me stare in horror at the realization that we are directly feeding the American dream of two cars in every garage at the expense of the earth. Not to mention the pollution of the Great Lakes that we directly contribute to with every shovelful of taconite that goes into the river as we clean the deck. I go about my job with mixed feelings, loving the work, yet concerned about its impact upon the earth that my shipmates seem oblivious to.

The swiftness of the ship ensures a lot more time at ports, loading and unloading, and several more trips a year than the smaller ships on the lakes. But the crew of the *Carnahan* are getting ready for the end of the season and there is much conjecture about when and where the last trip of the season will be. Because the destinations and cargoes are determined by the company and relayed to the captain on a need-to-know basis, there is much unfounded speculation as to where we are headed, often right up to and in some instances after the ship has departed the dock. Fortunately, the *Carnahan* crew is composed of some fairly sane characters who are a good cross between the schiz-

Hanna flagship *George M. Humphrey* making an offering to the Great
God Zug, Zug Island (Author's collection)

ophrenic club of the *Mercury* and the straight-laced group aboard the
Hulst. Even though we are down to our last trips of the season, several of the crew take the time to introduce themselves and have some
conversation with me. Among them I discover an uncle of my Beaver
Island friends, Jack Connaghan of the Beaver Island Connaghans.
Although an amiable fellow, Jack's eccentricities sometimes put him
at odds with other crew members. One evening he bursts into the rec
room where several crew are watching TV and demands to know who
has been spitting tobacco in the forward end garbage pail. His Silver
Star from Omaha Beach on D-Day earns him respect and tolerance.
Another character is Charley Hawkinson, a navy Vietnam vet and
now a deckwatch full of fast ideas. One evening in Cleveland I have
the task of standing on the dock to shift the cables. I am standing in
the dark December night, enjoying the cold and watching the con-
stellation Orion already well up in the sky. Along comes Charley with
a noncrew fellow in tow. Charley introduces him as a navy buddy
whom he has invited back to check out the *Carnahan*. I watch as first
Charley and then his buddy, both looking like they're feeling no pain,

negotiate the ladder up to the deck. My eyes wander back to the cable for a moment before I hear a loud splash nearby followed by the watchman's cry of "Man Overboard." I follow the ruckus and discover Charley's buddy paddling like a puppy and trying to figure out how to get back up the breakwall a good four feet higher than the water level. The watchman tosses down a life ring, which I catch and lower down to the fellow. Then he climbs down the ladder and, between the two of us, we manage to pull him up to the dock. By this time the first mate has joined us and agrees that the first thing the man needs is to get out of his freezing clothes and into a shower. We shepherd the guy up the ladder and he is put in the care of his buddy Charley, who promises to take care of him. When the ship departs the port an hour later, we have him as a guest all the way to the Soo, where he is finally allowed to get off.

Among all the excitement of being a deckhand come the dangers. There is much work among moving machinery under tension and the steel cables pose a constant hazard, especially in docking. Coming back from Allouez at the Soo, the *Carnahan* is proceeding too quickly toward the lock wall. The mate signals to me from the deck to throw my cable onto the next bollard to check the speed of the ship. I drop the cable on and, as I have been trained, stand clear. But even the distance of ten feet behind the bollard doesn't prepare me for the shock of the snapping cable that rings out like a shotgun as it whips through the crisp air. Because I have positioned myself away from the tension, the shards of steel spray in front of me and back toward the ship. I stand shocked by the violence of the moment before I hear the mate yelling for me to run forward to catch another line attached to a backup cable hanging from the bow. I manage to catch the line, haul the heavy cable down, and throw it onto the next bollard, where it succeeds in holding and checking the forward progress of the ship a hundred feet from the gates. Back on deck the crew are breathing noticeably easier and the mate pats me on the back and congratulates me on my swiftness in helping stop the ship.

I have been on the *Carnahan* just two weeks when the word comes down that the ship will lay up in Detroit after unloading at Zug. We have been working most of the night as the last of the cargo is swept up from the hold. Smiley and I join the first mate in driving to a nearby slip at the foot of Great Lakes Boulevard in Ecorse. He drops us here to catch the lines as the *Carnahan* makes her way in from Zug. To do this, we have to climb over the already laid-up *Joseph Thompson*, against which the *Carnahan* will be moored. After a half hour of waiting, the *Carnahan* hoves slowly into sight and we catch the lines and tie her up to the *Thompson*. In the interim, Mike, the boatswain, has been busy replacing the hatches with the help of the deckwatches, and we are informed that the decision has been made to lay the ship up immediately so that the deck crew can head home tomorrow—Christmas Eve. The motivation to complete the operation is high and groups of men team up to pull out the long lay-up cables and to secure the pilothouse and a variety of other tasks. With the cables in place, pilothouse shuttered, storage cabinets cleaned and locked, and ballast tanks cleared, we break for the night at eight o'clock. I find myself sitting on a cabinet in the rec room, watching some TV to unwind. The room swims around and I manage to catch myself as I almost fall from my perch, my mind having gone to sleep on me. I decide not to tempt fate any more and head to my bunk.

In the morning after breakfast, George, the first mate, surprises us by announcing that the lay-up is complete enough for the ship-keeper to finish after Christmas and he has lay-up checks to distribute before we are dismissed. Although I have not been a part of the crew to share in the end-of-season lay-up bonus, I am happy to accept a nice check and carry my bag off. I share a ride back to the east side with Jack and am glad to be home for Christmas with money in my pocket.

CHAPTER 9

1970

Fitting Out and Related Tragedies

The cold months pass quickly enough with an ongoing party scene developing at the apartment on Lincoln Street. We watch from the hallway as the apartments fill up with like-minded folk from all over the city. Frenchy, the landlord, has finally hired a guy named Gary to watch over things, although no one, including him, is quite sure what that should entail. Gary is nothing if not a street person, like the thousands of kids Sam and I had seen on the streets of Frisco the past spring. Along with his pregnant girlfriend, Kelly, and friend Ruben Rodriguez, he brings a nervous edge to the party scene that on weekends spills out from the apartment and into the hallways and up and down the stairs of the rambling dwelling. Hans, another high school friend, hangs with a group of Cass Tech alumni who have taken an upper apartment. Frenchy maintains a room for himself and his friends, Stafford, an ex-con, and Scotty, a meek schoolteacher. A couple of speed freak girls take over the front apartment with their boyfriend, Keith, a Vietnam vet with a psychotic streak.

While we listen to the music of Santana, Ten Years After, and Crosby, Stills, and Nash from the *Woodstock* album, the scene around us is at times more reminiscent of the Hell's Angels'–dominated massacre at Altamont. Fistfights are not infrequent as we realize that our brethren returned from 'Nam have some unresolved things to work out. Fortunately, they usually seek one another out to vent their frustrations and leave the rest of us to hug the walls as the combat ensues. It is not uncommon for one of these guys to flip and, with back to the wall, assume a lethal karate position. This is a situation that only another vet can respond to, as Rick often does in defense of our

217

apartment. Unfortunately, he is not a very good street fighter and usually winds up getting his ass kicked down the stairs or into the hallway and out the front door.

Watching these guys act out the horror of their lives, I only become more hardened in my opposition to the war. Even through his blackened eyes, Rick is capable of seeing the monstrosity he has been forced to be a part of. And so he joins us in our forays to Ann Arbor to march against the system. These events draw thousands of people and are mostly characterized by brief marches that culminate in hours of mediocre rock and roll and speeches that are exercises in overkill. Invisible on the opposite side are the majority of kids who choose to ignore the conflict and focus on having a good time and getting their degrees and making money by being a part of the war industry. A party on Lincoln Street is usually represented by all sides and, except for the war cries of the vets, we manage to get by pretty well.

On a personal level, I manage to represent both the establishment and anti-establishment camps. Winds of change since Nixon's election indicate that the end of the days of college-boy exemptions is fast approaching. I further explore the idea of expatriating to Canada but am sidelined in late February by the purchase of a '63 Triumph TR4 roadster that quickly becomes the love of my life. I even forgive it when I have to push it into the garage when the rack and pinion fails on my first attempts behind the wheel. However, the cost of the car, impending repairs, and a flat budget propel me to enter discussions with my Monteith advisors to explore a unique work-study scheme. To my surprise, I am quickly approved to research and write papers for eight credits over the next quarter. That out of the way, I quickly respond to a telegram I have received from the Hanna Mining Company asking me to report back to help fit out the *Carnahan* for my continuing deckhand assignment on March 19.

With a final round of parties at the house that is now known as Stonehead Manor, I bid adieu to my compatriots and head back down to the foot of Great Lakes Boulevard in Ecorse, where the *Paul H. Carnahan* and her sleeping sisters await me and my fellow harbingers of spring. I discover that most of the crew that laid her up at Christmas has returned, including Smiley, Charley Hawkinson, Mike the boatswain, and George the first mate. Beaver Island Jack is back too, but at his request is assigned to another ship in the fleet for the 1970 Great Lakes shipping season.

SS *Paul H. Carnahan*

Built	1945
Builder	Sun Shipbuilding, Chester, Pennsylvania
Owners	U.S. Maritime Commission (1945); Atlantic Refining Company (1946); National Steel Corporation (1961)
Names	*Honey Hill* (1945); *Atlantic Dealer* (1946); *Paul H. Carnahan* (1961)
Length	729'3"
Beam	75'1"
Draft	39'
Engine	Steam turbine
Boilers	Two Babcock and Wilcox oil-fired
Capacity	24,250 tons dwt
Cargo	Iron ore, taconite
Crew	30

While it took us only twenty-four hours to lay up the ship, it will probably take a couple of weeks for the *Carnahan* to be ready for the new year. The engine crew is working down below to crank up the turbines, so we rely on shore power for the first week or so. Much of our work is centered on cleaning, scrubbing, and painting areas of the ship that have been worked on by the winter gang in a variety of locations from stem to stern. Once these mop-up operations are completed, our attention is turned to painting the entire exterior of the vessel.

While we are doing this, the sisters of the *Carnahan* are receiving like treatment by their respective crews. The fleet of eight ships that operate under the red "H" in the white star on the black stack is divided among three companies. In addition to the *Carnahan*, the National Steel Corporation manages her identical twin the *Leon Falk Jr.*, the *Ernest T. Weir*, the *Thomas Millsop*, and the *George M. Humphrey*. Built in 1925 at the Great Lakes Engineering works in the Rouge, the *Millsop* is just over 600 feet and the third-oldest of the fleet. The ship was distinguished as the first lakes freighter to have been built with one-piece hatch covers. The *Weir* checked in

219

at 690 feet when built in 1953 in Lorain. She set a new cargo record in her first year by loading 21,270 tons at Allouez. This record was broken the next year by the newest National Steel ship, the *Humphrey*, also built at Lorain. Checking in at 710 feet, she carried over 22,600 tons down to Lake Erie. The *Humphrey* was also the first ship built on the lakes with a 75-foot beam. She is regarded as the flagship of the fleet.

Sailing for the Hanna Mining Company is the Toledo Shipbuilding Company's 1923 creation, the *George R. Fink*. The *Fink* has a 600-foot length and was previously known as the *Ernest T. Weir* until the newer ship was launched and took that name. Next-oldest in the fleet and built at the Rouge in 1924 is the 612-foot *Matthew Andrews*. The *Andrews* is still a coal burner, propelled by a quadruple-expansion steam engine. Rounding out the fleet for the Hansard Steamship Corporation is the *Joseph H. Thompson*. The *Thompson*, like the *Carnahan* and the *Falk*, is a converted Liberty ship, built in 1944 and brought into the lakes in 1952. At that time, at 714 feet, the *Thompson* held the title as the longest freight vessel in the world.

Of these eight vessels, five ships are berthed together here in Ecorse. To get to the *Carnahan*, it is necessary for us to climb over the *Thompson*. This gives us time to admire the plaque located near her forward cabin commemorating the heroics of the captain and crew of the ship as they rescued the crew from the *Henry Steinbrenner* after it broke up on the rocks of Isle Royale in the cold waters of Superior in 1953. The *Humphrey* and the *Weir* are tied together immediately behind us at the river's edge and the other three ships are wintered elsewhere around the lakes.

Our stem-to-stern paintfest continues for several bleak, chilly days as March plays out the last of the winter cards on our heads. We pull a Huck Finn–style raft around the stern under the massive propeller to get our rollers on the outside of the ship. As we pass under the engine room, someone decides to open a valve, releasing a gusher of cold water directly on Smiley, who is manning one of the poles. He is excused to take a hot shower while the rest of us struggle with the rollers.

As the fit out progresses, the Coast Guard visits to conduct an inspection. While every U.S. flagship is required to undergo a dry-dock inspection every five years, the Coast Guard inspects safety and communications equipment annually. They go through and cut into

The *Paul H. Carnahan* at lay-up next to the *Joseph Thompson* (Author's collection)

a few ring buoys to determine if the cork has lost its buoyancy and watch as we go through the motions of a fire and boat drill. But they seem to spend most of the time with the engineers who are trying to recalibrate the steam whistle. It is amazing to hear how out of shape a whistle can get in just a few months.

While we have pretty much been working every day without a break, we are reprieved at noon on Easter Sunday. I make arrangements to get home for dinner and spend a quiet afternoon visiting with family. Since we are expected back to work early on Monday, I decide to return to the ship later that evening. I arrive back to discover that many of the younger crew who are hundreds of miles from home have chosen to celebrate Easter by going up the street. As they filter back in during the wee hours, I am told by Charley that the highlight of the evening was being led through a whorehouse by a deckhand known as Little Swede, son of Big Swede—Arthur Johnson, a watchman on the *Carnahan* renowned for his marlinespike and accumulated lakes wisdom. News of the big night out and related exploits sweeps through the five ships as we slowly get back into the groove the following morning. Every time the word "stairs" is mentioned by one of the participants, its weighted meaning causes those in the know to convulse. This gives me cause to feel good. I am gratified to realize that we have life among the crews in this fleet and that we aren't a bunch of uniform-wearing, clock-punching, water factory rats. This is important as I contemplate spending the next several months among these people.

The routine of preparation finally gives way to news of our first trip. For the past couple nights we have noticed a few ships sliding past us upbound in the Detroit River. On the morning of April 2, we are given the order to haul the long-dead cables aboard. That evening the ships are tugged out into the Detroit River and begin taking ballast water while at anchor. The winter has been severe enough that there are reports of thick ice at both the St. Marys River and at the Straits of Mackinac, and Bob, the deckwatch, tells me that the captain isn't anxious to be the first one through. After a morning of fine tuning in the river, the Hanna fleet begins a slow cruise up the river, through Lake St. Clair and into the St. Clair River. The *Carnahan* takes on fuel near Sarnia and anchors below Lake Huron for the night with at least a dozen other ships around us, the captains universally preferring daylight for their first run into the big lake.

Shortly after the next dawn, the *Carnahan* slides under the Blue Water Bridge and, with a few other ships and hardy seagulls as traveling companions, begins the run up the Michigan coastline. Although the weather on the lake is cold to fierce cold, I find the work ethic much more pronounced than the one I recall on the same ship just before lay-up last December. Our daylong eight-hour shift is divided into a variety of tasks, including hosing down the deck and soojying the white-painted cabins and trim. Soojying employs cold water, a harsh detergent—called soojie—and stiff brushes. Although we wear rain gear, it is impossible to keep the solution from running down our arms when applied overhead. Our shirt sleeves are quickly soaked, allowing the concoction to slowly eat away at our skin. By evening, my arms are raw and red. Our day is also spent lugging and coiling the heavy lay-up cables in the forward locker, where they will be stored until the *Carnahan* again lays up. Perhaps the second-least appealing job finds us down in the holds, where we spend hours emptying out water that has seeped in over the winter. Because there is no such thing as a plug in the bottom to let the water out, the task requires hauling buckets one at a time to a compatriot on the deck above, who gets to dump them over the side. There are also hatch clamps that need to be oiled and adjusted and white paint spots on the pilothouse window that need removing.

While we are thus engaged, the *Carnahan* enters the Straits of Mackinac and meets a massive field of ice just west of the bridge. Even with the help of a Coast Guard cutter, we remain stuck for the next twelve hours in the field, which resists dynamite blasts placed in the pack immediately before us. Between deck tasks, it is unsettling to glance up and watch the cutter work its own way through the ice, one inch at a time. Every hour stuck out here is another hour of this boring work. We long for the relief in our schedule that making a port will bring. I simply can't imagine how deckhands aboard salties endure the three- to four-week periods between ports.

By late the next morning we are freed and bound for Escanaba. Because the ship's engines are still working out their own kinks, we crawl into Escanaba toward midnight. Fortunately for us deckhands, there is no midnight shift operating the ore conveyor at this dock this early in the year. So all we can do is tie up the ship, take off the hatch covers, and go back to our bunks until morning.

But the next morning, Sunday, brings fresh problems, as it is discovered that the taconite pellets are frozen together and can't be loaded onto the conveyor to the ship. This results in a delay of several hours while dockworkers figure out how to unstick them. Then the conveyor belt itself breaks down, not once, but repeatedly. It is now midafternoon and I am on shift detail. The boatswain has decided that, since nothing else is happening, I might as well earn my keep. So he sends me down to the dock with a large bucket of paint and a roller and I pass the time painting the side of the ship that we couldn't get to during the fit out. As I apply the rust-red paint to the ship, I can't help agreeing with him; I'd rather be out here in the weak sun of early spring than in the rec room watching TV and waiting for the system to start working.

However, when I am relieved at 4 PM, my immediate thoughts turn to a tavern located just the other side of the taconite pile at the end of the long dock. During my painting, I noticed several of the crew head that way and figure that might be a good way to pass a couple hours. Once inside the one-room bar, I discover a fair number of shipmates enjoying the cozy confines, content to watch the daylight

223

The *Paul H. Carnahan* in ice (Historical Collection of the Great Lakes/Bowling Green State University)

fade over Little Bay de Noc. I find a seat at a table and shout out my order for a beer to the bartender above the din. But I am surprised to hear myself outshouted by Ray, a bearded watchman who yells to the bartender, "Better check the age on this guy." The bartender takes one look at my peach face and asks for it. Since I'm still a month shy of my birthday, I am frozen in my embarrassment and, with a look of scorn at my so-called shipmate, quit the place. As I walk back to the ship, I find my thirst for a ten-cent beer overridden by my anger and disgust at being victimized by a fellow crew member. I am only slightly mollified when, at supper, Ray offers an apology, saying that he actually thought I was of age. I grudgingly accept, willing to take one for the good of the ship, but silently resolving to have as little to do as possible with that guy in the future.

Some thirty hours after we have arrived, the *Carnahan* finally takes its leave of Escanaba and glides out of Big Bay de Noc and through the Death's Door passage, out onto the cold lake. We manage to clamp down the hatches against the cold wind and spray that quickly ices the deck over, and the boatswain decides that it's too late to hose the deck down. The next morning we are completing that task as the *Carnahan* navigates the Straits of Mackinac without the aid of dynamite. We breeze through in five hours and are soon on our way across the "Blue Water" lake, heading toward Cleveland. We hit a patch of early spring warmth down here and the *Carnahan* experiences relatively few delays in unloading. Within the span of a day, we are heading back up for another load of Escanaba cold. We again encounter the thick ice of Mackinac, and the ship is once again at the mercy of the floes and the Coast Guard to get us out. With another less-than-perfect loading at the Escanaba dock, the *Carnahan* receives orders to try her luck with some red ore from Superior.

Compared to the Straits, the St. Marys River and the Soo Locks are a cakewalk. Although there is ice in Whitefish Bay, the *Carnahan* plows on through. At the harbor in Superior, Mike, the boatswain, equips us with grappling hooks to snag huge pieces of ice and maneuver them out of the path between ship and dock. It works and the *Carnahan* is soon sitting under the gigantic red chutes awaiting them to drop down and begin filling our hold. Unfortunately, the red ore of Allouez is no less frozen than the taconite marbles of Escanaba and, it is only after many hours of sitting and watching dockworkers unjam frozen blocks of ore from the chutes that we are able to proceed south. It is approaching the end of April and we are still waiting for our first normal trip of the year.

In the meantime, personnel changes are beginning to change the faces of the *Carnahan*'s crew. One of the deck watches has gone home and Smiley moves happily into his slot, leaving me as the "Bull"—or top-seniority—deckhand. This added responsibility means more opportunities for me to gain overtime work and to choose which of the watches I want to take while the ship is in port. The position is treated with humor by some, but is a genuine union-supported slot, which the boatswain and first mate take seriously.

The only drawback is that, as Smiley moves to new quarters in the deck watch cabin, the newest deckhand becomes my roommate, and he is a genuine loser. His name is Dave and he is short and stumpy with greasy black hair and a ham-bone scowl on his face. His habit of speech quickly earns him the nickname Mumbles. Mumbles is not a natural-born worker; he is one of those people who prefers to rise and dress at leisure and to blend into the background of a work situation. His lassitude is marked by both the first mate, George Baker, and Mike, the rotund boatswain. To make matters much worse, Mumbles is drawn to alcohol and is always in search of some beer or wine, neither of which he can handle. My feelings for him range from mild disgust at having to share my room with this slob to pity for his being unable to do more than sit next to my radio, swigging beer, smoking cigarettes, and listening to unhip CKLW. His presence also makes it all but impossible for me to use the room to pursue my course work.

I have arranged with two of my Monteith profs to register for eight hours this quarter. The deal obliges me to craft two essays of significant length on my research. The first topic is in the humanities area and gives me a chance to stretch out and explore the mythology surrounding works including the *Ring of the Neibelung, Beowulf, The Hobbit,* and *The Worm Ourobourus.* The second topic is more open ended and I try to spend my free time constructing a theme into which to fit my ideas. But life with Mumbles makes this effort next to impossible.

Fortunately for me and sadly for Mumbles, he fails to answer a call to work one evening in Escanaba. He has passed out, dead to the world, leaving his work for the other deckhand, Al, and me. The next morning the mate gives Mumbles notice that he will be let off in Cleveland. Mumbles is bitter about the mate's decision and talks about the next ship he'll catch out of the hall in a couple of days. As the saga of Mumbles recedes into the background chatter of the crew's mess, I am free to resume my scholarly contemplations—at least until my next roommate arrives.

His name is Jim and he comes to us through Cleveland by way of Kentucky. He is about thirty-five, balding, genial, fond of Kool-Aid and Vodka, and prone to goosing anyone who gets too close. When one of the guys gooses him back, he responds, "I'll give you five minutes to quit that." Jim serves as a magnet for rebels and their sympathizers aboard the *Carnahan,* making our cabin once again a social hub. I resign myself to the fact that the seagoing life doesn't always reconcile itself to the recluse writer. I sit at the desk in the cabin, a small party swirling around me, sipping Dixie cups full of cheap vodka and cherry Kool-Aid and wondering how the hell Conrad ever managed to get a single word on paper.

The ice in the rivers, straits, and harbors yields grudgingly to milder weather as we tie up for a load of red ore at Allouez on a breezy forenoon. It isn't long before the rain forces loading to cease and begins a thirty-two-hour marathon. Since everyone else, including the dockworkers, works a regular four- or eight-hour shift, the deckhands and first mate are the only crew who have the distinction of seeing the loading from start to finish. And so we take turns standing on the dock in the driving rain as night descends. The severity of the rain has already caused the mate to order all but a couple of hatches closed as a precaution against taking too much water directly into the holds. Occasionally, the rain relents enough for a chute to be lowered down and a pile of the loose ore to slide into the ship. But mostly, the *Carnahan* sits and rides out the weather through the long night while two deckhands stand on the dock, the driving cold rain penetrating our rain gear, waiting for orders to move cables to winch the ship forward or back along the dock. When the call does come to move the heavy cable from one bollard to the next, it is performed with extreme dread and caution. The dock, blackened by darkness and rain, is filled with puddles that hide holes and other hazards. It is an accident waiting to happen. When relieved by the third deckhand every couple of hours, the first thing I do is head to my cabin, strip off my sodden clothes, and hang them over the railings suspended on a catwalk over the engines to dry. By midmorning, the warm room has failed to keep up with demand; the railings are covered with damp clothes and I am down to my last set of dry clothes. My waterproof boots have long since been compromised and easily overcome the illusion of dry socks.

By that evening, as darkness descends and the *Carnahan* heads out into Lake Superior, we are three exhausted deckhands. We work slowly with the boatswain, putting the last of the hatch covers on, and drag ourselves toward the cabin for what we hope will be an undisturbed night of rest. George, the first mate, is all smiles, as he has beaten the elements and gotten out of Allouez with a full load with only a day lost to weather. As the first mate, he is responsible for all loading and unloading operations. He has to answer to the company owners for any slowdown on either end. To his defense, he can look back to the other ships at the docks, several of which arrived before the *Carnahan* and have yet to depart. He stops us in the galley and thanks us for the long hours we have just put in. He also tells us we will get full overtime for the night on the dock. We straggle to our bunks, looking forward to pleasant dreams plumped with money.

Perhaps the greatest advantage to life aboard a steamboat is that the money is good and there is really nowhere to spend it. It is not difficult for a deckhand to make a thousand dollars in a month—a decent wage—and, for a fellow like myself, to be able to live on two hundred a month or less on shore.

Twenty-four hours later, the *Carnahan* has reached Whitefish Bay and the entrance to the St. Marys River. The only problem is, except for the outline of the shore on the radar, there is no way to know where we are. A thick, white veil of fog envelops us and the *Carnahan* is forced to drop anchor and await the fog's lifting to allow us to proceed safely in. As a precaution, the ship's whistle automatically begins to hoot its fog signal—three blasts of one short, one long, and one short every minute. After a while, we discover that we are not alone; similar blasts from other ships come out of the fog from every quarter. The watchman on his break says that there are twenty other anchored ships blipping on the radar screen, invisible to our eyes but not our ears. Throughout the remainder of the day and all through the night, the various tones remind us that the fog has not lifted. The next day fails to dawn, with the fog occasionally lifting enough for us to make out the shrouded outlines of three or four of the other vessels surrounding us. Because the *Carnahan* is at anchor, the positions of the ships shift as the current moves us around in a circle. But the air is still and clammy and not relenting enough to lift the gloom, and the crew becomes increasingly irritated by the wait. It is a Saturday, a normal workday for the boatswain and the deckhands. We have been assigned to chip and scrape the ship's tunnels that run under the decks from fore to aft. These tunnels are narrow and lit only by occasional dim lights. They run alongside the ship's holds, right next to the water, and are always below the waterline. They are designed for emergency passage in bad weather and are usually not a part of the ship in regular use. Nevertheless, the tunnels are subject to corrosion as much as the rest of the ship—probably more so because of their proximity to moisture and lack of access to dry, warm air. Therefore, they must be chipped, scraped, sanded, and painted on a regular basis.

But the cold, clammy fog has driven the deckhands away from this task that is depressing and chilling to the soul on even the brightest of days. We have somehow migrated up to the forward dayroom,

where we have joined some of the other deck crew watching the baseball game of the week on what has become a prolonged break. Mike,
the boatswain, our foreman, has busied himself with some other task
and is nowhere around. So, when George, the mate, our erstwhile
champion, passes by the room for the third time and sees us settling
in for a long afternoon of baseball, it is more than he can bear. He
confirms the fact that we are supposed to be on duty and then sends
us off to find the boatswain. Within minutes we have located Mike,
but not before he has gotten word that we have wandered from our
workplace. He demands to know why we have vacated the tunnels.
When we complain that they are too cold and damp, he turns on me
as bull deckhand and immediately assigns me to scrape and paint a
shower located just off the dayroom. I am angry at being assigned
more busywork and take out my anger on the shower. I make such a
racket with the scraper that several of the crew complain that they
can't hear the baseball game because of the noise coming through the
wall. I work with such a fit of burning energy that the task is done in
a matter of minutes. When I emerge from the room sweating and my
face red with rage, no one, not even the boatswain, comes near me.
He inspects the work from a distance, nods his approval, and watches
me disappear from sight.

Although it takes a while to sink in, I have learned a valuable
labor lesson from this experience—never let the boss catch you not
appearing to work. In spite of this low drama, the fog refuses to lift
and the foghorn blares through another endless night that dawn fails
to resolve. For the first time I begin to feel a prisoner of the ship. To
compound the feeling, we are once again assigned out of sight to the
tunnels. These tunnels are so long and in need of paint at so many
points that it is easy to entertain the dispiriting thought that we could
be kept busy down in these tombs for the entire year. But, just as it
seems we can't tolerate another minute of this abuse, the fog relents
at the end of our third day just enough to allow us to haul anchor and
proceed. The *Carnahan* joins a long caravan of ships at last allowed
to enter the Soo Locks and takes its place in a slow parade down the
still-foggy St. Marys. By the time we have reached the DeTour Light
and Lake Huron, it has cleared enough for us to stop using the
foghorn. Tensions among crew members ease almost immediately.
As we pass down the lake and into more southerly climes, the weather
continues to improve. By the time we reach Buffalo, we are in shirt

229

sleeves and the boatswain has told us that the mate will minimize our time in the tunnels from now on to concentrate our efforts on the ship's exterior. We ride into Buffalo harbor reprieved.

As we pass upbound through the Soo, the relatively warm weather follows us back up and allows the deckhands to come into their own. Now there is a spring-fed audience of tourists in the viewing stands watching as we perform our struts with cables along the locks. Having prevailed through gales, ice, sleet, and fog, we are ready for something new in our lives. George, the mate, delivers another piece of interesting news when he confirms the rumor that Bob, the deck watch, will be getting off for a few trips to attend to family business.

This being steamboating, no one of the crew even thinks to ask him what the nature of his business is. The ship's company simply accepts it as his right and, before you know it, Bob is going over the railing, grinning, with a duffel bag in his hand, to catch a bus to somewhere in the hinterlands of Wisconsin. This means that I, as bull deckhand, am the first to have the position of deck watch offered to me. Even though the offering is only as a temp replacement for Bob, I jump at the chance to get a watch of my own. Although the twelve-to-four shift would not be my first choice, it is my only choice to step up the ladder of shipboard responsibility. Among other things, this means that I will have to figure out how to stay awake through the long nights and when to get my sleep. The mate tells me that Bob will be away for two to three trips—maybe two weeks. I will start at midnight tonight.

And so, at 11:45, a traditional fifteen minutes early, I report to the pilothouse. The *Carnahan* is in the middle of Lake Superior and the house is illuminated by only the eerie green glow of the compass and the orange reflection of the radar screen in the corner of the room. The mate on this watch is the second, a man named Jefferson Davis, who, obviously, comes from somewhere in the South. Davis is not an unfriendly sort, just one who doesn't make friends easily. The fact that he is twice my age has nothing to do with it. I have made friends out here with people three times my age. He just acts like a country bumpkin and has manners to match. Nevertheless, he is my watch mate and I listen as he runs down the duties. Since the ship is in the middle of the lake in the middle of the night, there is not a whole lot for the deck watch to do. The first task is to clean and mop the stern alleyway and forward dayroom. This takes me about an hour to do. Then there is dead time until, about halfway through the watch, I relieve the watchman for his fifteen-minute break. This happens either immediately before or after the watchman relieves the wheelsman for his break.

The watchman's primary responsibility while the ship is under way is to serve as lookout in the pilothouse. While the mate is plotting courses and communicating with the engine room and the wheelsman is focused on keeping the ship on course, the watchman is basically a third set of eyes looking out in front of and around the ship to make sure that there are no threats to safe navigation. This includes keeping an eye out for other ships as well as making sure that the ship's running lights and emergency gear are functioning properly. In reality, the three men—mate, wheelsman, and watchman—work as a team to make sure that the ship is running safely on course. The responsibilities are taken seriously by the entire crew and shipping community: all three positions require Coast Guard certification, with the mate needing to apprentice and pass an exam for his license and the watchman and wheelsman needing to have accumulated experience and their Able-Bodied (AB) Seaman's Certificate.

So it is one of the biggest thrills of my life when Ray, the watchman who was responsible for denying me beer in Escanaba, says, "I'm heading back aft for my break, mate." At a nod from Jefferson Davis, I walk up to the front window and take Ray's spot with my face to the blank, open darkness. I am the watchman, and, even though there is absolutely nothing to see for 360 degrees around the *Carnahan*, it is all mine.

After Ray's all-too-brief break, I am again free to disappear for a while. I simply make myself obscure in a back corner of the big room and stand and watch. None of the three crew with me are especially talkative and there is not a lot to discuss in relation to the course of the ship as we continue to plow in a straight line toward the lakehead well beyond our horizon. The sea is calm, broken by the occasional lights of other ships heading down on other courses that pass them no closer than ten miles to us.

At 3:15, I once again spring into action. My responsibility is to wake the first mate and the four-to-eight wheelsman, watchman, and deck watch for their upcoming shift. Then I go and make fresh coffee to help with their wake-up. My errands complete, I stand proudly in the pilothouse as George, the mate, climbs the inside stairs, cursing loudly. "What the hell is this stuff?" he demands of all of us. Ray, the wheelsman, says, "What?" George answers by waving his cup and then glaring at me. "This stuff. It's hot water. There's no goddamned coffee down there!" I shiver as the realization hits me that the coffee that I thought I'd made didn't make. Ray is quick to make amends and finds the mate some hot coffee still in the pilothouse thermos. George sips the stale brew sullenly and I take advantage of the calm to slip out and away. At my back I hear him say, "Next time make sure it's coffee. That's the most important part of your watch as far as I'm concerned." I slink into my bunk feeling bad until sleep overtakes me.

I am awakened by Jim, my roommate, a few hours later as he prepares to assume his deckhand duties. I lie awake groggily in my bunk, comfortable with the knowledge that I can sleep in for a few more hours. But then I realize I would miss breakfast and an opportunity to work on my papers while Jim is out of the room. So I drag myself out and into the galley located on the other side of the ship. I manage to walk in just as the deckhands are leaving to report to duty. I derive satisfaction from the simple fact that they see me as someone different from the person they knew yesterday.

With time to kill before my 11:45 reporting time, I retire to my cabin and spend a couple good hours writing at the tiny desk. For the first time, I feel confident that I can pull these papers together and complete my requirements for Monteith. My professors have asked for progress reports by mid-May. So I spend my time developing and copying outlines for their review. The fact that Wayne State is on a quarter system means that the final paper won't be due until mid-June.

When I report to the pilothouse before noon, the mate points to the approaching breakwall of the Duluth-Superior harbor and tells me I'll be needed on deck to help with the docking. This is no surprise, as the deck watch almost always assists in the removal of hatches with the boatswain and deckhands. When the ship approaches the dock, it is my role to help swing the deckhands over the side in the boatswain's chair and then to feed out the cable from the winches as I monitor their progress in attaching the lines to the bollards along the dock. While the watchman operates the steam winch that feeds the cable, I look over the railing and let him know by hand signals when enough cable has been paid out and when it is attached. Instead of being down there on the dock while the ship is being loaded, my role is to stay at the winch and work with the watchman to make sure the ship is shifted per the mate's directions. Basically, instead of being a deckhand on the dock, staring up at the ship, I am the deck watch on the ship, staring down at the dock. The fact that I don't have to lug the dangerous heavy cables to and fro is an added bonus. The best part is that at 3:45 I am relieved by Smiley, who is the four-to-eight deck watch. I luxuriate in the knowledge that I can enjoy my supper in the galley without having to rush back to work. While the deck-hands are still down on the dock as darkness descends, I find a couple more valuable hours to work on my papers. And even later, when the deckhands and the eight-to-twelve watch are buttoning up the hatches for the return to Lake Superior, I am catching a nap before my 11:15 wake-up call. I reach the pilothouse as the *Carnahan* enters the open lake, refreshed and having bid goodnight to the exhausted deckhands as they head to flop in their bunks. The way this loading has played out, I will probably come on watch tomorrow at noon just as they are completing hosing down the deck.

The daytime twelve-to-four watch is more active and the deck watch is often put to work helping to scrape and paint along with the deckhands. However, there is still the need to relieve the watchman in the pilothouse, and the mate will give the whistle a short toot to notify me whenever my services up there are requested. Another task that the deck watch is required to perform is to take ballast tank read-ings using a lead line. This involves walking down the deck and unscrewing the tops to tubes that descend to the tanks, measuring the amount of water in them, recording the results, and reporting them to the mate, who is responsible to recommend adjustments to the cap-tain. With all of these time-consuming tasks, it is the rare day that the deck watch manages to get much painting done. Except for the fact that I haven't figured out how to work out this sleep thing, I like the change of pace from the eight-to-four life of a deckhand to the posi-tion of deck watch. And the pages keep rolling off my notebook.

The night watches allow me the most fun of all. On Lake Huron the watchman and mate combine to show me how to take an azimuth reading and how to read the radar screen. At the watchman's break, the mate sends the wheelsman back to the galley to bring him a slice of pie and says, "Okay, kid. Your turn on the wheel." My heart pound-ing, I repeat the heading and grip the tiny metal wheel, smaller than the one on my TR4. My only previous experience on the *Mercury* proved near disastrous, as I couldn't keep the ship on course and spent the entire time correcting from one side to the other. This time I am more cautious and the *Carnahan* proves a more stable ship for me. I manage to keep the ship within three degrees of the course until the wheelsman returns to relieve me. To everyone's amusement, his first act is to turn on the "Iron Mike" that automatically controls the wheel and keeps the ship on course.

The following trip down finds the *Carnahan* in a shroud of fog, this time at the entrance to the narrow channel of the Detroit River. To make matters even more complex, it is night and, judging from the cacophony of foghorns, there is a lot of traffic. But the general consensus of the ships' captains is that their vessels can and will navigate through this and so the *Carnahan*, relying on radar and seamanship, joins the parade. Because Smiley had to go home for an emergency, I have been transferred to the eight-to-twelve watch. My watchman is none other than Arthur Johnson—known as "Big Swede" to distinguish him from his son "Little Swede," who works on the *Ernest Weir*. Swede, as we call him, is one of the most seasoned of the *Carnahan*'s crew. He is a jovial gruff sort of guy who keeps himself occupied off watch with marlinespike. It seems you can find him at almost any hour sitting in the dayroom splicing line or even thin cable with his mitt on to protect his grip. His limited speech is thickly accented and full of "Jah, jah's."

On this foggy night, I am on the bow with Swede as the *Carnahan* crawls through the dense soup. While on the open lake, the watchman is allowed to perform his duties in the shelter of the pilothouse. On rivers and channels, the Coast Guard mandates that there must be a lookout in the open air on the bow of the ship. And so we stand in the warm mist, blackness and whistles all around us, the occasional red flashing buoy crawling by to remind us that we are still in the channel. This is an area where a good number of ships who stray out of the channel run aground every year. Fog is usually a contributing factor. The sole purpose of the watchman is to watch and make sure that the mate, perched in an open window in the pilothouse twelve feet above, knows exactly what is happening on the river. Talking is strongly discouraged so as not to interfere with the sounds coming from all around us. Occasionally the fog lifts to reveal the dim outline of the lights around the fantail of whatever ship is in front of us. The fact that no two ship whistles sound the same allows Swede to distinguish the newer sounds from those of ships heading in our direction.

It is customary for ships to use their whistles to communicate with other ships, especially in the narrow rivers and channels. When passing to each others' port or left side, one toot of the ship's whistle means "I am passing to your port side." Two blasts signal a starboard-to-starboard passage. While it is customary for U.S.-flagged ships to thus signal, for some reason that no one has been able to explain to me, Canadian ships rarely answer a signal from another ship. I remember asking the mate on the *Hulst* about this a couple summers back. He explained that, before ship radios became commonplace, the whistles were the only way of signaling passage. Nowadays the mates are in communication by radio and can tell the other ship which side they will be passing each other on. Thus, the whistles are more a formality and a way for ships to salute each other. But Swede disagrees. "Can't tell these ships apart in the fog or the dark," he whispers, hawking a plug of tobacco over the side. "Specially on a night like this when ships are strung up and down the river. Better to use them goddam whistles." He breaks off his muted discussion to yell to the pilothouse, "Over to port there. She blew one." The mate quickly responds and the *Carnahan*'s whistle rattles sharply through the thick night air. "Answered one," Swede says to verify to the pilothouse that the *Carnahan*'s whistle on the smokestack sent one signal in response. While we can easily hear our own ship's whistle on a still night like this, Swede's response is born of practice and habit, anticipating a howling night when it might not be so easy to hear. He is also confirming that the white light above the pilothouse mast has flashed one time in conjunction with the whistle.

In addition to listening for ship's whistles, the watchman is responsible for ensuring that the ship's running lights are in working order. This means that, every half hour or so, Swede strolls to either side of the bow and peers toward the sides, to the top of the pilothouse and back toward the smokestack to observe the running lights. If the four lights are burning in place, as they are this night, he sings out to the mate, "Lights are bright!"

As the *Carnahan* creeps through the murk, Swede notes that we will soon be passing Detroit and we've got to get ready for the mail boat. This is the *J. W. Westcott*, the same ship I have used to catch and depart ships in the river. As the *Carnahan* makes her way past the barely visible buildings of downtown Detroit, we attach a line to a bucket and ready a ladder to lower over the side to pick up a wheels-man coming back after a couple trips off. I am sent to the forward dayroom to gather the outgoing mail from a box and transfer it to the bucket. The river is broad enough at this point to allow for easy passage of ships and, as we cruise under the Ambassador Bridge, the tiny shape of the *Westcott* pops out of the gloom and nestles under our starboard flank, well inside our wake. As soon as the ships are touching, an arm from inside the Westcott waves in a downward motion. That is our signal to lower the bucket down onto her deck. The bucket hasn't even hit the deck before a figure emerges to drag it inside and empty it out. A moment passes while the mailman tosses our mail in and adds any radioed requests for the *Detroit News* or *Detroit Free Press.* Then the bucket is on its way back up and onto the deck of the *Carnahan*.

While I have been handling the bucket, Swede and the twelve-to-four watchman have slid the ladder down to the *Westcott* and secured it to the *Carnahan*'s rails. Swede signals that it is secure and, almost immediately, a figure appears from the pilothouse of the *Westcott* and is scrambling up the ladder to our ship. Jerry, the wheelsman, is back, followed by Bob the twelve-to-four deck watch, whose job I have been minding. This means that, when Smiley comes back in Cleveland tomorrow, I will go back to being bull deck-hand. And I don't mind, having had enough of this two-shifts-a-day stuff. As soon as Bob's feet are safely on deck, the ladder is dragged back up and—with a toot of its whistle, answered by one from the *Carnahan*—the Westcott slips off into the night toward the steamer behind us to repeat the performance. The entire operation has taken place in less than two minutes without the *Carnahan* losing a revolution of her turbines.

The spring fogs, of course, are a harbinger of the approach of warmer weather. That is, weather warmer than it has been. The next trip down we spend a Friday afternoon in the St. Clair River watching the sun do its work on the human spirit. And even as we watch the kids bravely jumping in while their older sisters work on their tans, the rivers and lakes are consistently cool enough to make it feel like it will never get warm fast enough to compensate for the spring we have been through. The deck of the *Carnahan* is made of steel. A

The *Paul H. Carnahan* (Thomas Manse Collection)

steel that seems to hold forever the temperature of the earth from which it was mined. When we deckhands are on a rare daytime break and want to sit in the sun and watch the chicks in their swimsuits on the nearby rafts, we have no choice but to sit on the cool hatch covers. While our faces turn red from exposure to the full sun, we have goosebumps from exposure to the wind cooled by passing over the water. We also secretly worry about getting piles.

For the first time, I find myself missing the full beauty of spring days like this one because I am stuck on this ship. It is easy in my mind for me to trade places with those teens on the shore, working up a sweat playing Frisbee on the beach and then choosing to cool down either by jumping into the water or by pulling a cold one out of the cooler. And then lying down on the sand and talking to the chicks in the bathing suits and making plans for the party tonight—perhaps on this very beach where a bonfire will be lit and more beer brought out to cool the dance fever. And somebody will look out and say, "God, look at the lights on that ship going by." And one of the girls will hold up a beer and yell out, "Hey, sailor! C'mon and party down!" And, among their laughter, no one will hear the soft whoosh of a body hitting the water and swimming toward the fire as I strive to answer the invitation.

When the *Carnahan* ties up at Zug, it is just before six in the evening. Exercising my right as bull deckhand, I am taking the rest of the night to go up the street while my comrade deckhands, Jim and Al, mind the ship. I walk through Zug's churning machinery full of fire and brimstone and emerge at the gate to find my cousin Martinez—formerly known as Tom—and buddy Rick there with his green Bug ready for a night on the town. We proceed immediately to the house on Lincoln Street that now has a makeshift sign proclaiming it to be Stonehead Manor. In the two months I have been away, our lease has lapsed and there has been a transformation of residents away from student types and more toward the dropouts. But Rick and Martinez have maintained contacts with Gary the caretaker and Ruben Rodriguez. In a basement apartment, we sit on the floor, listen to some music, and share a large beer with Ruben, who still thinks that, because we call him Martinez, my cousin Tom is a brother Chicano.

We head off into the evening and a trip over to Louie's, where we drink more beer and watch the NBA playoffs. It is while watching Lew Alcindor's basketball move slowly, slowly toward the basket before going through, just as I absolutely knew it would, that I sense something is different. Noticing my confused state, Rick shakes his head, laughs, and says, "I wonder what those punks dropped in that beer." Around midnight we are back in the Bug, driving across town, singing with Kenny Rogers's "You picked a fine time to leave me, Lucille—with four hungry kids and a crop in the fields." And all too soon, we are back at the monster Zug and I am waving goodbye and walking past the gate guard, thinking, "Can't he tell I'm walking crooked? And he's allowing me to pass by as though everything's normal?" He does and I find myself walking through the maze of cavernous buildings illuminated by flashes of hell and sparks leaping out of blast furnaces. Somewhere above a siren goes off just as a crane zips overhead. Then a train's horn blasts as it rumbles through the midst of the maze. Underfoot, all is cinder and ash and I am constantly on guard to keep from tripping. Men in hard hats go about their business all around me, ignorant that I am doing all I can to keep one foot in front of the other. After what seems like an hour of walking through this hell on earth, I see the familiar outline of the *Carnahan*. The maws of the Hullett cranes are swooping into her hold and emerge dribbling taconite marbles that fall like black hail all around me. I make my way to the ladder and climb up and run into Al, the newest deckhand, who seems way too glad to see me. I discover that he, too, has been able to get up the street and is quite drunk. I manage to leave him to his devices and make my way to my cabin, where I decide to lay down and try and get some sleep. But, after much tossing and turning, I discover that sleep is the one thing that I can't do. To complicate matters, the cabin has become very claustrophobic and I begin to imagine myself squeezing out of the porthole to the freedom of the sky and river. It is a relief, then, when Smiley comes rapping on my door to summon the deckhands to join in buttoning up the hatches.

I pull on my pants and work boots and make my way back out onto the deck. We are a long way from dawn but the night is illuminated by bright orange fluorescent lights that dance in the ripples of the river. I find a wrench and try to stay as far out of the way of the deck crane as possible. I am sufficiently paranoid to avoid the open hatches by all means, recalling the stories of sailors who have fallen to their deaths. Sometime after five, the first streaks of morning become visible and I begin to feel better. I am relieved when Jim and Al volunteer to go over and release the cables from the dock and when all the hatch covers are in place and it is just a matter of wrenching the bolts down. The rigors of the night begin to catch up with me a while later as we begin the ritual of hosing down the deck and sweeping the piles of stray pellets into Lake St. Clair. A break for breakfast finds me totally uninterested in food but very attracted to crashing in any available corner. As the morning progresses, the warmth of the sun helps to pull me through the by now familiar routine. Amazingly, no one has been on my case about not pulling my weight. Perhaps the fact that I have consistently pulled my weight under far more difficult circumstances has cut me a little slack among my shipmates. Or it could well be that, hungover after a Friday night in Detroit, they don't even notice my spacey behavior. I am very relieved that, by the time noon rolls around, the boatswain passes the word that we are knocked off for the day.

In Superior, Charley Hawkinson, the eight-to-twelve deck watch, hauls aboard an ancient Harley he says he bought from a farmer for a hundred bucks. It will be his project to rebuild the engine and make a chopper out of it. His status goes from that of lowly Navy vet to that of demigod. He makes deals with the engineers to use their tools, torches, and compressed air and is soon spending much of his free time on the project. That is one of the beautiful things about sailing—with no lawn to cut, house to fix up, or car to repair, your time off watch is your own. Jim, my roommate, tends to spend it socializing and drinking. I try to write my term papers. The boatswain watches his new TV in his cabin. I am really floored by the idea that you can do this job, make good money, eat good food for free, and still have plenty of time to pursue your hobbies.

I spend my twenty-first birthday in the middle of Lake Superior, wishing I were with my friends partying at our favorite riverfront park. By the time we get to Cleveland, I am looking forward to making up for lost time. The festivities begin late at a lakefront bar not far from Municipal Stadium. After a couple of beers, we are wandering down the street when we come across Mike, the boatswain, parading in front of another bar with a sign he has borrowed from some union plumber he has met inside. The sign reads "On Strike— Plumbers Local 251" and Mike is busily picketing the sidewalk outside the bar, his face reflecting the plaids of his hunter's shirt. Everyone seems to get a good laugh out of his show of support and we join up with him and a few other crew as we roll up the street to another joint. It is difficult exactly to describe at this point how we got to the next place or the one after that. Or even when it got dark. The point is, that's all meaningless anyway, because we all get good and drunk and roll back to the ship late in the evening. It is Al's idea to head to the galley and raid the night lunch, where we make some fried egg sandwiches with lots of ketchup. The sandwiches go down real easy and, in my case, come back up the same way a little later as we are called out onto the deck. For the second time in a fortnight, I find myself struggling to stay out of harm's way as the dangerous work of cleaning up the cargo holds and replacing the hatches commences regardless of our condition. To demonstrate leadership, Mike runs the crane as though it were bright daylight and he is the soberest person on earth. It is only his singing that gives him away, a sign that George, the first mate, chooses to overlook.

The following week, on another run to Cleveland, we are nego-tiating the Detroit River as I try gamely to plug away at my papers. My plight has been eased somewhat by the departure of my room-mate, Jim, and the appearance of a new deckhand named Damon. Damon is almost exactly my age and we hit it off right away. He imme-diately understands what I am trying to do and finds other cabins to do his socializing in. Without being in party central, I find I am able to focus and actually get something done. Taking a break from my work on this late May morning, I wander into the dayroom and find Ed, one of the oilers, watching TV. Ed is about forty-five, with his crew cut going white and plastic-framed glasses in an era when the wire frames worn by John Lennon are all the rage. He is of average build with a wiry frame and is wearing his customary off-duty white T-shirt and green pants. He is normally pretty quiet and we have had no conversation of any merit since I've been on. The news on the tube is all about the college kids killed yesterday afternoon at Kent State. While I watch in stunned disbelief, Ed proclaims, "God-damned hippies. Communist punks! They shoulda shot every one of 'em. Teach 'em a lesson." It takes me only a second to take a look at him glaring at me before I decide to get the hell out of that room. I've heard enough stories from the crew of the *Mercury* to know that shipboard fights never really end and never bode well. And so I choose to socialize with Al, Damon, and many of the crew closer in age, who all understand the terrible injustice of what has happened. I soon dis-cover that there is not a whole lot more discussion among other mem-bers of the crew about this massacre and I become increasingly agitated as the pictures shown on TV sink into my consciousness. It becomes apparent to me that Ed has verbalized what a number of the older crew are probably feeling but, at the risk of bringing the civil war aboard the *Carnahan*, refrain from doing so. I bury myself in my writing, feeling the pull of the land and my friends more strongly than at any other time since I got on this spring. All the antiwar feelings come out in a rush as I think of my friend Raymond, buried under friendly fire and the lukewarm words of the minister before the six-gun salute in that cemetery in Detroit. I seethe with anger at the wrongness of what my government is doing to the world. And I feel worthless and out of the scene as the *Carnahan* moves swiftly through the river to deliver iron ore for the industry of our country's death machine.

It is at dark times such as this that the upper lakes come to my rescue. Back on Lake Superior, it is a tranquil, unusually warm early June evening. I sit on deck, basking in the evening sun, painting some bookshelves for my cabin. I take a break every so often to look over the placid waters and admire the vast, seemingly endless beauty that the big lake presents. The *Carnahan* itself seems to float on a single wave across the stillness of the ocean world. Off the port side, the distant Keeweenaw Peninsula is represented by a purplish line of haze. There are no other signs of life around us. This, I reflect, is the way the world should be. Not that crazed, industry-mad society epitomized by the crushed ore and dashed human spirits perpetuated by Zug Island, the very place that is responsible for our being out here, to provide its sustenance. I realize that I have traveled a long way from my first trip to Expo 67 aboard the *South American*. I also know that, even though I am planning to be off this ship in less than a month, I am most probably not through with either Lake Superior or Zug Island.

Summer sailing is a whole different breed of animal, as Swede would say it. The threat of snow and sleet is, for the most part, behind us. The mornings and evenings, especially in the north country, are long and we find plenty of time on our hands. With the new deckhands, Damon, from Iron Mountain, and Al, I have forged an easygoing relationship. We are able to get the job done with minimum exertion. If the boatswain puts us down in the tunnels for a morning of painting, it is understood that we don't want to finish the job too quickly and deprive future deckhands of this great opportunity.

I find plenty of time now to complete my Monteith papers, and send them to my mother to type and send in for grading. One of the papers is titled "The Six-Day War" but has more to do with the American war machine, the biblical account of creation, and the writing of Dos Passos than the event in the Middle East. Although there were days when I thought I would never be able to find quiet space to write on the *Carnahan*, the departure of Jim the party man changed everything.

With the good weather, the ship's crew begins to take advantage of the conjugal visiting policy offered by National Steel. Second mate, Jefferson Davis, brings his wife aboard for the trip, providing many of the crew their first proximity to womanhood since the visit to the whorehouse at Easter time. We deckhands are not impressed.

"Look at her over there picking her teeth," observes Damon one evening on deck after supper as we cruise into Cleveland's harbor. "Looks like some farm wife."

Seeing nothing more worthwhile there to mine, Al turns his gaze to the downtown seawall and says, "Hey, look at that. Is that a U-boat?" I respond quickly, turning the question to Damon with, "No, that's notta my boat. Is thatta you boat?" Damon takes the baton and passes it to Jim, the young, friendly third mate. And thus the joke gets passed on from crewman to crewman all the way up the river to the steel dock.

A cursory calculation of my assets leads me to believe that I have made and saved enough money out here to be able to cruise ashore through the rest of the year. But now the difficulty is in leaving the *Carnahan* just when the fun is really beginning. I have come to relish my role as bull deckhand and the perks that go with the job, like being the first to swing from the boatswain's chair at the Soo Locks and be oohed at by the swelling number of tourists. Or the easy eight-hour-long port shifts, basically being paid to watch the ship being loaded or unloaded. Or the nights going up the street to get pissed and rolling back to the ship, laughing with my buddies. Or the three squares a day. And, while the *Carnahan* can't touch Johnny's galley from the *Columbia*, they do a good job day in and day out. In short, the good, comfortable life of the *Carnahan* has captured me and I have a really hard time deciding to leave it after going through the not-so-nice spring season so fresh in my memory.

It is only after telling the mate twice of my decision to get off at the next port that I'm able to follow through on the third try. I get off where I got on the *Carnahan* for the first time way back in December. Winter or summer, stoned or straight, Zug Island is the same nightmare at any point in our stroll through the universe. With my good-byes behind me, I climb down the ladder and meander through the maze, unfazed now by the hissing, belching, sulfur-drenched plumes of soot and ash that engulf me. I have made it through here under much worse condition and I know that, with only a good coating of dust to show where I've been, I will emerge back onto the streets of the Motor City, ready for summer.

My prolonged departure from the *Carnahan* has made it possible for me to add to my transportation empire and I waste little time in acquiring a Yamaha motorcycle to complement the TR4 in my stable. It is on the way to check out the cycle that Rick informs me of the multiple murders that took place at Stonehead Manor a few weeks prior. Apparently the father of a girl broke into the place, firing at and killing his daughter and three others in the middle of the night. This is much more real to me than far away Kent State and the Vietnam protests. I am not sorry to be free of that tragic place.

I spend the early days of summer a young man of leisure, motoring about. I take great pleasure in these vehicles and yet am occasionally aware of the absence of being in my life. It is a part of my character that I have not yet come to terms with. I possess many of the trappings of what most young men of my age desire, yet I find nothing in those possessions. My TR4 and Yamaha are vehicles that I mostly ride in alone, although I find I'm happier when I'm with others.

I take the Yamaha up to my brother's place in the Upper Peninsula. The ride is arduous and by the time I reach Mackinaw City, my back is sore from carrying a knapsack and my face is pocked with the remains of bugs. Even though it is full summer, the rules of the road dictate that I wear full cycling regalia and abstain from bathing. I find a little churchyard on the outskirts of the busy tourist town and curl up in my too-hot sleeping bag. The next day I reach brother Jim's, where I find nothing much to do but read, listen to music, take woodsy walks, and help his wife, Joan, with meals while the four kids scurry about underfoot. This is a place of respite for me where I can stop and think about things going on in my life. My brother, nine years my senior, is just far enough away from my tempestuous world to be able to talk with me. Our late-night conversations, usually held over a beer or two, are a balm to me. The clear northern skies are a perfect place to learn astronomy and develop a sense of poetry. With my studies at Monteith becoming more focused on the natural sciences and humanities, I find that my polar moods tend to balance out after my northern sojourns. After a few days I am joined by my friend Roger, who is, like me, seeking salvation through a motorcycle. Except his is a BMW and rides circles around mine. We spend a few days together tripping around the back roads, stopping in the occasional tavern to share a legal brew (although we've been doing so illegally since we were fifteen), and arguing about the meaning of life (which we've been doing since we were fourteen). Roger and I share suspicions of the behavior of our fellow Americans, each other included. While we enjoy each other's company, I know that the day he gets on his bike and rides away, we are both a little happier for being apart again.

My trip back down to Detroit takes me by Charlevoix, where I resist the temptation to hop the ferry over to Beaver Island. I decide against it partly because I don't want to blow the money and partly because I've had enough of drunken partying to last me awhile. I decide instead, on a whim, to visit my boyhood camp, Sancta Maria near Gaylord. I am amazed when I am welcomed as an ex-camper and invited to spend the night in a cabin full of impressionable twelve-year-olds who ooh and ah at the Hell's Angel in their midst. I am moved to find life at camp almost the same as when I left it eight summers ago. Yet I feel very out of place and I wonder if there is any place in the world where I can become myself, truly myself, and be at home with others.

My return to Detroit only invites me to keep on moving. I cannot be comfortable in my parents' home, even though they are among the most tolerant creatures on the planet. Away from home, the east side party scene is pretty much relegated to nights in Angel Park until the cops kick us out and we all drive to another nearby park. In near desperation, I decide to return to one of my favorite spots, Montreal, where I first tasted the joy of freedom via the *South American* at Expo 67.

I have always wanted to take the train and so I do. A five-hour ride takes me to Toronto and another five hours to Montreal. Only after alighting at the train station at 11 PM do I realize that I have landed as a tourist in a big city with no idea of where to stay. I walk up and down the downtown streets, looking for a cheap pension. Finding none and aware that the hour is getting very late, I cast about for a spot on the ground and find a likely haven behind the wrought iron gates of a churchyard. Like a good hippie, I have brought a sleeping tarp and spread it on the ground. I roll up my blue jean jacket and use it as a pillow. Then I commence to toss and turn for the next five hours as the noises of the city refuse to stop. At dawn, I straggle up and resume my march along the now quiet streets. I wind up at the quay where the *South American* tied up just three summers ago. I feel the warmth of the sun give strength to my bones and I wander into a nearby restaurant, where I use my weak French to order breakfast *ouefs* served with the customary sliced tomatoes. Feeling all right, I hop the Metro to the Expo site that is still open on a diminished scale. I wander around the island fondling the souvenirs in my memory bank but feeling very empty at the awareness of being alone and having no one to share them with. The summer of '67 I was never alone. There were always at least a couple of shipboard companions up for a quick fling at Expo 67 or anywhere around this town. To deepen my mood, I encounter a new exhibit on Youth Culture that features at its entrance statues of a forlorn-looking hippie boy and chick. Their lost eyes lead me into an exhibit that displays drug paraphernalia and a video-synthesized "acid trip." I emerge feeling somewhat the worse for wear only to hear the refrain from the new Crosby, Stills, Nash, and Young song playing over the Expo loudspeakers with the refrain "Four dead in O-hi-o." Realizing that Expo 67 is over and maybe it wasn't so great an idea to come here alone, I trudge back toward downtown and the train station. I ride the train all night back to Detroit.

Before too many more evenings in the park have passed, I realize that I am just as bored with the scene in summer Detroit with friends as I was alone in Montreal. I share my complaints with Rick, who agrees that it sucks and he suggests we go again to Montreal and to the East Coast in his green Beetle. Within a few days we are on the road and rolling through the cornfields of Ontario. We have brought camping gear and have picked up a bottle of duty-free whiskey for the campfires. Within a couple of days we have done Montreal and Quebec City as well. Still, not feeling welcome in the Francophone bars as hippies, we decide to get the hell back to the U.S.A. We enter the border through Maine, where the customs agents treat us with a barely concealed contempt as they methodically tear apart the vehicle. It is when one of them carefully unrolls my head bandana to reveal nothing hidden that I realize these guys are playing for keeps. It is less than a minute later that the other agent yells out "Got it" and waves a plastic bag that has magically appeared in his hand from somewhere under the floor mat. From that instant I understand we are in some deep shit. The agent proudly displays the bag to the other and we see three or four hand-rolled joints tucked neatly inside. At that moment, my bowels turn to jelly and I race to the john, where everything inside me rushes out in one pathetic whoosh. Thus cleansed, I rejoin the guards and Rick and we go into their office, where the agent unrolls one of the joints, puts some in a tube, adds a liquid chemical to it, and proudly shows us the orange color while smugly proclaiming "positive." Surprise, surprise.

The state police are called and escort us to the nearest town, about sixty miles away. The trooper lets us know that everything will be okay for us if we cooperate and that it won't if we try anything smart ass. Rick, as the owner of the offending vehicle, is incarcerated and I am left to figure out how to get some money to pay the anticipated fine. I find a Western Union and wire home that the engine has blown on the car and we need six hundred dollars. That accomplished, I realize that I am facing a night in a strange town with no money and no camping gear, it having been confiscated along with the car. I dejectedly walk around until I end up back at the jail, where the constable processes me so that I can sleep in the drunk tank. I make myself as comfortable as possible, again using my blue jean jacket for all it's worth.

Morning finds both Rick and myself bedraggled and looking much the worse for the wear. The state trooper has prepped us for the appearance, advising a guilty plea and an expected fine that matches to the penny the amount I have received through the Western Union. The judge admonishes Rick and threatens to put him in jail if he catches him in Maine again. The fact that he is looking at me as he passes this judgment does not go unnoticed by me. The trooper helps arrange for a logger to truck us back to the border, where the customs agents give us a hard time about impounding the car. They finally let us go and we console ourselves with a beer in a nearby café while we plan the rest of our trip. But we never get any further than agreeing on getting the hell out of Maine as the first thing we need to do. Although we don't quite make it out of the state before finding a campground that evening, our campfire thoughts are definitely locked on home. We spend the better part of the next couple days driving and wind up at Angel Park with stories from the front to tell.

While I am grateful that we survived to tell the tale, I am also aware that the experience has left me with a serious cash flow problem. The cushion I had to ride me through at least the first part of the year has shrunk significantly with my share of the fine.

CHAPTER 10

Steamboat VII

The Summertime Blues on the SS *Bethlehem*

And so, with a few short weeks to go before classes recommence, I find myself calling the Steelworkers' Hall in Toledo. At least here my luck is in, as the dispatcher offers to ship me out this very afternoon from the foot of Grand Boulevard on the *Bethlehem*. I make quick work of throwing a duffel bag together and scrounge a ride down to the dock, where I arrive just in time to catch the *Westcott* motoring out to meet the ship. Within seconds of leaving the dock the *Westcott* surfs the wake thrown by the ship and nestles up alongside her at ten miles an hour. A ladder is quickly thrust down and secured and I look out and up to see a couple of faces peering down. I hesitate when I see a duffel bag at the ship's rail, thinking I should wait until the person has come off before climbing up. But the man is beckoning me so up the ladder and over the railing I go. The mate pulls me over the top, claps me on the back, and says, laughing, "That's always my rule: new crew get on before old crew get off. That way there's no surprises." He then leads me to his cabin to verify my "Z" card and to have me sign the ship's papers. Then I am assigned to quarters back aft, where I will report to the steward for my assignment. The fact that I will be working galley again doesn't faze me at all. I'm happy to be able to work and make some money, especially for only a couple weeks. To make matters better, the steward tells me that, since there's also a porter spot open, the second cook and I can split the job and make some extra money. Better and better, I think as I quickly adjust to life in the galley of the *Bethlehem*, slipping into virtually the same roles I had a couple summers ago aboard the *Mercury* and *John Hulst*.

The *Bethlehem* (Dossin Great Lakes Museum)

The *Bethlehem* is an old vessel. She was built in 1917 in Ashtabula and launched as the *Midvale*. The present name was given her in 1925 and she has worn it on her six-hundred-foot length up and down these lakes carrying ore for Bethlehem Steel. She is still in good shape, from what I can see as we move at a moderate ten miles an hour through Lake Huron toward Drummond Island in the St. Marys River. The *Bethlehem* is one of a fleet of eight ships sailing for Bethlehem Steel. Two older ships, the *Cambria* and the *Donner*, have been converted to crane ships and I have seen them tied up at the Bethlehem works in Lackawanna. The flagship of the fleet is the *Arthur Homer*, built in 1960, the last hull to roll off the ways at the Rouge yard of Great Lakes Engineering and the only ship in the fleet in excess of seven hundred feet.

The *Bethlehem* is also unique to me in another way. She is the first ship I've been on that has a Skinner Unaflow engine. Upon first hearing this from an oiler, I can't wait to get down to the engine room to check it out. But, in going down there, I discover a machine operating basically in a cover with all the works thrusting away out of sight, like a car engine. What gets me over this disappointment is seeing the other end of the engine room where the boilers are open for the world to see, not hidden away like on all the other steamers I have worked. And, in front of the boilers, a man in a filthy T-shirt, his face blackened by dust, is thrusting big shovelsful of coal into the fierce fire. Not only is the *Bethlehem* a coal burner, she still has coalpassers! I am hypnotized by this scene and would stay longer if the coalpasser weren't working quite so hard in front of me.

The *Bethlehem* ties up at a dock on Drummond Island, where a conveyor begins to fill her up with limestone. The conveyor is small and not very fast. It drops the limestone into the holds from a height of about ten feet above so that the breeze distributes the powdery substance freely about the ship. The loading process will take about fourteen hours. A crewman confides to me that it will take at least that much time to get the dust off the ship and out of our clothes, hair, and noses. He also points out the thirty-five hatches that will need to be secured—almost twice as many as on newer ships.

The island itself doesn't seem to offer any attractions beyond hills of limestone, so I am content to nap until the evening meal is called. When I awake, the deck looks like a snow squall has hit and, because the conveyor has broken a belt, we will be here longer than expected. Perhaps because the *Bethlehem* is older, I don't sense the same pressure I felt on the *Carnahan* to stay on schedule. The crew, including the first mate, who has the responsibility for loading and unloading the vessel, walk about the deck quite nonchalantly, enjoying the summer evening and the respite from the dust. After dark, when the conveyor comes back on, I go to sleep listening to the drone of the machine and the slow whoosh of the pulverized limestone as it slowly fills the hold.

The next day on Lake Huron is brisk, an early reminder that our short Michigan summer will not last much longer. The day is full of a north wind and fleeting clouds that give a grey cast to the Blue Water lake. But by the time we reach the St. Clair and Detroit Rivers, the breeze has abated and we enjoy full summer once again. I have discovered that the crew loves to hang out in a space on deck between the hatches and the after cabins on evenings like this. There is a much-sought-for wooden swing that is made for such idyllic days and nights.

251

SS *Bethlehem*

Built	1917
Builder	Great Lakes Engineering Works, Ashtabula, Ohio
Owners	Johnstown Steamship Company (1917); Bethlehem Transportation Corporation (1925)
Names	*Midvale* (1917); *Bethlehem* (1925)
Length	600'
Beam	60'
Draft	32'
Engine	Skinner Unaflow steam
Boilers	Two Babcock and Wilcox coal-fired
Capacity	13,500 tons dwt
Cargo	Stone
Crew	32

Because of the time of year, most college-aged kids have already quit their summer jobs and are enjoying the last days of summer on shore, preparing to head back to campus. This means that the *Bethlehem* has no other crew members who are my age. My only social entertainment is playing chess with a guy in his mid-twenties named Willard. But, try as I might, I can't give him the level of competition he needs at the game, so I reach my limit with him after a few tries.

The *Bethlehem* unloads her stone at Sandusky, home of Cedar Point. I have been coming here to ride the Blue Streak since I was fourteen and am a little disappointed that none of the crew are even interested in going there while the ship discharges her load. The crew of the *Bethlehem* reminds me more of the crew of the *John Hulst*— just a bunch of working stiffs who treat this like any other factory job. No real love of the water and no sense of adventure at being sailors.

But there is Dan, the coalpasser. He is quiet and aloof to the rest of the crew. He, too, looks to be in his mid-twenties. The second cook mentions something about his being back from Vietnam. I imagine that he is out here trying to get as far away from society as possible and I envy him the experiences that have formed his serious, dark demeanor. I imagine him to be someone who has actually seen it, been through it, survived the hell of it and has come back to haunt us with his firsthand knowledge of evil, something I can only infer.

Dan doesn't order large portions of food from the galley, and I get the impression that he is sort of fasting like a Buddhist monk might. He has by far the most energy-consuming task on the ship, passing shovel after shovel of coal into the boiler for most of his four-hour shifts. When not doing that, he has to hose down the clinkers and cart them away in a bucket to be thrown overboard later. All this in hundred-plus-degree heat. He shows not the least amount of concern for anyone else around him and seems perfectly content to be where he is. More than his experience, I envy him that. Dan's presence touches a chord in my soul. I realize that I can march and fight the police oppressors until I am black and blue, but I will command no respect from the Silent Majority that will change the way they think. Yet one word from a guy like Dan carries immense gravity and could change hundreds of attitudes because he has been there and can speak from that perspective. People respect experience. I am frustrated in my lack of experience and stifled in the knowledge that my protests against the war will not gain respect until I become a part of it, thus defeating my antiwar purpose.

When I do manage to converse with Dan, the topic of war and peace does not surface. I am left with the impression of talking with the lake itself. He conveys and communicates his detachment from man at the same time that he is part of the earth around him. I go away from my conversations with him puzzled and amazed and find myself staring over the railing at the lake in a trance. He conveys to me that one can float through time as effortlessly as the *Bethlehem* carries us through water.

On our next run up to Drummond Island, the *Bethlehem* has to tack in a beam sea up near the Straits of Mackinac. The captain has warned us of this impending move, so we have secured everything in the galley before the tack. Although we are only in eight-foot seas, the ship pitches and rolls until on her new course. The loading procedure for limestone is much like the first time out. This time I pass the time playing a couple games of chess with Willard and then meandering among the stone piles before clambering back on board. The fact that I know I will be getting off soon also prevents me from bonding with these guys. They are also aware that I will be getting off soon, so, except for some of the expected casual banter, I'm left to myself.

Because the *Bethlehem* is such a slow loader and unloader, I am faced with a decision to disembark after our second trip to Sandusky. But rather than drop me here with a long, costly bus ride home, the captain generously agrees to drop me off where I got on—the *Westcott* mail boat in Detroit. On the morning of my departure, the captain asks me to visit him in his quarters, where we talk about my program and experiences at Monteith. I gather that he has sons around my own age and is happy to have a chance to have contact with my generation, painful as it might be. He wishes me well and reminds the mate to make sure the new crew gets on before allowing me off. I scale down the ladder to the deck of the *Westcott* and, within seconds, am back on the dock at the foot of West Grand Boulevard with a check for $300 in my pocket to help wipe out this summer's bad memory. I walk to downtown and arrive at the *Free Press* building in time to catch a ride from my sister, Cathy, who works there.

I am also in time to begin my fourth year at Monteith. I am now more than a trifle jaded at this college life and, although my classes are occasionally stimulating and challenging, I enter this year of 1971 with the outlook of a Christian scheduled to meet the lions. At the conclusion of this year I will lose my protective student status and be fully exposed to the draft. Since Richard Nixon decided to get even with my ilk by imposing a draft lottery and since my assigned number is 137—the round my birth date was picked out of the hopper— chances are very good that I shall be summoned.

This knowledge combined with the recent incident at the border create a smog that hovers over my being as the quarter begins. I consult with a friend who is a certified draft counselor who advises me on the requisites of the conscientious objector and the options of forsaking these United States to begin life anew elsewhere. I am not cheered or especially emboldened by this information. I tell my friend Louie that, if my number doesn't come up, I will join the Peace Corps. Even though I strongly oppose our government's actions in Vietnam, I haven't become a total cynic like some of my Monteith associates and denizens of the Cass Corridor. I would still like to do something good for the world. That old St. Bernard's altar boy mentality still lingers within. And perhaps that might help the rest of the world understand that we aren't all warmongers.

A breakthrough of sorts arrives when I read a brochure proclaiming the Free University, a loosely organized assortment of nontraditional pursuits taught by professors and would-be professors. The classes are eclectic, to say the least, and range from witchcraft to Tai Chi. The class that catches my eye is titled Backpacking and Related Interests. As part of my mental preparations to break free from mothership America, I realize that I will have to start learning how to survive in all types of situations. Definitely something that will relate to backpacking—carrying your world on your own shoulders. If that's what it takes to break free from the war machine that feeds me, I'm for it. Who knows, this might even be the key to moving out of my parents' house again.

It turns out that the class is being offered by one of my Monteith classmates, and he invites me to the first meeting at 904 W. Forest, an apartment just off campus. Since my classes are mostly colloquiums and seminars and I'm not working, I have no problem fitting the Wednesday night meetings into my schedule.

The first thing that grabs me about the class is the ultra-relaxed flow of the ten or twelve folks sitting in the living room of the apartment house. Paul begins the class with an easygoing talk about the types of things he likes to do in the out of doors. Copies of the *Whole Earth Catalog, Recreation Coop*, and other outdoor catalogs are scattered on the dark, wooden coffee table. Paul suggests that the group convene every Wednesday and a different person do a presentation on something they love that is outdoors related. Everyone nods in agreement and then Paul further suggests that those who would like can follow him down to the Bronx Café, a neighborhood bar located a couple of blocks from here. I join the small group and am soon ensconced around a black formica table with a pitcher of beer and some peanuts in front of me. This could be heaven if it weren't quite so funky, I think. The Bronx is not your typical campus bar with students falling from the rafters, awash in foam. It is truly a crossroads for university types and the denizens of the adjacent Cass Corridor, including longtime Depression hobos, failed Ph.D. candidates, and dropout hippies, as well as some blue-collar working stiffs. The jukebox is a mix of hippie and country with some Sinatra thrown in. The bar has a couple of pool tables and a nude of Marilyn Monroe embossed in a mirror. To top it off, George, the owner, makes a great burger, which I find myself plunging into well after the midnight hour I'd planned to be home. I cruise home feeling good. The Backpacking and Related Interests group might be that something of value I have been seeking in my devalued world. I become a regular to the group and at the extracurricular meetings at the Bronx. We are abuzz with plans to purchase U.S. Army surplus cross-country skis and to build a sauna for the basement of 904 West Forest.

Yet somehow in late November, as the gold of autumn yields to the pre-winter overcast, I find myself once again enveloped in gloom. I am too aware of the future to enjoy the present and, when one afternoon I leave campus to discover a parking ticket on my car windshield, I cannot help but feel a sense of rage at the system of law and order that is controlling my life far too much.

On a Monday night before finals, I visit my friend Sam and his father at a Belgian bar on Mack Avenue. After a few beers, I bid everyone a good evening, planning on getting home to do some studying before I turn in. I am in a hurry to get home so that I can both study and get enough sleep. I drive through the mostly empty streets without much care. When I cruise toward McNichols, I decide that I don't want to wait for the light to turn green. There are no cars near me anywhere, save for one three or four blocks away. I let the clutch out of the TR4 and cruise across. I am comfortably into the home stretch when a car roars up behind me and I see the bright flashing lights in my rearview mirror. It is at that very instant that I decide not to stop but instead turn at the next side street. As the car follows me, I continue to turn until I have recrossed Hoover and am gaining velocity down side streets toward Seven Mile. I realize that I am now in the midst of a chase and time almost stands still. Every passing house is etched in fire on the coal-black night. But my plan to reach home is cut short at a turn where the TR4 spins out and ends up facing the wrong way. Before I can do anything to get back on course, the police car is on top of me. I switch off the ignition and sit behind the wheel, stunned—amazed at myself and full of wonder at what is going to happen to me.

It is only a matter of seconds before I find out. One of the cops pulls me out of the car, takes a swing at my face, and pushes me up against the cop car for a frisking before tossing me into the backseat.

"Jesus Christ. You coulda been killed. You coulda killed somebody goin' them speeds down those side streets . . . runnin' those stop signs. What the hell were you doin'?"

I stammer out a few syllables that make no sense to them and less to me. What the hell was I doin' anyway? I only wanted to get home to study.

While I ponder that question, the two cops discuss what to do with me. It turns out that the younger one, whose turn it is to be arresting officer, decides against writing a ticket and to run me into the station.

It is a relatively short drive to the Conner Precinct house. I am brought before the desk sergeant, who listens to the officer's complaint. The sergeant takes a quick glance at me, ignoring the scratch on my face. He dismisses me with a shrug, saying, "Let's throw the book at him." I use my single phone call and am lucky when my sister answers. She takes it calmly when she learns where I am and promises to get a lawyer for me to arrange bail tomorrow.

After fingerprinting, I am led back through a dark corridor to the holding cells, where I am shoved into one. There is a plank board that I lay down on using my trusty blue jean jacket for a pillow. At dawn an officer serves me a piece of bologna between two pieces of white bread for breakfast. Shortly after, I am loaded into a paddy wagon for the ride downtown to the courthouse. At the arraignment I am accused of a felony—fleeing and eluding the police. A blackboard in the courtroom informs me that this, along with drunken driving, is a jailable offense. The lawyer that my sister has arranged enters a not-guilty plea on my behalf. With a trial date set for March, we begin discussion with a bail bondsman. When I begin to identify my occupation as sailor, my lawyer quickly pulls me aside, letting me know that bondsmen generally don't give bail to those in the Merchant Marine. I vaguely recall Jimmy in the pilothouse of the *Mercury* bragging about never having to answer a drunken driving charge in Michigan as long as he stays out on the lakes.

With the bond arranged, I am back on the streets of Detroit, and a couple of bus rides bring me near home. I retrieve my car and head home to lick my wounds, waiting for the next round.

A couple nights later I am the toast of the Bronx as I relate my encounter with the pigs to the wonderment of my peers. Dick, one of the co-teachers of the class, mentions that he has space in his apartment and I make the move to campus. Symbolically, I leave the vehicle of my problems in the garage along with the motorcycle. I forget about my troubles in that world and immerse myself in the good life of Wayne State University. And the world opens itself up to me in ways that I never imagined. My confreres of the backpacking group adopt me as a new family member. I am soon absorbed in helping to liberate the middle rails of the wooden fence at Louis Stone Park for the walls of the new sauna under construction in the basement of 904. Then the cross-country skis come in, packed in huge wooden crates. The story is that they were made for U.S. Army troops' use in the Alps in their anti-Nazi efforts. We set to work under Paul's direction fitting the bindings.

When I'm not totally dedicated at 904, I partake of the good life of the campus, including art galleries, poetry readings, film screenings, and concerts within easy walking distance. I become a habitue of the Bronx, no longer worried about having to drive home after closing the place. Often enough, after closing the bar, we go to Tom the bouncer's place to drink some more and continue the high philosophical discussions that have been meandering along for hours. These sessions include people like Harvey, the disgraced Yale prof, and Carlyle, who carries all his poetry around in a shopping bag, not to mention Tabu, the snake fetishist. On Sunday afternoons we pile into cars and head out to the country for long strolls in the woods before heading back for a Bronxburger. When the snow finally falls, we pack the skis along and learn cross-country skiing the hardest way imaginable, with lots of falls and broken poles and bindings.

CHAPTER 11

1971

The Last Trip up the Lakes

A ray of sunshine enters my life a few weeks later when Dick asks if I can help him out as a bar boy at a Saturday night bash at the Engineering Society of Detroit on Warren. I report for duty and am given a red-patterned vest and put to work setting up bars around the three-floor facility. The rest of the evening is spent hustling from one floor to the next, servicing the bartenders at the twelve bars, making sure that they have enough of everything to keep the hundreds of revelers reveling. Great work for a college boy, rolling gallons of liquor and kegs of beer up and down elevators, into chandeliered ballrooms, pausing every so often in the long corridors to sample the wares and help keep the sweat down to a torrent. We end up at the Bronx for last call, having had at least as much fun as the partygoers, who didn't even get paid for going. We are each $20 wealthier, which, in a world of $40 monthly rents, is pretty damn good.

As the winter wears on, I am called to work at the ESD, as we call it, more often, and eventually end up working as much as Dick. My Monteith studies have slowed to a crawl at this point as I am facing the reality of my senior essay—the last step between me and graduation. The essay is designed to be a yearlong effort and requires approval by a faculty adviser and a great deal of research. I am enjoying myself too much to take this final step toward graduation, noting that Monteith has plenty of students like Dick who are threatening to double the normal amount of years it takes to graduate. I think about my essay while taking a lot of humanities classes on subjects like Shakespeare and the Renaissance and weaving and ceramics, which I think I could do forever. I am also developing an interest in the world of ideas through poetry and am considering devoting a portion of my essay to the works and enigma of Wallace Stevens. I say that because I am thoroughly baffled at how an individual working for a major insurance company could at the same time be a poet. There is something that is basically strange about it that deserves closer inspection.

At the conclusion of winter term my court appearance for the fleeing and alluding charge approaches. I dutifully head downtown on the cold March morning with my parents and brother Larry in attendance. My lawyer now advises me to plead guilty to a charge that he has bargained down from a felony to a misdemeanor. I stand accused and cannot believe my ears when the judge still sentences me to two weeks in the Detroit House of Corrections and a $500 fine, as well as a year probation. Although the jail time will be suspended upon payment of the fine, I stand stunned, awaiting transfer to a detention cell, forlornly watching my parents watching me. I reemerge on the streets of downtown Detroit virtually broke and some the worse for the wear to discover a blustery spring afternoon. I am a little cheered to see a ship steaming upbound on the river. But the following weeks are difficult for me as I struggle to deal with a sense of enveloping depression. I am confused and full of dread at what I have done to my life. I ask myself whether I should see a psychiatrist to help answer the big Why. But the feeling of residual anger in my breast forces me to forgo that option. There is a part of me that knows rage and understands its potentially limitless consequences. It is something that I am loathe to explore too deeply, afraid of what I will discover.

So, in lieu of analysis, I allow life to go on. The job at the Engineering Society develops into an everyday gig cutting grass and doing general landscaping with bar boy duties on the weekends. Dick has quit the place and vacated the apartment to head out west with a girl. While one of the terms of the sentence has placed me on one-year probation with no driving, I am fortunate enough to have friends with cars. In a class on the history of jazz, I meet Marshall, who introduces me to Sue. The three of us start going to jazz clubs around the city to catch some of the amazing people coming through Detroit and from the city itself. Yusef Lateef, Rahsaan Roland Kirk, and Archie Shepp are a few of the cats we catch at little clubs here and there. Another class I am taking focuses on urban culture. I have decided to write on the types of bars in Detroit but am hampered by lack of transportation. This need fortifies my shy character. One night at the ESD I am introduced to a brown-eyed girl named Janet who is sent to help inventory the liquor supply at the end of a party. She is so beautiful I am speechless and can only stand and stare at her from across the room. Later that night, as we close up the place and have a beer, I work up the courage to tell her about my project to study the bars of Detroit. To my eternal amazement, she agrees to take me to these places in her little black Corvair.

These friends, classes, and experiences help me to weather the disturbances that make me wonder if I need some help to get me through this life. Spring continues to blossom and my dark thoughts slowly dissipate with the first soft warm breezes that carry the scent of the river to the air I breathe. I thrive on my studies and enjoy my early-morning gardening and late-night bar research with Janet. I discover myself alive and okay and, with the coming of summer, hope for the best. This mood culminates in a June morning, shortly after classes have ended, when I answer the phone in the basement of my parents' home. On the other end is a woman who represents herself as part of the Selective Service. She says:

"We are calling to inform you to report to headquarters next Tuesday for induction into the United States Armed Forces."

After a few moments of silence, I ask, "Do I have to come if I'm on probation?"

A pause. "You're on probation?" Another pause. "How long?"

"For another year."

"No, you don't have to bother coming. We don't want you. Guess this is your lucky day. Bye."

I stand in the basement, phone in my hand, as the truth slowly bursts like a rocket in slow motion through my being. I replace the receiver, wondering if I heard the woman right, and become a little convinced that maybe there was method in my madness after all. I am free of the dreaded draft that has haunted me since the day I turned eighteen. Free of the bloody army and death in 'Nam. I think back to my buddy Sam telling me about his cousin Caesar, who was rejected for similar reasons when he tried to join. I wonder now if I never entirely forgot that story and that I have lived it in order to avoid the slaughterhouse in Asia. In my euphoria, I don't forget my pledge to join the Peace Corps if I'm not drafted. Even though I could cop out on a technicality, I feel obliged now to follow through.

My work at the ESD has allowed me to finish the quarter without being in dire need of money. I travel with Marshall and his girlfriend, Karen, to the Porcupine Mountains, where we try out our backpacking skills for a week among the blackflies on the shores of Superior. The rest of the summer moves mellowly along, with many hitchhiking excursions to the Upper Peninsula that culminate in a bicycle journey from Marquette to my brother Walt's in Madison on a beautiful Schwinn ten-speed I purchased from a high school buddy for $30. From Madison I pedal down to Milwaukee, where I catch a midnight car ferry across the lake to Ludington and continue pedaling the slow back roads home. Between backpacking and biking, I am discovering a freedom and peace of mind that was always somewhere ahead of me in the TR4 or on the motorcycle.

My periodic returns to Detroit are laced with wild parties on campus and the east side. The swirl of parties quickly yields to a hunger for the solitude of the Upper Peninsula and the quiet of my brother's farm. Generally, I last no longer than a week at a time in the city before I'm on the road north again.

The summer comes to a perfect head when Marshal, Peter, and I travel to Isle Royale in the sweetness of early September. With overflowing backpacks, we travel the trails, eating rice and lentils and trail mix, for ten blessed days. We spot moose and loons and stumble through swamps and enchanted forests. When we get back to civilization in Hancock we head to the Library Bar to scarf chili and burgers and beer before heading back to rendezvous with my brother near Marquette. This experience makes for a near-perfect summer and I emerge on the first day of fall feeling whole once again.

CHAPTER 12

Steamboat VIII

Laying Up the SS *Champlain*

As fall eclipses summer, I recollect that I have yet to complete my senior essay to graduate from Monteith. Although I have completed all the course work, I am left with this trifling thing that has created an unwashed horde of seventh- and eighth-year Monteith under-grads. I am a bit forlorn to discover that the summer parties have once again given way to dreary life in the city. Janet has fallen from the face of the earth and my other friends are all back into the college thing. This feeling, accompanied by a growing need for money, compels me to telephone the Steelworkers' Hall in Toledo one late October morning. Within three days I am driving with my friends Louie and his wife, Joan, down to the foot of West Grand Boulevard. My army issue duffel is full and I am ready to board the *Westcott* that will carry me to the Cleveland Cliffs steamer *Champlain*.

The sky is bright and the river full of friskiness as the tiny mail boat chops and plows through whitecaps and wake to the side of the giant steamer. The climb up the ladder is long onto the empty upbound ship, at least fifteen feet higher than she would be when full. Seconds after I hit the deck, the first mate shakes my hand and intro-duces himself as Al Flood. Although it is midafternoon, he wants to know if I want to get a day's work in. My eagerness to make a buck has me in foul-weather gear, helping the deckwatch hose down the bottom of the first hold before the ship has even passed Belle Isle. Our task is to clean out the remnants of a shipment of taconite pel-lets in preparation for a load of wheat. This will be the first cargo of grain that I will have assisted in carrying and I am surprised to learn that ships that carry loads of ore would even be considered as food

The *Champlain* under way (Dossin Great Lakes Museum)

haulers. The government apparently shares my concern, as the cleaning of the holds is a long and arduous one.

During a quick supper break I meet the other two deckhands and am pleased to find them both of my age. The *Champlain* also offers my first experience at having a berth in the bow of the ship along with the rest of the deck crew. We three deckhands share a spacious room located about fifteen feet above the waterline just off the port bow. A cabin in the bow. After seven ships, my bunk is finally removed from the ever-present thumping and throbbing of the ship's engine. When I finally collapse into my lower bunk sometime after midnight, I am lulled to sleep by the sound of rippling water against the hull as the *Champlain* leaves the St. Clair River for Lake Huron.

I encounter no difficulties in readjusting to shipboard life. My roommates share my madness at being cast afloat in an insane, uncaring world. Jim is a native Kentuckian who has been aboard much of the season. He wears his straight brown hair shoulder length and is

SS *Champlain*

Built	1942
Builder	American Shipbuilding Company, Cleveland, Ohio
Names	*Belle Isle* (1942); *Champlain* 1943
Owner	U.S. Maritime Commission (1942); Cleveland-Cliffs Iron Company(1943)
Length	620'
Beam	60'2"
Draft	35'
Engine	Lentz-Poppet double compound steam
Boilers	Two oil-fired
Capacity	15,825 tons dwt
Cargo	Iron ore; taconite; grain
Crew	30

interested in the season ending sooner than it will. Kim is just eighteen and has been on the *Champlain*, his first ship, for just over a week. He has curly blond hair and can't wait to get off and back to his girlfriend, who has given him something he has desperately longed for. As the cold air precludes late-night deck lounging, we spend much of our free evenings in our comfortable three-bunk room, talking about the lives we've left behind. Jim explains that he's here to earn enough money to buy a piece of property in West Virginia, build a cabin on it, and retire from the world. Kim is here because his girlfriend's parents have threatened to murder him if they catch him around her again. When my turn comes I answer that I am out here because of a woman. They nod sagely.

It turns out that my fellow deckhands also share a predilection for beer, which helps make our evening sessions become meaningful events as we sail across uncharted seas, oblivious to the cold deep surrounding us. Charlie, a young deck watch from Ecorse, joins us on our forays as we sail away on the night *Champlain*.

As the ship works her way up to Superior, I get to know the rest of the crew. The forward-end bunch is a generally pleasant group,

265

highlighted by watchmen Buck and Early. Buck is a burly Georgian who lives in his white coveralls with the Cleveland Cliffs name embossed in red letters across the top left pocket. He has a penchant for chewing tobacco and sipping sour mash bourbon and is ready to laugh at just about anything and anyone. He has taken to riding young Kim with the curly locks by calling him "Kim-ber-ly." Yet he manages to do it in such a way that even Kim can't help but laugh along. On one storm-tossed eve, Buck staggers uninvited into our quarters and, noticing a picture of Popeye on the wall, exclaims, "Popeye! . . . Is that Popeye? I heard he wuz a queer." Then he stumbles out of the room on his merry rounds of the ship's company. On another eve, he mesmerizes us with a vivid detailed description of his intimate knowledge of sheep and swine. "You get your rubber boots on, set yourself good into the ground, and push the pig toward the creek and it backs up right to you. Whooooe!"

Early, Buck's roommate, is downright dim by contrast and therefore an interesting study. He is a small, soft-spoken man who seems to shave about once a week. His quiet and amiable personality blends easily into the plasterboard woodwork of our cabin. But he is way too quiet. It isn't long before we have declared him certifiably insane and therefore a minor star in the rotating cast of our favorite deranged shipboard characters.

The *Champlain* measures 620 feet in overall length and is a pleasant working ship. She was built in Cleveland by American Shipbuilding in 1942 as one of sixteen Maritime-class ships for the war effort. Even at that age, she is among the newer ships in the Cliffs fleet. Her sister, built to the same dimensions the same year at the Rouge by Great Lakes Engineering, is the *Cadillac*. The primary difference between the two, aside from slightly different stacks and fantails, is the engine. The *Cadillac* is powered by my favorite triple expansion that provides for lots of excitement in the engine room, while the *Champlain* has a slightly less dynamic Lentz-Poppet double compound. That engine, while similar to the triple expansion, simply doesn't provide the overall mesmerizing effect.

Also built by Great Lakes in Ecorse in 1917 is the oldest ship in the fleet, the *Pontiac*. It boasts a whistle that is distinctive among all ships on the lakes. The *Frontenac* and the *William Mather*, built at the Great Lakes Engineering River Rouge yards in 1923 and 1925, respectively, round out the younger siblings of the *Champlain* and don't travel in our circles.

Although technically constructed in 1942, the *Walter Sterling* was given its name when it was lengthened to 730 feet in 1961 and joined the fleet. The *Sterling*, because of its capacity and size, is considered by many to be the unofficial flagship of the Cliffs line. Then there is the *Cliffs Victory*. The *Victory* is unique among Great Lakes ships and is always a favorite to watch en passant. Built in 1945 in Portland, Oregon, as a Victory-class ship, the *Cliffs Victory* joined the fleet in 1951 when she was towed up the Mississippi and entered the Great Lakes through the back door in Chicago. Purchased to help meet demand for increased steel production during the Korean War, the *Victory* proved such a fast ship that the company lengthened her in 1957. But they didn't do it by cutting out the midbody and adding to her in that mundane way. No, they decided to add footage to the after section of the *Victory*, thereby making her the only ship on the Great Lakes with hatches behind her stern section and thus recognizable from many miles away. But, in addition to her unique design, the *Victory* is noted for her speed as the fastest ship on the Great Lakes.

Rounding out the fleet is the *Edward B. Greene*, built by American Shipbuilding in 1952 in Toledo. Although the newest built, the *Greene* is shorter than both the *Sterling* and the *Victory*. Nevertheless, the *Greene* is a handsome vessel and the official flagship—a fitting complement to what is considered to be the strongest fleet of ships on the Great Lakes. The Cleveland-Cliffs Iron Company goes back to the nineteenth century and the beginnings of the industry in the lakes area. The name identifies the connection between the cliffs of the iron ore mines of the north country and the home of the blast furnaces that line the shores of the southern lakes. The company takes great pride in its ships and their appearances along the lakes. Every ship is recognizable by its black hull and lime cabin-deck coloring. If that isn't enough, the name Cleveland-Cliffs is emblazoned in ten-foot-high letters along the length of each and every hull. The black smokestacks sport a large red "C" that is floodlit at night. Also, when the whistle blows in the dark, the light on the forward mast above the pilothouse illuminates a white "C" in a diamond to let the other ship know who's coming at them. Cliffs is not a shabby outfit, I realize, as the first mate presents me with my own set of white coveralls emblazoned with the company's name even at this late date in the season.

The *Champlain* at ore docks in Lake Superior (Author's collection)

Through the month of November, the *Champlain* takes us to Superior for grain, Duluth for taconite, and Escanaba for red ore. We take the grain to Buffalo and the iron ore to Cleveland or Detroit.

While I am very familiar with the iron ore end of the business, I find the grain shipments to be a great diversion from the ordinary. After having the holds pass an inspection by the U.S. Department of Agriculture in order to handle food, the *Champlain* ties up at the huge grain elevators in Superior to take on her load. Instead of railroad cars and chutes, there is a long cylinder that descends from the elevator directly into the ship's hold. The cylinders are attached to each elevator, so the ship doesn't need to shift up and down the dock, resulting in less work for us deckhands. Grain, being much lighter than iron ore, allows us to fill to the tops of the holds. To compensate for the reduced work in shifting, it is necessary to wrap and secure a tarp around each of the eighteen hatches to make them watertight. No mixing of liquids with grains. Bad combination until you're ready to eat. On the lower lakes, when we tie up at the Pillsbury elevator in Buffalo, the operation is reversed. The tarps and hatches are taken off one at a time as security against rain, a cylinder is lowered from a dockside silo, and the grain company workers handle the offloading. The *Champlain* deck crew is not involved and is on hand only to uncover and cover hatches. Standing on deck, looking into the hold, I notice a lot of water stains on the inside walls. I ask Buck, who confirms with a juicy chortle that those guys don't get potty breaks and, when they have to go, they do. Of course Buck does everything to imply that these guys'll do both numbers down there and, by the way, what's my favorite cereal? Where are the inspectors now, I wonder.

For us deckhands who have to be around the ship for various tasks during loading, it is hardly worth our while to go up the street during the limited time afforded us in the upper lake ports. We discover that greater opportunities are available in the unloading ports of Cleveland or Buffalo, where the ship is stationary at the dock and our workload is reduced. Yet, since I have turned twenty-one, I find myself less drawn to those pursuits, more content to stay aboard and immerse myself in reading and writing and sleeping in the cozy cabin rather than wandering from bar to bar along the mean November downtown streets of those cities. So I compromise, especially in Buffalo, where young Kim can legally join us. We head to a bar just off one of the campuses where the clientele is more our age, have a few beers, shoot some pool, and head back to the ship around ten for some winding down before some reading and pleasant dreams. This formula works well for me. I am rested and hangover-free to enjoy the next day.

Instead of working on my senior essay for Monteith, I decide to keep track of life aboard the *Champlain* for an article I will submit to *Telescope* magazine. Most of the crew are aware of this, and many go out of their way to offer helpful advice. The second mate, a young guy also named Al, provides me with old photos and information about the ship and her cargoes. He is the first to inform me that the *Champlain* almost split in two while being built in the Cleveland shipyard for the war effort in 1943. He shows me a picture of the side of the ship with a large crack running from top to bottom, enough to make me wonder about the seaworthiness of these ships I have been blithely sailing aboard for the past five seasons. His love of ships and steamboating has led him to a career on the lakes, while my romance seems to be cooling with the season. As the end of the season comes into sight and is part of the crew's everyday conversation, I commiserate with my roommate, Jim, who hopes for an early lay-up so that he can return to his old Kentucky home.

I retreat to the lifeboat deck one cold, but still, night, beer in hand. I sip the brew and watch as the *Champlain* glides by Bob-Lo Island. Except for the hiss of steam escaping the whistle on the smoke-stack, all is silent and dark. I can barely make out the silhouettes of the rides, and the monstrous dance hall looms like some German cas-tle from the woods. Even the large sailors' monument appears ghostly in the gloom. I watch and reflect on all the years of my life that I played on that monument, walked through that dance hall, and rode those rides. And then my dream came true—I actually worked on the *Columbia* coming here to Bob-Lo three times a day. And I reflect on all the days that I have lived out that dream since the summer of 1967, and all I have been through. Yet the silent island gives me no solace on this chill November night. There is no life there and I am agitated at the thought of what has happened to my life since those careless days. Even though I am no longer draftable, the war in Asia is still a great monster looming out of a foreign and far darker place. Disconsolate, I throw my empty bottle toward the monument and head back toward the warmth and security of my cabin.

Part of my problem, I realize, is that my discomfort at being in any one place too long has followed me out onto the lakes. I am approaching a point in life that will be filled with great changes, and I am anxious to cast off the old trappings and seek the new. But my urge to move on from the *Champlain* is tempered significantly by the news that I will qualify for a 10 percent lay-up bonus if the season extends beyond December 15.

Thanksgiving Day blooms cool and grey as the *Champlain* enters the Detroit River from unloading in Cleveland. The deck watch, Charlie, provides our wake-up call by entering our cabin puff-ing on a cigarette that turns out to be a joint. He explains noncha-lantly that he is celebrating early. Of the eight ships I have worked on since 1967, the *Champlain* is the first on which I have witnessed the use of pot. This is not too surprising, as its use has become fairly ubiquitous ashore over that same period. As in the broader society, pot is pretty much in the domain of the younger crew members, and I never observe any of the crew from wheelsmen on up even being aware of it, let alone using the stuff.

While the rest of the crew are on duty to perform their watches and earning overtime, the deckhands, with no docking called for, receive the day off. As the ship steams past Detroit, I stand on deck in the frosty air, straining to hear music and see the tops of floats as the Thanksgiving Day parade moves down Woodward to Jefferson.

Shortly after noon, the captain assembles nonessential crew in the mess for a few words of thanks before we sit down to a sumptuous feast put together by the excellent galley crew, who have spent the better part of the night preparing for this moment. The menu is presented to us on fancy cover stock and features the names of the ship's crew on one side and the goodies on the other.

Even before this event, I have recognized the *Champlain*'s galley as one of the best I've ever seen on the lakes. I think the only galley that surpasses this is that of the *Columbia*, and she has the advantage of fresh stores every day. Moreover, I think the Cleveland Cliffs company is the best overall outfit I've worked for out here. In general, we are treated well and with consideration. Although I have a run-in with Ed, the third mate, who wants me to lift a heavy metal grocery basket by myself against all safety regulations, I find the mates are a fair bunch of guys. The captain, John Johnson, knows how to keep his distance and let the crew run the ship. While it's not all fun and games, the attitude of the crew is quite positive, especially this late in the year.

My friendship with Al, the second mate, grows and he often will call me up to the pilothouse to share in the magic of sailing. One Sunday afternoon as the *Champlain* is laboring through a storm on Superior, Al sends word down to me to come up to the pilothouse. When I get there he is beaming. Pointing toward the shore, he says, "See that? Know what that is?" I hazard a guess that it's probably the Keweenaw Peninsula of the Michigan shoreline.

He nods in agreement and then says, "And guess what? Because of the weather, the captain has agreed that we are going through the Keweenaw Passage. Ships never do that anymore!" he laughs. So the rest of the afternoon I hang around the pilothouse as the *Champlain* negotiates the passage, snapping pictures with Jim's camera. Although the day is storm-struck and gloomy and the pictures probably won't show much more than land and water, I am thrilled to be recording Great Lakes history.

But as the leaden days of late fall become more immersed in darkness, the deckhands are sorely tested and found wanting. Kim is the first to take the plunge, choosing to risk parental wrath for the certainty of a girl's warm body. Jim and I, jealous and hurting, gnaw away at each other. When he learns that another trip has been added

Thanksgiving Day

Aboard The
STEAMER CHAMPLAIN

November 25, 1971

"Thanksgiving aboard the Steamer *Champlain*," cover of day's bill of fare, November 25, 1971 (Author's collection)

STEAMER CHAMPLAIN

DECK OFFICERS
JOHN JOHNSON—
  Captain
ALLEN GLANTZ—
  First Mate
ALLEN FLOOD—
  Second Mate
EDWARD GALLAGHER—
  Third Mate

ENGINEERS
D. E. HOLLISTER—
  Chief Engineer
ART WALROOS—
  First Asst.
VICTOR SCHWARTZKOPF—
  Second Asst.
MICHAEL MUCINO—
  Third Asst.
EDWARD FAJTAK—
  Third Asst.

MELVIN OLSON—
  Steward

UNLICENSED SEAMEN

DECK DEPARTMENT
JUD BRASWELL
GERALD PALESOTTI
DONALD MORROW
LARRY NEECE
ERVIN EARLEY
JAMES F. SMITH
DONALD SHATTUCK
DAVID MARSHALL
CHARLESE MC INTYRE
JAMES E. ROGERS
KIM W. SHORT
PATRICK LIVINGSTON

ENGINE DEPARTMENT
GERALD MC DONALD
ROBERT BONDY
WILLIAM RUDDER
HARLEY SKIFF
JOHN T. HAYES

STEWARDS DEPARTMENT
CLARENCE DEN HOUTER
HOMER YATES
HARRISON MC CABE

**THE STEWARDS DEPARTMENT WISHES
ALL A HAPPY THANKSGIVING**

THANKSGIVING DAY - - - NOVEMBER 25, 1971

Aboard

STEAMER CHAMPLAIN

MENU

Shrimp Cocktail

Roast Turkey   Chicken

Ham   Duck

Giblet Gravy   Mashed Potatoes

Squash   Peas   Corn

Stuffed Celery   Cranberry Sauce   Olives and Pickles

Apple Pie with Ice Cream   Pumpkin Pie with Whipped Cream

Mince Meat Pie   Plum Pudding

Assorted Fig Tray   Chocolate Candy

Hard Candy   Mixed Nuts

Fruits   Cake   Fruit Cake

Gum   Cigarettes   Cigars

After Dinner Mints

Coffee   Tea   Milk   Beverages

THE CLEVELAND-CLIFFS IRON COMPANY

Thanksgiving menu (Author's collection)

to the *Champlain*'s season, he flies into a rage and storms down the deck as the ship is being unloaded in Buffalo. In his anger, he brushes past the captain and mate conferring on the deck, almost knocking the old man into the hold in his zeal to get off the ship. Later that night, as the *Champlain* prepares to batten down her hatches for another northern trip, I catch up with him in a dockside bar and convince him to weather just one more trip, that we can do it.

Late that night, while standing on deck, holding a rubber tire to cushion the ship against contact with the concrete walls that line the river, I hear the most melodious ship's whistle I have ever heard. Al pokes his head out of the pilothouse, exultant, and yells down, "Did you hear that?" That's the *Sidney Smith Jr.* coming this way. I'll try to get her to salute us. She'll pass us at this bend coming up when we tie up." I am as excited as Al to watch the old steamer creep up out of the mist of the river toward the *Champlain* and am downright thrilled to hear the triple chimes answer Al's salute at 3 AM.

Before turning in an hour later, I decide that I will record the events of this last trip of the season as it unfolds.

Buffalo: Thursday, December 9: The hour is approaching 2300 and the SS *Champlain* is once again preparing to sail, her cargo holds free of the iron ore she has delivered from Superior. The night is relatively mild, although overcast, and the threat of rain mirrors the mood of much of the crew who have just learned that their next destination is not the lay-up dock in Toledo as had been rumored, but to Escanaba on Lake Michigan for another load of taconite that will bring us back here.

The three deckhands are dispatched to cast off the cables that marry the ship to the dock. At a signal from the mate, the cables are slackened and, after we wrestle them from their bollards, we are left to race for a ladder hanging over the side that is our one remaining link to the eleven thousand hulking tons of steel that has become home.

The deckhands have been working off and on all day and evening and much of the deck paraphernalia has already been secured. The eighteen hatch covers are replaced over the holds and secured by the fifty-six clamps on each hatch. Our duty is now to stand by amidships with tires suspended by lines to cushion the ship against inadvertent contact with the concrete banks as the *Champlain* negotiates her way through a narrow bridge-opening that separates us from the harbor.

We wait patiently as a tug nudges into our stern to guide us through and turn us so that our bow is pointed toward Lake Erie. All that remains for us to do is secure the tow line in the aft deck locker and lash the shore ladder to its rack on the boat deck.

As the 2500 double-compound reciprocating engines power the *Champlain* at thirteen miles an hour into the inky darkness of the lake, the deckhands are knocked off for sleep. We nod off knowing full well that the morning will bring us the task of hosing down the deck to rid it of iron ore remnants and cleaning it for the next load.

This is the life of a deckhand on the Great Lakes, an existence often encapsulated in one frustrating hour, say 0300, when he must stumble out of a too-comfortable bunk to battle a blizzard and the hundreds of clamps that must be wrenched off one at a time so that the ship may be loaded. At other times, however, the deckhand's lot is relieved considerably by a rare awareness of the beauty of a Lake Superior sunset or the awesomeness of the Keweenaw Peninsula. Waves lashing against the bow induce excellent dreams and, at these times, majesty is in the deckhand's back pocket. Years ago, around the age of ten, one of my chief preoccupations was to gaze at the steam-boats rounding Belle Isle and to fantasize them as valiant guardians of a glamorous era past when ships were the principal communica-tors that linked different modes of thought and life about the earth. Since I have begun gazing at Belle Isle from their steel decks, I have discovered that these steamboats have lost much of their allure.

Back on deck the next morning, we discover that the quantity of ore spilled is moderate and the watchman, deck watch, and deck-hands have the deck hosed down by noon, in time for dinner. The day is far from complete, unfortunately, as the deckhands, although on twenty-four-hour call, generally work a straight eight-hour day. The rest of the crew are on established watches of four hours on, eight hours off. After dinner, with the help of a different watchman and deck watch, we begin hauling three dead cables, each four hundred feet in length, from the boat deck aft to a space between two hatches midships. Although difficult and wearisome, this task is tempered by the knowledge that these cables will be employed a week hence at lay-up. At 1630, our services rendered for the day, we are released to supper and a return to the room that the three of us share.

Evenings on the lakes or rivers are free time for the deckhand. He can do whatever his interests dictate although the usual pattern

Hosing down the deck (Author's collection)

is to read, talk, or watch TV in the rec room, listen to the radio, wash clothes, or take a walk back to the galley. Of course, the most popular diversions seem to be playing poker, tipping a few beers, and sleeping. Since the deckhands occupy relatively spacious quarters, it is often our office to entertain whoever elects to drop by on any given evening. It is essential to keep one's mind in some semblance of working order out here, so I usually anticipate the conversations, arguments, and head games that comprise these floating soirees.

On this particular evening, I am still a bit stunned that the *Champlain* is embarking on another trip this late in December. This will extend our season by one week, a short period of time unless you were expecting to be home a week sooner. Anticipation is a way of life for sailors, and seven unplanned-for days can be a burden on the mind, which must now work overtime to employ this void gainfully. The challenge is to make the hours pass as painlessly as possible. I decide to sleep on it.

Friday, December 10: The deckhands are awakened at 0700, the usual time, by the deck watch. We troop back to the galley for breakfast and prepare for work at 0800. Since the weather is warm but wet, our jobs are trivial inside chores, such as scrubbing down bulkheads and mopping inside passages. No painting remains to be done this late in the season so our work is of the "keep busy" nature. In the meantime, the *Champlain* is passing Detroit and Belle Isle, affording some relief from the endless stretch of water encountered on the open lake. Simply viewing familiar terrain gives me strength.

Dinner comes and goes and the day becomes warmer and stormier. We stop at Sarnia at 1400 for fuel and, although every other ship in the river has gone to anchor rather than risk the wrath of Lake Huron on this day, Stormin' John Johnson, our captain, elects to challenge the elements once more. He orders more water in the ballast tanks and everything on the ship battened down and secured, and moments later we are on the lake. Beyond supper, in the darkness of 1800, the *Champlain* is rolling with the edges of a gale that intensifies as we press on. The evening is passed tensely and climaxes when we hit the Saginaw Bay around 2200. I hunker down in my bunk with a book, trying not to think about the *Daniel Morrell* that met her fate a few years before at this very spot.

Saturday, December 11: The storm is still raging at 0700 when I rise and, as the waves have made the deck impassable, take the tunnel back aft for breakfast. The tunnel is dimly lit, dank and silent. As we walk through, we are very aware that the reason that we can't feel the waves is that we are beneath the waterline. The storm has caused the *Champlain* to lose much time and the Mackinac Bridge does not come into sight until noon, a good four hours behind schedule. Our afternoon is filled with menial, meaningless chores, although near the end of the shift the waves subside enough to allow us to drag out four more of the long cables for lay-up. The remainder of the day is spent watching the storm, reading, or talking. We hear that the *Champlain* will go to anchor in Escanaba Harbor around midnight because another ship will beat us to the dock. This means that we may not begin to load until as late as eight o'clock Sunday morning. There is considerable grumbling and muttering among the forward-end crew related to time. We are all now acutely aware that the sooner the *Champlain* completes this trip, the sooner she will reach lay-up, releasing us to our respective homes.

There are, however, a considerable number of men aboard, mostly from the engine department, who express some consternation at the prospect of lay-up. When steamboating becomes a way of life for a man, he requires nothing else. It is with some degree of seriousness that a Great Lakes freighter is referred to as a "steel womb." There is often friction in the crew's mess when one of the "lifers" will taunt one of the deckhands or some other nonprofessional with eulogies of the sailing life and its obvious advantages over life "on the beach." At times like this, I can only scowl and count the days until I can once again join the ranks of the living on solid ground. I am not a steamboater.

Lake Michigan proves equal to Lake Huron in its tempestuousness. By now, we have adapted to the rolling of the ship that has continued pretty much nonstop since we entered Lake Huron. But the occasional big breaker smashing over the bow will shake the vessel and jar us out of our complacency. To take our minds away from the potentially ship-cracking "sickening thud" that signals disaster, I look forward to watching the movie *The Big Country* that the ship's antenna is able to pick up from Escanaba's TV transmitter. Although the wind plays havoc with the reception, the story softens the blows against the hull and our psyches.

Sunday, December 12: Surprised once again. I turn in at 2300, expecting a full night's sleep with the ship safely at anchor in Escanaba's Little Bay de Noc. Abruptly at 0030, the deck watch raises us with the news that we are going into the dock now and our services are requested. The night is cold and evil looking and my head is still in my bunk when I reach the deck. Lines and cables must be prepared, the ladder readied on the boat deck aft, and the landing boom, our ride to the dock, swung out. At 0115, the ship is docked, held fast by six winch-controlled cables. The deckhands immediately climb the ladder back onto the deck, where the hatch covers need to be unclamped and removed, the grocery hoist rigged on the fantail, and one cable repositioned before we are knocked off at 0330. By this time, I am fully awake and enjoying the star display on this crisp, clean northern night. We return to our bunks, where we are allowed to sleep until the third mate wakes us at 1000 for more work.

To our surprise when we hit the deck, the *Champlain* is well on her way to being loaded on this brilliant but freezing Sunday. We go right to work replacing hatches and clamping them onto the hold covers. At about 1230, two deckhands are dispatched to the dock to

The *Champlain* loading in Escanaba (Author's collection)

cast off the lines. This accomplished, we are once again heading into
Lake Michigan. The smooth lake today is no kin to that rocking and
rolling mass of motion that we crossed last evening. The sun is warm
and the work on deck is quite pleasant as the steamboat wends her
way through the scenic St. Martins Island passage of the Green Bay
toward the Mackinac Bridge some twelve hours ahead. The deckhands remain on duty until all deck apparatus is secured and then we
drag out the hoses to clean the forward and after cabins of taconite
dust. Then the hoses are turned on the port and starboard walkways.
Although the water streaming from the hose is hot, it freezes almost
instantly. Only nonskid paint saves the deck from becoming treach-
erously icy. At 1730, we abandon that hopeless task and are knocked
off for the second time this day. I return to the room for some reading and writing while the other guys join the off-duty crew at the TV
for the remainder of another big football Sunday. Exercise and a
shower are next on my agenda as I slowly, deliberately exult in the
realization that we are en route to our last port before lay-up.

Monday, December 13: Another big day as the *Champlain* surges across
a relatively calm Lake Huron. The 0700 call is followed by breakfast

and the work entails scrubbing down bulkheads until it's warm enough to finish the hosing down of the decks begun yesterday. The day is frigid but tempered by a late fall sun trying to nurse us back from freezing. By afternoon, the captain decides that the day is warm enough and we throw on the foul-weather gear and lug out the hoses. We spend the next five hours battling piles of frozen taconite dust and a bitter wind that combines with high humidity to chill us to our souls. We knock off for the day in time for supper at 1745. The air is clear and we are close enough to pick up radio and TV from Detroit for our evening's entertainment. While there are crew TV's on both ends of the ship, the after-end set is located in the galley, which makes it much more the social center. Besides the three squares a day provided by the four-man galley crew, there is an endless supply of snacks and refreshments for sustenance at the in-between times. Immediate security is the least of one's concerns on a steamboat. There are those professional seamen who would prefer to sail year-round rather than be forced to fend for themselves over the harsh winter months. The Great Lakes have been referred to as a rest home for old sailors by more than a few of the saltwater brethren I have encountered. These fellows slyly insinuate or boldly proclaim, depending on how much they've drunk, that, once a saltwater seaman has tired of the adventures of the high seas, he retires to the restful confines of the Great Lakes. I have myself seen little to counter this theory and am sometimes honestly frightened by the prospect that I, too, could find relative happiness and a lot of security out here until retirement or until the Coast Guard carries me off on a stretcher. As young Kim remarked before jumping ship to chase after his girlfriend, "I have to get off. If I stay any longer, I might get to like it and not mind spending the rest of my life out here." Work is rarely strenuous physically or mentally for the sailor who has graduated from the deckhand stage on deck or the wiper stage of the engine room. Although the galley department's work is the lightest physically, the greatest amount of anxiety is theirs in trying to keep the crew satisfied both food and morale wise. If a man can convince himself that he does not need cars, cities, hordes of people, honest work, or life as most individuals know it, the Great Lakes is a superb refuge. There are thousands of seamen who will testify that life "isn't all that bad" because they have already accepted this excuse for existence.

On the other hand, the sun went down through a powder blue sky and burst into brilliance as it set over the Michigan shoreline above Port Huron. We are exiting the upper lakes for the final time this season and we go on with our lives.

Tuesday, December 14: 0700 call followed by breakfast followed by work at 0800. Preparations for lay-up are intensifying: the fire hoses are drained and stowed away; the life boat covers are readied back aft; three more cables are dragged out from the lower dunnage rooms two decks below the main deck. It is a real team effort to bring that dead weight up two flights. Since our ETA in Buffalo is 2000, the deckhands are knocked off after dinner to rest for what could be a long night ahead. Because the *Champlain* has to travel a few miles up Buffalo Creek and because the tugs navigate only during daylight hours this time of year, the possibility exists that we may go to anchor in the harbor for the night. The afternoon is filled with gossip and concern about this new factor and its effects on our approaching lay-up. The weather turns cold, grey, and snowy to match our mood.

At 1930, the decision is made that Buffalo Creek cannot be navigated without a tug. The anchor rumbles down the hull and our lay-up is postponed for another night. The forward end crew is somber. Time is tension.

Wednesday, December 15: At 0800 a tug takes our line and begins a five-hour tow up Buffalo Creek, passing at least two dozen ships already laid up. Along the way, the deckhands alternately remove hatches and stand along the side at tight turns with tires in hand to cushion the ship's sides from scraping the concrete walls. We reach the Republic Steel dock at 1300 and, after a wind-delayed tying up procedure, the deckhands are knocked off on the condition that we report back by ten o'clock.

The wind has brought unseasonably warm temperatures and the bars of Chippewa Street are only a taxi ride away. We spend the remainder of the afternoon and early evening going from one place to another up and down the street, enjoying the warm winds and a few cold ones. Although the crew as a whole are not a going-up-the-street bunch, we young deckhands try to uphold the public's expectation of the rapaciousness associated with our lot. Chippewa Street, in the heart of downtown, is notorious around the lakes for its grease and action. There are lots of bouncing lights, bouncing boob-filled go-go joints, and bouncers ready to give you the heave-ho back onto the street. We are a peaceful bunch, in general, and are happy to pay a buck for a beer, a few laughs, and a look-see. As we wend our way back toward the steel mills and docks in the darkness of early evening, the bars descend into the hard-hat and working-class variety of gloomy gin mills full of male faces hardened and creased by life and labor. We quit the one closest to the Republic dock and climb the ladder soberly and steadily back onto the *Champlain* at the appointed 2200. Although we had anticipated the ship being close to unloaded at this point, those same winds that have brought warmth from the Gulf have delayed the Hullett unloaders. We go to our bunks without definite word of when the unloading will recommence.

Thursday, December 16: The winds persist through the night and our call to the deck doesn't come until 1000. And I am the only deckhand called at this time for light standby duties. I help take on a few groceries, aid the watchman in securing the welding machine, and sweep a few stray taconite pellets. At 1400 the cargo holds are near empty and ready to be swept out. Steel brooms are the tools and the remaining pellets and dust are accumulated in piles for the crane. This is time consuming. At 2100 we're working on the last of the four cargo holds, which will be hosed down as soon as they are free of the last remnants of the dust.

Around this time, I am feeling exhausted and dreading the long night of work ahead. Jim comes around and offers me a Dexedrine, which he assures will help me get through. I break a personal rule and accept. This changes everything. I become Superman on top of the world. I find myself just a split second away from having the answer to the riddle of life and the universe to boot, even before the question enters my mind. It is only when I begin my final descent into the hold well after midnight that I look down to see Jim at the bottom, glaring up ruefully while giving me the finger for no reason that I can figure. Except maybe the speed. Sensing a darker side to the drug, I make a point to avoid all contact with him. I have been fortunate all these years to avoid any physical confrontations on these ships, and now's not the time to start.

By midnight the holds are empty and the hoses are ready for the final cleanup. Because the mate anticipates another long day tomorrow, he knocks me off to get some rest. I take a warm shower and retire to my bunk, where sleep proves elusive. My mind is focused

281

more on the stories I have heard over the years related to the days before sailors became unionized. I remember Rodger D. Rodgers from the *Mercury* who told me that there was a time in the not-too-remote past that deckhands were paid a flat $72.50 per month and were expected to be on call twenty-four hours a day with no overtime benefits. Today, the union presence has altered the pay scale considerably and any work beyond eight hours in a day as well as Saturdays and Sundays counts as time and a half on an hourly scale.

The Lake Carriers Local 5000 of the United Steel Workers represents the Cleveland Cliffs fleet and the majority of iron ore carriers on the lakes, including the massive fifty-ship U.S. Steel Pittsburgh fleet. While the Lake Carriers Union is restricted to the Great Lakes, the other two unions, the National Maritime and the Seafarers International, represent several other Great Lakes fleets as well as national oceangoing fleets. Initiation fees range from $100 at Lake Carriers to $350 at SIU, supposedly reflecting the degree of security provided by the respective union. Lake Carriers offers nondiscriminatory employment and virtually anyone can sail their vessels. On the *Champlain*, Kim has been replaced by Donald, the first black I have sailed with since the *South American*. On the other hand, the SIU, with the exception of the *South American*, is notorious for their strong discouragement of blacks and rumor has it that their leadership has voted to also deny employment to long-hairs. I have heard shipmates boast to one another that they prefer shipping with the Arabs in the NMU to shipping with blacks in our union. In my bunk I ponder this and wonder how much a man will pay to escape the things he least understands and, consequently, most fears and hates.

I feel the Lake Carriers to be the most representative of the three unions I have sailed under over the past five years. The plight of the professional sailor is a key point of interest to the Lake Carriers leadership. An excerpt from the *Compass*, the union newsletter, documents this concern in a letter from a seaman to the editor:

> I would never accuse you of being naive, but perhaps like myself blissfully unaware of the general attitude towards seamen. Fortunately, this blissful state was suddenly and rudely dispelled when a young deckhand, fresh from upper-class suburbia, told me, "You guys out here are nothing but a bunch of mentally retarded morons without the nerve of a rabbit or the backbone of a snake."

The letter goes on to lament the misadventures of sailors in trying to establish credit with banks and trying to understand why their insurance was raised 25 percent simply on the basis of their being a sailor. The writer closes the letter with the question "Why?"

I myself ponder that question in my warm bunk as the wind blows and the Hulletts struggle to finish their work on the *Champlain*. I drift off to sleep only to be awakened at 0330 on Friday morning, December 17. I struggle through the darkness and the mammoth cobwebs in my head. At 0400, when I reach the deck, I am happy to see the hatches being replaced and clamped and the deck in the final stages of being hosed down. This and other preparing-to-leave-port tasks occupy me until 0900, when Donald and I are sent down to the dock to cast off the lines for the last time. The weather has turned and the day is cold with threat of snow as we wind our way with the assist of a tug down Buffalo Creek toward our newly assigned lay-up dock in Cleveland. By noon we have reached the breakwall and are headed into Lake Erie, impervious to an impendng gale and blizzard. We are on our way home.

Unfortunately, what should be a trip of less than eight hours turns into a trial for both ship and crew on the smallest and shallowest of the Great Lakes. Lake Erie on this afternoon lives up to her reputation as the most wicked of the lakes. With its shallow bottom, the waves build strangely and contrive to keep the *Champlain* off balance. A whipping snow squall forces us to get a canvas to place on the railing for visibility for the pilothouse crew. A group of us charge the railing en masse but within seconds my fingers are numb and I have trouble tying the simplest hitch. After several bone-chilling minutes, the task is done and we retreat inside, humbled by this small lake. The storm intensifies to the point where our cap, Stormin' John Johnson himself, retreats and takes the *Champlain* to shelter behind Long Point on the Canadian side of the lake. Here we sit out the night at anchor, listening to the howling wind while the steward complains of running out of stores to feed us. The fact that Cleveland sits a normally easy four-hour run across the lake does nothing to ease our mood.

Saturday, December 18: The storm shows no signs of abating as we sit and mope around through the long morning. The coast of Long Point is snow-covered and the deck of the *Champlain* has six inches of snow, making the trek back to breakfast an adventure with few takers. However, by afternoon, Captain Johnson decides to risk making the run in daylight rather than wait out another night. The *Champlain* heads back out into the storm-tossed lake with the pilothouse crew running by compass through the still blinding snow squall. Although the vast majority of ships have cleared the lakes and are already safely in their lay-up berths, the watchman Early is given the unpleasant task of standing on the bow, looking out for shadows of other ships while the *Champlain* dutifully blows her foghorn in the whiteout.

Although we cannot travel at full speed due to the visibility, the *Champlain* manages to make Cleveland harbor in the early evening hours. We are glad when the captain makes the call to go to anchor rather than risk trying to find a strange dock in the dark. We go to our bunks happy to be resting up for what we believe will be a full day of lay-up tomorrow.

Sunday, December 19: The *Champlain* waits for plenty of daylight before proceeding into the dock. Because there are company reps there to catch the lines, the deckhands are spared being lowered over in the boatswain's chair one last time.

With the ship tied up, we get to work. The most onerous tasks fall to the deckhands, of course. We climb the ladder down to the dock to receive the long-dead cables that will secure the ship through hell or high water. It is more than difficult to lug these things hundreds of feet along the crumbling dock and then to secure them over bollards. Each cable takes a major team effort to secure, and most of the day is spent getting all eight cables attached.

It is in the process of helping lower one of these monsters to the dock that I am called to the deck to lend a hand. It takes a file of men to lower the cable the forty-foot drop to the dock where Jim and Don are waiting to receive it. But, somewhere along the line, someone lets the cable get away and it begins whipping along the deck untended, scattering crew members in its path. But, in the instant it takes for me to see what is happening, the cable whips by my legs and attempts to catch my ankle and drag me over the side with it. When I get up from the deck where I have been knocked, a couple of guys are looking over with shock in their eyes to see if I'm OK. Even as I wave a hand to reassure them, I can feel the stab of pain in my ankle. To my astonishment, the first mate, whose job it is to make sure the operation is running safely, is not looking my way at all. He and several of the senior deck crew are gazing over the railing to determine if the cable can be salvaged. I make it to my feet and hobble along the deck. Other than the pain in the back of my foot that forces me to lean on a hatch, I'm fine. When the mate eventually notices, he asks me how it is. I tell him it hurts and I need to soak the foot in cold water. He reluctantly gives me the OK to go below and soak it. But there's something in the way he tells me he needs me back on the dock as soon as possible that sets a slow burner going in my mind. As I soak my foot in the cylinder of the ship's wringer-washing machine, I recall all of the shipboard insults, major and minor, I have had to take from these yo-yo's over the years. I calm myself with the awareness that I have been treated fairly for the most part and am further relieved that, aside from a large bump on the back of the ankle, there doesn't seem to be anything broken. After a half hour or so I squeeze my foot back into sock and boot and hobble back to the deck. For the rest of the day I pitch in with the tasks, taking care to keep well out of harm's way. The first mate seems to be too bent on accomplishing today's lay-up tasks to pay much attention to me. By sunset in late afternoon, the mate announces that the majority of the chores to secure the *Champlain* have been taken care of. He knocks the crew off, saying that he thinks tomorrow morning we should be in position to release most of the deck crew. I go to bed hurting and excited. Jim and I share plans for the morrow including travel plans and the first things we'll do when we get home. As always, I look forward to seeing my family and friends, especially during the holidays. I'm thrilled that I'll have a good paycheck to buy presents for friends and some good albums for myself.

Monday, December 20: The morning arrives grey and with the threat of snow. A typical last day of autumn around the Great Lakes. After breakfast, we are surprised to find that the mate doesn't have a whole lot for us to do, save for mundane tasks like lashing down the tarps over the holds and securing line in the rope locker deep in the forward hull that reeks of sweet tar pitch. We lower bags of refuse over the side and, shortly before dinner, he tells us to report to his cabin so that he can sign our certificates and pay us off. We line up like schoolboys going on holiday to receive the documents signed by the captain attesting to our length of service given to the U.S. Merchant Marine aboard the *Champlain*. Captain John Johnson is on hand and

The Cleveland-Cliffs Iron Company
MARINE DEPARTMENT

STEAMER_____

LOCATION_____

_____19___

Signing off the *Champlain:* the author with Second Mate Allen Flood (Author's collection)

happily poses for final pictures with us deckhands. Even though I'm still hobbling around on my foot, I can't stay mad at these guys. The Cliffs company has treated us well and I can now see why they are regarded as one of the best outfits to sail for on the lakes.

After a farewell hot roast beef sandwich, we thank the galley crew and bid farewell to some of the engine room crew that will be on for a couple more days shutting down the boilers and engines. Then we return forward to our cabin to grab our gear and head toward the ladder. My duffel is slightly heavier with my Cleveland-Cliffs coveralls and a length of line resting in there as souvenirs of this trip. Buck, the watchman, who will not be released until tomorrow with the watchmen and wheelsmen, helps lower the gear down to the dock, where a taxi is waiting to take us downtown. I drop Jim at the Greyhound station and continue on to the lakefront airport that offers direct service to Detroit City Airport on the east side.

I look out the window of the small plane as it heads out across the lake for the short flight. I can see the shoreline far below. There is the Terminal Tower, Municipal Stadium, and the bridges over the Cuyahoga. Further along, I make out the slips and am thrilled to see the tiny red "C" on the stack of the *Champlain* one last time this year. My ankle throbs in sympathy as I imagine what the remaining crew members are doing as the afternoon creeps toward early darkness on this shortest day of the year. Within a short time the plane is whisking over the Southeast Shoal light and then over the Windsor shoreline as it descends for landing.

Back in Detroit as darkness falls I catch a cab to surprise my parents at supper time. The next morning I am at the store, buying some albums for myself as reward for completing the season. By afternoon I am at the hospital, having my ankle x-rayed. Other than a bruise and a sprain, there is nothing serious and I am free to begin enjoying the holidays with family and friends. Having laid up the *Carnahan* a couple years before, I savor the sweetness of coming home with stories to share with everyone.

CHAPTER 13

1972

Last Call

During the winter months I move onto a couch at Marshall and Sue's place on Fourth Street and I spend the lengthening afternoons sequestered in the Wayne State University library, alternately reading Norman Mailer and then writing my senior essay for Monteith titled *Wallace Stevens, Robinson Jeffers, and Mind Control*, an exploration of two American poets and their relationship to a Silva mind control course I am taking with my two friends on a lark.

My moment of truth comes a couple months later by way of a Western Union telegram. The note informs me that I have been assigned to the Cleveland Cliffs steamer *Cadillac*, and need to report April 10. I think about the sailing life that has carried me through these past five years, all the friends I have made, and all the great places I have seen. But I am in the midst of this essay and really don't feel like waiting another quarter to graduate. I pass on the offer.

But, still in need of money, I accept my dad's offer to get me a job on the line at Dodge Truck in Warren. I work the afternoon shift and in the process gain enormous respect for my father, who has spent twenty-five years in that place. I have difficulty making it through a single eight-hour shift of welding frames for front ends of trucks. The shop scene is hot, hellish, and relentless, exactly what people have been telling me for years. At lunch, many guys make it as far as the six-pack and joints in their cars in the parking lot. After lunch there are often accidents that shut down the line. This gives us a breather to reflect on just what the hell we are doing here in the first place. One night, a coworker on a machine called the merry-go-round gets his leg trapped in its moving underbody. By the time the red button is pushed to stop the line, he is on his back, crying in pain, unable to move. When I go over to offer support, other workers caution me to be careful, implying that he might do anything in his state of mind. It takes several minutes for a hi-lo to make its way over and lift the machine so that the medical team can extract his leg. By the time he is carried off on a stretcher, I have had more than enough time to reflect. I quit the plant the next day and invest a chunk of my pay in parts so that my dad and I can finish rebuilding the engine of the TR4, which I will soon be able to drive again.

In late June I receive my Bachelor of Philosophy degree from Monteith and move out into the world, which is a lot like my college life because I don't go anywhere except to see the Rolling Stones in July and then to my friend Gretta's place on a lake where we skinny-dip until dawn. The days and nights of this summer are filled with seemingly endless parties and good times. Friends seem to be everywhere. For cash, instead of catching a ship, I accept a call from Hare Cartage, who wants me to join a crew collecting voting machines from school and church basements throughout the city of Detroit, which has decided to go to a computerized system. The work is grueling, hard, and exhausting but the pay is good and so I am able to go with Sue to visit Marshall at the University of Michigan Biological Station in Pellston in August. After a couple days of visiting, I convince Sue to drive me and my trusty bike to the Soo, where I peddle across the International Bridge and begin a two-week tour around the north shore of Superior. I push my Schwinn into uncharted territory and eat, sleep, and dream bicycling, stopping wherever and whenever the mood catches me. I have a sleeping bag and supply pack on the back of the bike and depend upon little markets along the way for whatever food I can scrounge. I am seeking some kind of purification on this trip and vow to stay away from beer, a pledge I am able to keep for almost three whole days. In addition to some of the most beautiful country I have ever seen, I encounter all-night rains without shelter, hippie communes, black flies, black bears, government youth hostels, sleeping giants, and some of the biggest hills anywhere. Yet I persevere and wind up the trip on Highway 61, cruising into Duluth and Superior by land for the first time. By the time I get the bike back to my brother Jim's place near

Marquette, I suck down grateful beer after beer and think to myself, "Summer . . . Aaah!

As Wayne State reconvenes, I realize that I no longer have a purpose in life. There are no more courses to take and the campus life in and of itself cannot keep me. The antiwar movement has become increasingly represented by legions of recently returned veterans in wheelchairs and the marches and protest rallies are somber affairs with the look and feel of ragtag armies led by no one. There is a hopeless feeling in the air, fed in part by the dawning awareness that the Nixon/Agnew government, helped into office in part by the Chicago riots, has succeeded in neutralizing the get-out-of-Vietnam movement. The rallies come off like weak, tired efforts at resistance as the White House machine methodically and routinely rolls over the opposition. The leadership of the Students for a Democratic Society has been labeled as Communist and is in disarray. The Black Power movement has been similarly infiltrated and demonized and kept in the ghetto. The White Panther Party head, John Sinclair, has been recently released from prison after serving part of a ten-year sentence on the charge of providing two joints of marijuana to an undercover agent. The meteoric career of Jimi Hendrix has smashed into earth, leaving behind sound without life. Rock and roll has slipped into a narcissistic comatoid state reflecting the ennui of day-to-day existence. The underground press, like the *Fifth Estate*, is having a difficult time maintaining coverage of the systematic decimation of both the antiwar and countercultural movements with their rants of the too-sensational-to-be-believed truth. And all the while I have become used to the routine nightly television accounts of our army's successful skirmishes with the Viet Cong accompanied by the footnoted body counts of our own troops lost.

The 1972 presidential election, the first in which I will have the right to vote, offers a glimmer of hope with the advent of "Clean" Eugene McCarthy. I attend a rally at the University of Detroit, where I actually shake the hand of the antiwar Democratic candidate. But my newly budding cynicism is rewarded over the subsequent weeks as his campaign is minimized by the mainstream press and Democratic Party infighting. The Nixon/Agnew juggernaut is on a roll and out of control heading clear across America.

I am amazed in the midst of all this to get a note from the Peace Corps. I applied to join several months before, fulfilling my vow to do so if my lottery number did not come up. Even though it did, the fact that I was not drafted still counts and I feel obligated to do something with my life now that Vietnam is no longer a threat and I don't have to relocate to Vancouver. I fly to a late-summer meeting in Chicago, where a couple of recruiters tell me and a roomful of college grads about life as agricultural technicians in Nepal. Apparently, my experience as a backyard gardener both in the Upper Peninsula and in Detroit have been deemed acceptable qualifications. Even though the FBI does a background check, the Peace Corps does not consider my criminal record sufficient reason to veto my application. The fact that my government has determined that I may serve it in peace but not in war restores my confidence in democracy a little. Returning to Detroit, I am faced with the reality of leaving the only place I have ever really known for the absolute unknown of Asia. The fact that Marshall, Gretta, as well as my brother Walt have relocated to the Pacific Northwest makes me realize that the Detroit I have known is already changing. I run out there to cavort among the rivers, waterfalls, and sand dunes with them before finally deciding to cast my fate with the mysterious Far East.

The November election comes and goes. I celebrate my right by casting my first vote for Eldridge Cleaver, fully aware of its waste. I am twenty-one years old and am jaded. I reflect on how my growing cynicism may well have influenced my seemingly stupid decisions of the past and am forced to acknowledge the truth. But I have learned the hard way that the life of the pure cynic offers only bitter fruit. I am aware of enough people my own age who are sequestered in jails or whose lives are ruined because they allowed their cynicism to flower. I have come perilously close to that same outcome.

So I force myself to temper my dark side with forays into the good things the world beyond bad government can offer. I spend some late-autumn days bidding farewell to the wilds of the Upper Peninsula and my favorite Detroit haunts. Although my friend Janet has come back into the picture, the time is right for me to leave, not stay. I struggle through an endless series of goodbye parties, already homesick and wondering how I can stay away from here for even six months. I truly question how I will be able to leave such good friends.

In mid-November, shortly before Thanksgiving, I am shocked to see a small article tucked into the midsection of the *Free Press*. The headline reads:

Captain Killed in Seaway Blast.

Massena, N.Y. — Two explosions wrecked a vessel in the fog-bound St. Lawrence Seaway early Thursday, killing the ship's captain and injuring four crewmen.

The 344-foot tanker *Venus* had unloaded its cargo of petroleum products only a few hours earlier.

The initial blast ripped through the No. 1 hold directly beneath the captain's cabin. It touched off a fire which was extinguished in less than an hour.

The second blast tore a 50-foot hole in the port side. However, reports indicated the hole was above the waterline and the ship was not in danger of sinking.

Killed in the explosion was Capt. Charles Stanley, 53, of Cleveland.

The vessel's third officer, Edward S. Marek, 38, of Sturgeon Bay, Wis., was seriously burned on the face and the hands. The other three were less seriously hurt. The rest of the 23-member crew escaped injury.

Cause of the blast was not known and an investigation was under way.

Captain Charlie Stanley, the man who I remember drunkenly trying to navigate the *Mercury* down the Saginaw River just a few years ago. The pure insanity of that crew comes back to me in a flash along with the heat and bugs of Lake Erie. I drive the TR4 to my favorite parking spot just outside the Dossin Museum on Belle Isle and sit and watch the Canadian shore and the freighter traffic through the cloud-laden day. I say a silent prayer for Captain Stanley and all my friends out there on the lakes and for those in warm bars as well. I put the car in gear and cruise around the empty island as darkness descends, looking out past the Livingstone Lighthouse onto the expanse of Lake St. Clair. As I drive back to the mainland across the bridge, I realize that each of these adventures aboard eight steamboats helped to prepare me in their own way for the most difficult voyage faced by any man—leaving home.

AFTERWORD
Shadows of Our Forgotten Ancestors

Much water has flowed through the Soo Locks and over Niagara Falls and out to the Atlantic since I decided to forgo the sailing life and seek my fortune in the landlocked kingdom of Nepal. It is sad to report that of the eight ships accounted for here, only the *Columbia* survives.

In the decades that have passed since the period of *Eight Steamboats*, most of the ships in the Great Lakes fleet have become obsolete. Hundreds of smaller ships, many the largest and quickest of their day, have been replaced by a much smaller fleet with single ships capable of carrying three times the cargo with fewer crew. Also missing today are ships powered by triple-expansion engines—the type still intact on the *Columbia*. Today's ships have efficient diesel engines and motors, steam turbines, and even a few Skinner Unaflows.

Here is a review of what became of the eight steamboats:

SS *South American:* Sold to the Seafarer International Union, fall 1967. Towed to Piney Point, Maryland, for conversion to training ship. (She was purchased to replace her sister, the *North American*, which sank en route to Piney Point, September 13, 1967.) Never used and languished in a slip until finally being towed to Baltimore and cut up for scrap in 1992.

SS *Columbia:* Laid up 1991 at Nicholson's shipyard in Ecorse, Michigan, with her sister, the *Ste. Claire*. While the *Claire* has been restored and is awaiting a new career, the *Columbia* is in a state of disrepair, and her fate at this writing is unknown.

The *South American* in
New Jersey, 1982
(Chuck Truscott)

The *Columbia* in Ecorse, February 2003 (Author's collection)

Thursday, June 5, 1975   WAYNE STATE UNIVERSITY   VOL. VIII NO. 164

BY KITTY WATSON
South End Staff Writer

Monteith College Getting the Axe In U Budget Cuts

The Board of Governors, in a closed meeting Tuesday night, voted 6-2 to phase out Monteith College by eliminating next year's freshman class.

The Board's action must still be formally approved at its public meeting next Friday before it becomes official.

BUT SINCE all eight board members participated in Tuesday's vote to kill Monteith, the prospects for the "experimental" liberal arts school are doubtful.

The board also voted 7-1 to recommend the approval of a main budget proposal which would include a $200,000 reduction in the $800,000 Monteith College budget, according to Michael Einheuser, a board member.

"One of the main assumptions behind this budget is that there will be no entering freshmen class at Monteith next fall," Einheuser told a meeting of Monteith faculty and students yesterday.

Einheuser, a recent graduate of Monteith, was the one dissenting vote on the budget proposal.

Yates Hafner, Dean of Monteith, told the same group that he spoke with President George Gullen yesterday morning concerning the matter.

"President Gullen told me that the Executive Committee of the Board of Governor's had considered Monteith's status Tuesday night, that an extensive discussion had occurred, but that no final decision had been made," Hafner said.

Hafner said Gullen told him, "I'm not playing games with you, Yates. No decision will be made except in the public meeting."

Augustus Calloway, a board member, said yesterday that the board was having a difficult time drawing up a budget which would please everyone, but did not answer any of the specific questions asked him concerning Monteith.

All he would say about the college's closing is, "It's a possibility. Monteith is being examined along with a lot of other programs. It is not alone."

"No agency in the State of Michigan is allowed to operate at a deficit. We

Monteith College cut up for scrap. Clipping from the *South End*, Wayne State University's student newspaper, June 5, 1975 (Walter P. Reuther Library, Wayne State University)

The author's "Z" card (Author's collection)

SS *Mercury:* Scrapped, 1976. Remains of hull converted to derrick barge by Roen Salvage, 1978.

SS *John Hulst:* Laid up 1979, Duluth, Minnesota. Towed to Thunder Bay, Wisconsin, 1983. Scrapping began in 1984 and, due to the dissolution of the Western Metals company, lasted until 1986.

MV *Henry Ford II:* Laid up December 1988 in the Rouge River. Sold to Lakes Shipping Company of Cleveland and name changed to *Samuel Mather* in 1989. Towed to the Frog Pond, Toledo, Ohio, but never sailed again. Scrapped in Port Maitland, Ontario, 1994.

SS *Paul H. Carnahan:* Laid up 1985, Ecorse, Michigan. Sold for scrapping with the *George M. Humphrey* in Taiwan, 1986. Unlike the other scrapped ships, the *Carnahan* left the Seaway under her own steam, crewed by retired captains and engineers to Quebec City, Canada.

SS *Bethlehem:* Last trip, November 1973. Wintered in Quebec and scrapped in Santander, Spain, 1974.

SS *Champlain:* Laid up 1981 in Toledo, Ohio. Towed with her sister *Cadillac* to Aliaga, Turkey, where she was scrapped in 1987.

Created in 1959 by the Wayne State University Board of Governors, Monteith College was modeled on the College of the University of Chicago to offer 800 students some of the advantages of a small college within the larger university. The brilliant and eccentric Monteith faculty challenged students to use the academic, social, and cultural resources of the city and university to comprehend, challenge, and change the world around them.

In 1976 the Wayne State University Board of Governors, perhaps tired of being challenged, and thus using the pretext of budget cuts, voted to eliminate the college. Monteith College was towed from Wayne State University to the ideological scrapyard near the Bronx café where she was cut apart and laid to rest.

Index